P9-DGN-871

MIRIAM'S KITCHEN

Miriam's Kitchen

A MEMOIR

Elizabeth Ehrlich

VIKING

VIKING
Published by the Penguin Group
Penguin Putnam Inc., 375 Hudson Street,
New York, New York 10014, U.S.A.
Penguin Books Ltd, 27 Wrights Lane,
London W8 5TZ, England
Penguin Books Australia Ltd, Ringwood,
Victoria, Australia
Penguin Books Canada Ltd, 10 Alcorn Avenue,
Toronto, Ontario, Canada M4V 3B2
Penguin Books (N.Z.) Ltd, 182–190 Wairau Road,
Auckland 10, New Zealand

Penguin Books Ltd, Registered Offices:
Harmondsworth, Middlesex, England

First published in 1997 by Viking Penguin,
a member of Penguin Putnam Inc.

7   9   10   8   6

Copyright © Elizabeth Ehrlich, 1997
All rights reserved

PUBLISHER'S NOTE
The recipes contained in this book are to be followed exactly as written.
The Publisher is not responsible for addressing your specific allergy or
other health-related needs which require medical supervision. The
Publisher is not responsible for any adverse reactions to the recipes
contained in this book.

LIBRARY OF CONGRESS CATALOGING IN PUBLICATION DATA
Ehrlich, Elizabeth.
  Miriam's kitchen / Elizabeth Ehrlich.
    p.   cm.
  ISBN 0–670–86908–2   (alk. paper)
  1. Cookery, Jewish.   I. Title.
TX724.E37   1997
641.5'676—dc21   97–11473

This book is printed on acid-free paper.

Printed in the United States of America
Set in Bembo
Designed by Jaye Zimet

Without limiting the rights under copyright
reserved above, no part of this publication
may be reproduced, stored in or introduced into
a retrieval system, or transmitted, in any form
or by any means (electronic, mechanical, photo-
copying, recording or otherwise), without the prior
written permission of both the copyright
owner and the above publisher of this book.

For Leon
and the three who joined us

CONTENTS

INTRODUCTION

$\mathcal{M}$y grandmother used to sit before her stove on a tall, four-legged stool, stirring sweet-and-sour cabbage soup in a white enamel pot, dishing out salty perceptions of life. She was a capable woman. She carried herself with dignity about the neighborhood, as befitted the pharmacist's wife. Widowed in her fifties, she went back to work in the millinery trade she had learned as a nineteen-year-old immigrant in New York—proud to pay a cleaning woman, carry a union card, and earn health insurance on her own. With her proper passport case tucked into her two-handled pocketbook, she journeyed to Europe, at home in the world.

But my grandmother's blue-and-white tiled Brooklyn kitchen, in which so much life had been lived, was her truest sphere. There she chopped, grated, salted, peppered. There she handed on traditions brought from the Old World and translated amidst the exigencies of the New. Much of my valuable learning took place in that kitchen and in other rooms like it.

I grew up at a distance from my two immigrant grandmothers. In our Detroit neighborhood, my family became an idiosyncratic minority: Left wing, bookish, hypersensitive, white, Jewish, anti–middle class. A time came when we alone on our street lit Friday-night candles, and we lit them while holding few institutional ties to The Faith. My parents, first-generation Americans, selected from and approximated the traditions they took for granted. Still, they did so with affection for the old ways. They never stopped telling the stories that distilled immigrant essence and adaptation.

I knew who we were, and that stayed with me, even during years when I would have preferred otherwise. For a long time, though, there was much that I forgot.

I forgot the childhood appetites that could only be satisfied in my grandmothers' kosher kitchens. I forgot the practical, mystical teachings, spiraling back through time, that the grandmothers had once dished out with their soup. I forgot the dignity my immigrants had, that comes with the connection to something larger than everyday life, even when you are doing nothing more than stirring soup. I had the bequest of my grand-mothers' details, but I devalued all this for many years, as one does.

It came back to me when I became a mother. I wondered what to teach my children. I wanted to build a floor under my children, something strong and solid.

Then I remembered and unwrapped a bundle of family tales, many located in or near the kitchen. In these I found wisdom and innovation and the fading rituals and habits of an assimilating clan. I had been carrying that bundle all my life.

What made me value my inheritance as treasure, not burden? The luck that has placed me, as an adult, in range of Miriam's kitchen. My mother-in-law Miriam, born in a small village in Jewish Poland, survived the Holocaust. A keeper of rituals and recipes, and of stories, she cooks to recreate a lost world, and to prove that unimaginable loss is not the end of everything. She is motivated by duty to ancestors and descendants, by memory and obligation and an impossible wish to make the world whole.

When I am with Miriam in the kitchen, she speaks of the past. I listen, trying to imagine the world from which her cuisine came. I know gefilte fish tastes different when you chop it by hand; I'm sure the flavor is altered when you have lived Miriam's life. Yet serious cooking is an essentially optimistic act. It reaches into the future, vanishes into memory, and creates the desire for another meal.

I am trying to learn Miriam's recipes now. For me, it is a voyage of discontinuity and connection. Some of her dishes, and expressions, and perceptions, I remember from the kitchens of my childhood. The cadence is different—reflecting the differences, finally, between refugees like Miriam, and those like my grandmothers who emigrated at least somewhat by choice, and those who, like my parents, leave their immigrant homes to seek their own Americas.

The cadence is evolving for me now, as I seek to bring tradition home. With ambivalence and some sense of irony, I light a candle, recite a prayer, grate a potato, and move toward making my kitchen kosher. Thus, I forge links from my grandparents, and my husband's grandparents, to my children, who wear their ancestors' Hebrew names.

I think about it as I go, from a sinkside, stoveside, personal perspec-tive, not a rabbinical one. I turn over the old stories in my mind and col-lect new ones. I choose my own history, deciding which snapshots, decades, recipes, versions of arguments and events are to be discarded, and which will stand for the whole. That history is my own little temple where I measure my life against a reliable standard. Increasingly, I find meaning there.

It is a many-colored history, and it is one small strand in an intricate old ever-changing tapestry of migrations, extremes, accommodations, observances, contradictions. My father is part of it: Marxist, atheist, he collected signs and omens, lit memorial candles for the dead. As is my mother, who did not love to cook, who studied Chekhov, covered her head for a Friday night prayer, and could recite poetry at the drop of a hat. And at a distance, the grandmothers in their kitchens, preserving complicated rites in adopted cities, not only for the sake of the past.

I embrace them all. I consider the law, the restrictions, the presumptions of holiness, the doubt. I inventory layers of translucent recollection evoking food, love, home, apocrypha, anger, ritual, laughter, conflict, and regret. The result is a collage, but also a way of life. That collage is my religion, and it is what I am passing on.

September

LONGING

September

Work and house and errands and physical fitness and activities and things. The expediencies of every day. This cannot be all there is.

Something more is calling. It is of the past, it embodies tradition, yet tradition is only the vehicle. It is of the heart, but it is more than diffuse sentiment. Some of it is dimly remembered, yet remembered for a reason.

It is a coherent way of life and the taste of home. It is a way to teach the children right and wrong, consciousness, history, and appreciation of all we have. It connects them to their grandparents and mine.

It is an ancient religion. It beckons, and half the time I am not even sure why. Its rituals tantalize and will not be denied.

What is the lure of ritual when passionate belief is hardly ever to be found, when fulfillment of ritual is a matter of choice? It is more than the pre-servation of an empty vessel. It is the conviction, deep and unspoken, that ritual, the vessel, contains a precious substance, though I cannot name it. My ignorance is my problem, not that of the vessel.

Why do I, having long ignored the rituals, yearn in their direction? Some of its caretakers have been those I loved best and respected most. I cannot forget them. I start from there.

A COAL STOVE

$\mathcal{I}$ write to my mother about this and that. There are things I need to know. Such as, "Did your mother, our *bubbe,* cook on a coal stove, when you were a girl?"

I have forgotten the question two months later, when I open an envelope and read:

> Yes, she cooked on a coal stove.
>
> How she got the delicious results from an unpredictable flame is a wonder.
>
> Her vegetable and barley soup, chicken soup, *gedemfte fleysh* (pot roast), chicken roasted with potatoes or lima beans, potato *kneydlekh* (dumplings), *kreplekh* (filled dumplings), *lungen un milts* (chopped and sautéed lung and spleen), roast *heldzl* (stuffed poultry neck), chicken fricassee, *gefilte milts* (stuffed spleen), meat loaf, *konkletn* (spiced ground-beef patties fried in oil), *meyrn tsimes* (carrots simmered in honey), chopped liver, roasted *kishke* (stuffed derma), baked fish with string beans, baked carp, gefilte fish, potato pudding, rice pudding, noodle pudding, potato pancakes, cheese blintzes, chili sauce, sour pickles, pickled green tomatoes, canned fruit, farmer cheese, chocolate cake, spice cake, apple pies, apple strudel, and cookies were legendary.
>
> Let me not forget the marvelous beet and spinach and cabbage borshts.
>
> Cholent she made in the furnace. It was divine. The pea soup lives on in memory.
>
> We had heard about knishes, but never seen one.
>
> The farmer cheeses used to hang from the corners of chairs in cheesecloth bags, and drip, drip, drip all day. Then we'd slice them and spread with sweet butter—Paradise regained! We were young and very hungry.
>
> I am so sorry I failed to ask for the recipes.

EGG SALAD

It is a Friday morning, five o'clock in the morning. Miriam, my mother-in-law, has begun to cook. I am not there. I am fifteen miles away in my bed. I lie awake knowing that Miriam is moving about her kitchen on soft slippers.

Miriam's son, my husband, is beside me, asleep. Down the hall, our daughter is sleeping, mouth slightly agape, burrowed among numerous pillows, stuffed animals, dolls, and books. Our son sleeps with covers thrown off. There are droplets of perspiration on his upper lip and down his fuzzy little back.

Jacob, my father-in-law, is still resting, but he will be out of bed and downstairs to the kitchen soon. Miriam waits for him before making the instant coffee. In the meantime, she will begin. She will prepare tonight's dinner, which can be warmed again for supper on Saturday night. She will assemble her salads for Saturday lunch, to eat when her husband comes home from the synagogue, before his predictable afternoon nap.

She will make egg salad. I lie in bed thinking of Miriam's egg salad, which she has mixed for our parties and brunches and served with a bagel when we come to her house for lunch. It is her mother's recipe, and her grandmother's before her, as with so much of the food we eat. Over the course of a year's Fridays, Miriam cooks through a repertoire the rest of the world has nearly forgotten: potato dumplings called *kluskis,* flourless egg noodles, pickled fish, cauliflower soup.

Miriam's mother owned a restaurant in Poland, before the war. The tables were full. Middle-class Jewish families from the village came to dine, travelers between trains, Polish officers from the army base nearby. The fish dishes were famous. Miriam, as a little girl, would be shooed from the hot, busy kitchen, where two peasant girls helped her mother and a man opened barrels of beer.

Her father delivered the beer. He held the bottling concession at the brewery nearby, a license bestowed by the local lord and landowner, good for twenty years.

"No wonder," Miriam has told me, "the Poles didn't want us back."

After the war, she and other survivors returned to the village, crossing the Vistula River in the first civilian train back. A school chum was living in her parents' house.

"I thought they got you all," said the friend, closing the door.

A family of cousins was shot and killed before they could leave the village again.

It is still dark on this Friday morning, out beyond Miriam's white kitchen curtains. Only the necessary number of lights are turned on within, when my mother-in-law begins to make egg salad. She starts ten eggs in cold water with a spoonful of salt so they will not burst. Carefully, deliberately, she removes a large frying pan from a low cupboard with barely a metal sound.

She cuts onions, three medium-sized onions, scoring them in her hand, holding the onions one by one over the pan and bringing the knife toward her through the crisp white bulb. The pale, veined squares and triangles fall into the pan. She sprinkles pepper on the diced onions. To dry them a bit, and remove the bitter taste, she cooks the onions for a minute on a low flame. Then she pours oil on the onions, and lets them fry.

If I were there, in her kitchen, I would be slightly alarmed, as I always am, by the quantity of oil poured over onions, the basis for much in my mother-in-law's cuisine.

"I like raw onions in egg salad," I have said to her.

"Really?" Miriam has answered, tongue rolling over the "r," voice holding genuine surprise. "And my mother told me the more fried onions, the better it tastes."

I lie in my bed, in the dawn of an autumn morning. Miriam has already opened a can of mushrooms and drained them over the sink and patted them dry. She doesn't like the fresh white mushrooms sold in America. She liked the many wild mushrooms that grew in the Polish woods. She adds the canned buttons and stems to the pan, and there will be that smell in a moment, the onions and mushrooms and pepper sizzling gently in oil.

Upstairs, Jacob is washing and dressing, possibly making the bed. Downstairs, Miriam is peeling the hard-boiled eggs under cold running water. She cradles a wooden chopping bowl on a dishtowel, as my mother does, as her mother did, to keep the bowl from slipping, to hold the bowl secure.

In the bowl Miriam places the fixings—the eggs, the fried mushrooms and onions, a dose of salt, a bit of mayonnaise, a tiny sprig of dill. Real mayonnaise, none of your low-fat versions. Deep down, I suspect she believes that foods labeled "light" or "lite" are only a way to give less value for the dollar.

With a black-handled hand chopper, Miriam chops. The shiny chopping blade pulverizes the bowl's contents until the texture is of a fine spread. She does not trawl the refrigerator for a stalk of celery, a taste of parsley, something new that might work just this once. The egg salad, always delicious, always comes out exactly the same. The taste is not of invention, but of a moment lost, a moment recovered, a moment in time.

When cooking, Miriam rarely tastes. She knows the ingredients, the proportions. Even more, she knows the proper look in the pan or the bowl. She knows the turn of the spoon that will produce that look. She often tells me, "take that recipe," as if the mere taking would be enough. I know I should be there to see it, to fix her process in my mind. But dawn creeps into my bedroom, and the egg salad takes its anointed form without me.

It is egg salad transported, egg salad rescued from a vanished place. Once it all seemed eternal: In a restaurant in a small Polish village, officers raised their glasses, and hungry travelers relished such food as this. Now Miriam cooks for her husband, and for my family, hoping only that those at her table will ask for more.

It is just past six in the morning. My father-in-law must be stepping down the stairs. The salads, completed, will have been set aside. The oatmeal for breakfast is ready, and the kettle boils. When the breakfast dishes are washed and the sink is scoured, Miriam will start on the evening meal. I should be there, drinking an instant coffee beside her. I should be there to measure and stir and see for myself, before that particular salt is gone. I should be in Miriam's kitchen.

YOM KIPPUR

*W*e were out in a rented rowboat, on a small, serene lake. My father pulled the oars with the light muscled splash of rhythm, the gentle metal percussion of oar pin within oarlock. We attained a point near the center of the water, under a dome of blue sky. My father tucked up the wooden oars, and we were adrift.

My sister and brother sat facing my father. I sat behind him in the prow, my hand trailing in cool lake water scented faintly of algae and freshwater weed. My mother was elsewhere, perhaps at the shore with a book; she did not like boats.

It was a still, Indian summer day. All the spirits of the earth seemed in repose. Michigan pines, just-turning maples and elms sheltered the lake, throwing reflections of amber, garnet, shadow, and green on its silvered surface.

It was a school day, but we were excused from school. It was Yom Kippur, the day when God, having considered the fate of every Jew in the coming year, would sign and seal the Book of Life. The day was solemn, the day was huge. A tiny fish jumped and flashed, then disappeared.

For the devout, Yom Kippur is a day of turbulence, of climax. It is for fasting, prayer, searing self-examination, repentance. It is the culmination of a whole long year of trying to meet a standard that can never be met—to fulfill all obligations, to live by the commandments, to appreciate the earth and its bounty. On Yom Kippur, devout Jews take unblinking inventory of moral shortfall. They resolve on better thoughts, on selfless deeds, during the cycle of seasons to come.

For the merely traditional, Yom Kippur is at least a day of connection, of remembering ancestors and mourning the dead, a day of identifying oneself as a Jew, of celebrating continuity and belonging, of marking another year gone in a mortal life. There is purpose to this, a kind of psychic perspective, even without pious worship—and who is to know where on the asymptote stretching between spirituality and tradition, a given soul may at a given moment be fixed?

My own location is a blur, a point moving through four dimensions.

There has been bleak autumn and there have been brilliant frost-tipped skies in the Yom Kippur mornings of my life. Mostly I wake to fast, recognizing the salty taste of thirst, remembering too late last year's caffeine-deprived headache, which will strike again soon. Pregnancy subtracted some fasting years, and once or twice, as a young and angry person, I took myself out of the calculus.

My parents always fasted, as did we, the children, as soon as we figured we could. There was no food in the rowboat. No picnic waited in our car, parked in weekday, post-season solitude beside the boat house. An observant person, however, would not drive on Yom Kippur, a day more fearsome, and as holy, as the weekly Sabbath itself.

Yom Kippur holds *Yiskor,* memorial prayers. Four times a year are these prayers said, with a fifth recital on the anniversary of the loved one's death. On the eve of Yom Kippur my parents lit memorial candles. These *yahrzeit* candles, stubby, small glasses filled with white wax and wick, and stocked on a bottom shelf in the supermarket, burn at least twenty-four hours. They last throughout the Jewish day, which begins at evening, and ends with the following sundown.

Once, visiting my grandmother's house for the high holidays, I tiptoed down the hall in pajamas at night, on Yom Kippur. Irene, my grandmother, sat alone in the darkness, beside her dining room sideboard, on which a tray full of *yahrzeit* flames flickered and blazed. There seemed to be dozens, a whole night city of lost relations.

"I hope you never have so many *yahrzeit* candles to light," my grandmother said to me, pulling me close. Then she wept so hard her nose began to bleed.

We children accepted the fasting with no complaint. We welcomed anything outside the ordinary realm. We ate our meal of chicken, challah, honey. We cleared away the dishes before dark; we lit the candles. Young children tried skipping breakfast next morning. Older ones made it through lunch, proud of their hunger pangs.

We didn't go to synagogue as a family. Some years my sister and I went alone. We sat in a row of girls in new dresses and pastel-colored vinyl shoes, girls trying not to fidget or giggle or cross their legs, self-conscious in fishnet stockings held up by that first set of garters. My sister and I felt solemn, and we walked home the half mile from *shul* in a quiet mood. We did this one autumn and another and the next, until the *shul* was sold to a church group, most of the congregation having moved away.

We took walks as a family, read quietly at home or conversed on Yom Kippur; once we went out in a rented rowboat. At sundown always we broke the fast with a piece of honey cake and a cup of strong coffee, *farkhapn dos harts*—to give the heart a lift—as my mother's mother, *Bubbe* Malke, used to say.

As I grew up I saw it as mainly symbolic, the fasting, an annual cleansing of corporeal concerns, and incidentally would drop a pound or two. "I'm atoning," said a friend once in a jest, "for sins of gluttony." Medieval echo, that, more Christian than Jewish, even a bit irreverent, perhaps, but brave to say it right out. This is who we are.

We are a disparate people, often lacing up tennis shoes of a Yom Kippur morning. There is a tradition against wearing leather that day. I have thought, perhaps heard, that to wear the skins of once-living creatures, while God is judging, indicates a careless attitude. Or did the high priests of Judea enjoin us against the comfort of leather sandals on a day strewn with sharp stones of remorse? Is the leaving behind of leather shoes a way to cast off vanity? Comparing my feet with those of other penitents over the years—now my feet on Yom Kippur are always in synagogue—all interpretations seem possible: The people sit, they stand, they sway, in sneakers, sandals, beach clogs, canvas espadrilles, and sometimes new leather dress shoes, which for all I know may most mortify the flesh.

The repetitions of prayer and emotion echo and rise in every place of Jewish worship: We will die, we are sinful, we are not worthy of the privilege of life. But sincere repentance, works of charity, and acts of loving-kindness will avert the stern decree, untimely death, or so the believers believe. Not that God can be bribed, or that the wicked will be literally struck down, but that heartfelt return to the teachings is the affirmative stuff of life.

Emotions are heightened by the old Hebrew prayers and the building hunger. Tears are wrung out of thirsty bodies. Stomachs rumble. In my grandparents' time, there was no toothbrushing, no bathing; there was a preview of putrefaction, decay, a one-day's token of how futile is vanity, indeed, of the futility of all our busy activity, day in and out.

Flawed humans though we are, come Yom Kippur we have a moment to turn God's mirror on ourselves, if there is a God. Or it is a moment to think about something larger than everyday life, to contemplate obligations to other people, to regret our failures, to renounce our shallowness. Within all the nattering activity, this day is a silent space. In a whole year of watching rain fall, one day to dwell inside the water droplet, small and fragile, resolving to be better before the next deluge of daily life.

Any Jew who goes to synagogue, or to temple, if at all, will go on Yom Kippur. For years I did not go, sometimes calm with alienation, sometimes beset with longing for the small glowing flame of specialness I remembered, one that had had little to do with ritual worship. I never forgot that pristine day in the rowboat, surrounded by the huge affirmative power of sky and tree and vista, and that feeling of suspension between all the past failures and failings and the nascent beginnings to be.

Some years I dressed in the scraps of that longing, and went forth with few expectations to houses of worship. Perhaps my alienation exceeded that of other congregants, perhaps not. What others felt I cannot know. Yom Kippur is a motley heart assembly, my soul a Swiss cheese of misgiving and hunger and doubt.

I have taken a friend to her first temple, a sight on the way in a touring time of our lives. Heedless of Yom Kippur prohibitions on handling money, a beadle passed a collection plate to the strains of pipe organ chords. I could not explain; I was baffled. She likened it to a Lutheran church. I did not fast. I belonged neither there, nor anywhere.

And what was I doing, another year, young woman that I was, in a veterans' hall among strip malls and corn fields, observing Yom Kippur from a back row of folding chairs? The quality of prayer, the rabbi's words, the cantor's voice, my own inner voices that day, all have slipped away. Even how I got there is mysterious.

Only a satirist's recollection remains: the late-hour entrance of local gentry, a couple tanned and trim, dyed and scalpeled, and their regal procession down the center aisle to front row seats evidently reserved. Unworthy and evil thoughts were mine, judging a raiment of animal skin, the height of secular fashion that year, including violet suede boots and a leather hat to match. Did Jews somewhere still look within and tremble? Remembering my impression of this discrepant sight into eternity is its own fit punishment.

My father took me to synagogue on Yom Kippur only once, or so I remember. My hand in his, we passed through the trash-blown foyer of his boyhood Brooklyn *shul*. Perhaps his arrival enabled the remnants of the congregation to attain a *minyan,* the quorum of ten needed to open the Torah and commence the public prayers. I moved my eyes to names on a wall, and there found names I knew, grandfather and great-grandfather on plaques of green bronze, beside a dimmed eternal light.

"That was the women's gallery," my father whispered. I looked up to the balcony, empty but for its rouged, behatted ghosts. I sat behind a grimy sheet rigged to divide the few pious women, the few pious men.

At the buoyant center of memory, I had this: a small wooden rowboat out on the lake, an Indian summer day, a warm and clear Yom Kippur. Tomorrow at school the children might ask where I had been, and the matter of what I would answer troubled me. I did not know what I would say. I trailed my hand in the water and dipped it out. Drops of lake water sparkled as they fell. My father spoke.

"So where is God?" my father asked. "Inside a synagogue or out here?"

I know I shivered, and I thought I knew.

HOW TO KEEP A
KOSHER KITCHEN

*Y*ou need a lot of things. Meat dishes, dairy dishes, coffee cups two ways. You need ladles for cream soup and ladles for beef stew, knives for steak and knives for butter. A cutting board for cheese, and a different one for turkey. You need a lot of cupboards if you're going to have a kosher kitchen.

You need a meat pot for meat soup and a dairy pot for dairy soup, and separate soup bowls, each of their kind. You must never mix any food derived from animal flesh with any sort of milk product, neither in pot, nor plate, nor meal. You may not seethe a kid in its mother's milk. You may not seethe a chicken in a calf's mother's milk. So God said, so the rabbis elaborated. You may not eat chicken à la king.

The pots have their essences. These cannot be denied. Cook vegetable soup in a meat pot, and that soup itself becomes practically *fleyshik,* a thing of flesh. You must eat it with a *fleyshik* spoon. You may not dust it with grated cheese. That soup is branded by its provenance, until the end, the moldy end two weeks from now in a plastic container marked MEAT. If you want soup to be neutral, neither dairy nor meat, you'd better have a separate pot that you call *pareve,* and a ladle and a stirrer and containers to match.

It's not utensils only. You need distinctive tools to clean with. You can't use the sponge that wiped sour cream at luncheon, to scrub beef drippings from the broiler pan that night. You need a separate meat sponge for the broiler pan. While you're at it, get another broiler pan.

You need two sinks or you need to alternate two plastic racks in a single sink. You set your ice cream dish on the dairy rack to keep it above any lingering residue of meat. Your meat rack elevates the chicken soup pot above the coffee cream poured down the drain this morning.

You fill the dishwasher with dairy or meat plates, never with both at one time. Between meat and dairy you *kasher,* make kosher, the dishwasher's innards with water and heat. Heat and water, soap and water and heat: Burn your oven, destroy every particle of baked-on meat. Scour the counter, get every molecule that once was milk.

You need kosher food in a kosher kitchen. The mammals you eat must be the kosher kind, with cloven hooves and ruminating stomachs. You may not eat pig, rabbit, dog, or horse. You may eat cow, sheep, goat, or deer, if you can find a kosher butcher to chase down a deer. These animals may not be killed with a blow to the head nor by a bullet as they run, but by a quick slash to the throat, so that the blood drains out. You don't have to do this yourself, but someone must. You must not eat the life fluid, blood.

Fowl are O.K. but not birds of carrion or prey. Don't eat crow, eat a nice roast chicken. Snakes and snails and lobster are off the list. Your water creatures must have fins and scales, never shells or tentacles. You may eat whitefish. You may eat smoked salmon, and at every possible opportunity. You must not eat shrimp, ever again.

In the supermarket you will stalk groceries, alert to characteristics, markings, derivations. You will squint at the ingredients on a box, you will track down seals of certified approval. You reject the frijoles refried in lard. You note the dairy extracts in a cookie, disqualify it as dessert after meat. You will suddenly wonder what to do about cheeses cured with rennet, an enzyme processed from the stomach of a pig. I can't advise you; ask a rabbi. Some see the enzyme, some see the pig.

And what about foods that are neither meat nor dairy, but may be used with either type of meal? I'm talking about the jars of mayonnaise and bottles of dressing, the mustards and olives and *salsa verde*. Dip a dairy spoon and *presto!* that mayonnaise, depending on how wrapped up you're getting, may take on qualities of dairy in itself. I wouldn't use that mayonnaise later on a turkey sandwich if I were you. You need two different jars or a spoon that is *pareve*.

You need a third set of some things. You need more storage space. You had better get a bigger kitchen.

My mother didn't have two sets of dishes, much less three. She bought kosher meat, and never mixed it with dairy in a meal. But a single dishrag, a one lonely *shmate,* hung on our kitchen faucet when I was a girl. My mother soaped it and scalded it, wrung it out with red hands, and rubbed it in scouring powder to clean the sink.

My mother's mother, an immigrant, had two *shmates*. My mother, child of the New World, sat on the fence. A can of scouring powder sat on the sink. My mother taught us to scour after every meal.

My immigrants, the grandmothers, kept kosher kitchens. They had dairy spatulas and meat spatulas, and they always knew which were which.

They had enamel pots, *milikhdike,* for creamy fish soup, and wooden bowls to chop liver, and glasses for tea. They rendered chicken fat in one pan and fried cheese blintzes in another. They had dishtowels trimmed in blue to dry plates after blintzes, and red-bordered towels to dry after meat.

My father's mother had six sets of dishes. Behind the glass breakfront she stored the yellow scallop-edged crockery, with its frieze of burnt-orange blossoms, dishes that cried out for oatmeal with whole milk, potatoes with butter, and coffee ice cream. She had everyday meat things and the good meat dishes, for Sabbath and holidays during the year.

She had Passover dishes, *milkhik* and *fleyshik,* and also the grand Passover dinner set. These were white bone china edged with a thick band of gold. The platters, gravy boat, soup tureen, and covered vegetable dishes had dressy gold handles. They never held dairy, but were dedicated to meat. Nor had one crumb of bread ever touched them, only the Passover matzo of her Seder meals.

The dairy silverware lived in a red-handled drawer in the tin-topped kitchen table. The Passover dishes were stored in the basement fifty-one weeks of the year. She had blue glass bowls in the shape of fish, in which nothing but freshly cooked, pink, lemony applesauce was served. So expertly was that applesauce heaped that it rose in a convex meniscus above the bowls' edges, and yet not a drop ever spilled.

Glass can be used for meat or dairy. Glass is *pareve.* You'll want a few glass things in a kosher kitchen.

There is a heightened sense of reality in a kosher kitchen. You have to think about where your food comes from, at least somewhat, at least slightly. You need awareness in a kosher kitchen. You draw lines, and say, Some things I will not eat. You set limits on appetite. That seems to me not a bad thing, but of value in a society bloated with excess.

You don't keep kosher for heightened awareness. Keeping kosher is in the Torah. It's an obligation. It's not an opinion.

It's discipline, a kosher kitchen. It is an encompassing way of life, in which discipline and meaning, the mundane and the spiritual, are inextricably tied. You are only washing your dishes, but you are doing something more. You are tending something ancient, and it matters. That meat knife matters. Your work matters.

Zen tea-making must be something like this.

I think my grandmothers knew their work mattered. They knew they were bringing forth more than food from their kitchens. They cooked twenty-one meals a week, fifty-two weeks a year, all their adult lives. On the menu, however, were other things too: history, tradition, community connection, anger, humor, and just about anything else worth conveying. I sat there fiddling with the silverware drawer in the kitchen table. They served me emotion and substance on a dairy plate.

You don't keep kosher to honor emotion, or even for history's sake. You do it to keep a commandment. You shouldn't romanticize. Do you even believe in commandments?

It's a lot of work. It's a real pain. Who wants a kosher kitchen?

I do. I mean I might. I'm thinking maybe I'll try.

HONEY CAKE

*W*hen I was a girl growing up in Detroit in the 1960s, autumn brought, as predictably as cold weather and crisp leaves, a bulky brown parcel to our door. It was for my father, sent by his Aunt Dora, who lived in a third-floor walk-up apartment on Featherbed Lane in the Bronx. He was her favorite nephew, away in some dimly understood exile. In the package were history, family, culture, tradition, heart. This gave off a smell of cinnamon, waiting on the kitchen table, as we kids twirled about the house until the dad got home.

In a ceremony of unwrapping, he untied string, opened shoe boxes, folded back leaves of foil and waxed paper. There was never a letter. I don't know if she ever learned to write English, beyond her own name and whatever the citizenship test required. But the long roll of strudel, its dough stretched to transparent perfection, expressed much. There were crescent-shaped butter horns, *rugelekh* pastries, a brown sheet candy called *nundt,* made of pounded walnuts and honey. At last there was my father's loaf of honey cake, almond halves buttoned into its shiny top.

For an atheist raised in ritual, this stood fast, year to year: Seated, he asked for a knife. Thin shavings of honey cake, glittering with bits of fruit, fanned out on a plate. He lifted a shot of schnapps in a green crystal glass. Then he wrapped the honey cake gently, and set it atop the refrigerator, invisible to all but himself, my tall father. Aunt Dora's candy, strudel, cookies might vanish swiftly in my mother's charge, but his honey cake would last.

Slivered, portioned, precise, it tasted rich through the celebrations of fall, gave pale sweetness to winter feast days, and it lasted, being no naive honey cake.

Summers, Aunt Dora made *vishnik,* a home-brew liqueur, marinating fresh cherries in a vat of Four Roses whiskey. Working, this *vishnik* perfumed the cramped, embroidered, patched apartment, the dark, sweaty hall, and by August, the stairwell and lobby of her Bronx tenement.

She boiled lemon peels and orange peels in sugar syrup. She mixed the peelings and drunken cherries with strong coffee, honey, flour, eggs, and—what else? Well, the whiskey must have preserved it through the long cold midwestern months, until the last dry crumbs were taken, just before Passover, in the spring.

Each spring, we would go to New York, and visit Aunt Dora, bearing bottles of Four Roses whiskey.

One year the usual package arrived. The ritual was enacted, the honey cake unwrapped, tasted, wrapped, and raised on high. Two weeks later, the loaf turned green. My father immediately picked up the phone, calling not Dora, but Dora's daughter, Sylvia, by then living in Buffalo, another scattered remnant of a once-coherent tribe.

Yes, she admitted at last, her mother had not been well, but Dora had refused to upset the family. She, Sylvia, had made the honey cake. What made him wonder, anyway? Didn't it taste the same?

October

DIASPORA

October

A new year in the Jewish calendar. I pause to consider it. I give myself this year to this calendar, to see where it takes me. I have been so mixed in my own mind.

Not so much a brand-new beginning as intensifying. We have been lighting candles at least some Friday nights for some years, though self-consciously. The children like it. So do I. What is the meaning of the lights? Weekday darkness, Sabbath illumination. The world out there, the spirit in here. Lights of the city versus lights of home.

Recently we light candles more often. Every Friday, more or less. We aim the week in their direction. Subtly, the week incorporates their shape. Friday evening becomes a time to gather, a family island, a quietness in the week's flutter and noise. We are staying home most Saturdays, venturing to synagogue now and again, a family together.

The candles, at first, were purely of the past, a way to bring tradition tangibly home. It was a nice way to remember, to gather those scattered Friday nights of candles strewn over childhood's inconsistent terrain. A token of memory, and also of history, the collective remembrance far beyond memory's reach.

Now the rhythm is itself compelling. Sabbath is becoming a gift to us, one we are choosing and wrapping ourselves and then opening with a kind of astonished surprise. I can't say precisely when it happened. All I know is this: Saturday morning cartoons, errands, and bill-paying once were the standard. Now such mornings seem empty, barren, a cheat.

We will try for a Sabbath more often, think about holidays in advance. But I remain cautious. I long drew from observant households a metaphor never written in the Book: the symbolic sacrifice not of Isaac but the Mother. The mother who bends the course of life to have everything ready for that Friday night, who brings in the Sabbath but never rests.

And always, I have feared my own obsessions. I fear losing myself and then discovering my location is a point of no return.

The Sabbath, one of Ten Commandments. As important as not murdering, as ancient as the knowledge that envy can tear the heart out of human life. Are the Rules still rules to live by, for those such as me, raised to pick and choose, raised without God? Does the peace of Sabbath pertain, without the Divine to enforce it? I have never been much interested in whether God is, or is not. I have not believed it matters, either way.

Piety aside, I cherish the cultural forms. I don't like to see them fade away. But I don't know if regret contains meaning, in this great wide universe of ours. There are so many sources of wistful regret to choose from, so many different clocks to mark time.

For the moment I will try Sabbath, and stop all our clocks, step out of time. I will light the candles and watch them burn, and think about it. So far with no sense of obligation, no sense of commandment. I will recite prayers, but to What or to Whom?

CHOLENT

I came to New York to meet the family of the man I was seeing, the man I would one day marry. I still have the dress I wore to dinner that Friday evening so many years ago. With this dress, navy blue and yellow, I have not been able to part. It is stowed away in the attic in a dusty cardboard box.

In the clean, light, family home I met a constellation of handsome faces: Miriam and Jacob, my boyfriend's parents, and Miriam's mother, Rivke, who always lived with Miriam after the war. The other relatives had gathered from far places—Israel, Paris, Cleveland—for the wedding of a cousin, to be held the following night. I heard four languages. I could but count to ten in three.

Miriam welcomed me with hope, excitement. She wanted to do right; I wanted to do right. We were nervous, Miriam and I.

Why nervous? I was planning never to marry, intended to live as a free and untamed spirit. But faced with Miriam's Yiddish accent, and the family, and the look in Miriam's eyes that plainly asked, *Are you the one for my only son?,* my position felt suddenly confused, and I wanted only to please.

The house dazzled clean. I took in the yellow sofa, the sparkling crystal, the china figurines. My boyfriend's relatives nibbled grapes and almonds. They smiled warm and bright in my direction. I perched on a tawny velour-covered chair, under a painting of Jaffa-by-the-Sea.

We were summoned to dine. Rivke, the *savta*—grandmother in Hebrew, for my husband had lived childhood in Israel—labored with her steel walking cane, and reached her dining chair. Her platinum hair was beautifully waved, her careful outfit a pastel paleness, lavender or blue. Small old diamonds set in white gold adorned her. The grandmother settled regally, and we all sat down.

We made a blessing, shared a *l'chaim*. We drank a schnapps, Cherry Heering in delicate small stemmed goblets of etched glass. Radiating pleasure, Miriam set a large steaming bowl in the center of the table, to appreciative murmurs. It was cholent, the famous Sabbath dish of the Ashkenazic

Jews. In Miriam's house it was *chulent,* pronounced with a long "u" in the Polish way.

I had heard tell of cholent. During my childhood my mother spoke of cholent as of lost wealth, a piece of the glistering past. Her mother used to make it. Although no two cholents or *chulents* are exactly alike, my mother's mother was said to prepare one very like this: beans, barley, potatoes, onions, and meat, baked in a crock for hours. I had never partaken, only imagined.

In Europe, the housewives brought their cholent pots to the baker on Fridays. The thick brick walls of the baker's big bread oven held the heat overnight and into the next day, without the addition of fuel, allowing the casserole-stew-pudding to bake hot and slow—*chaud* and *lent,* perhaps. This afforded a warm, savory meal on Sabbath, when no fire could be lit in the stoves at home. When my mother was a child, in her mother's Canadian outpost, the Sabbath dish was slow-cooked in the basement furnace, on a bed of glowing coal.

All that was past, gone, unrecoverable. But Miriam never let it go. Under her mother's eye, Miriam established cholent for the present. Her mother, the silvery matriarch of the dinner table, had guarded culinary specialties in her mind during years when possessions and certainties were ripped from her hands. The family cooking reprised the village past. But it also came to mark the rhythm of the life Miriam now lived for its own sake.

That first Friday night was all thrilling impressions. Later I learned other things. This cholent began at five in the morning and baked in a low gas oven all day. Miriam, once a girl eating dinner in her mother's restaurant, became through chance and conviction over the years, a woman who gets up at five in the morning to fry onions, because a cholent needs onions both raw and fried, and a cholent must bake for hours.

CHOLENT

(Miriam uses the same $20 ovenproof pot to fry the onion, boil the barley, and bake the cholent.)

1 lb. beef flanken (short ribs)
3 to 4 beef or veal marrow bones
1 raw onion, chopped
3 to 4 Idaho potatoes, diced into
   1½-inch pieces
Paprika
1 tbsp. salt
1 onion, diced for sautéeing

Pepper
Oil
1 carrot, grated
¾ to 1 cup barley, rinsed
1 stalk celery, thinly sliced or
   grated
½ to ¾ cup dried kidney beans,
   rinsed

Place the beef flanken and marrow bones into a large pot. Cover with water. Bring to a boil; drain, rinse the bones and the meat, then set both aside.

Mix together the chopped raw onion, potatoes, and paprika. Set the mixture aside.

Dissolve 1 tbsp. salt in ½ cup water.

Put onions in an ovenproof pot or casserole. Sprinkle with pepper and cook over low heat until dry. Cover onion with oil and fry over medium heat until golden crisp. Stir in the carrot and turn off heat.

Add 2 cups water, barley, and celery to the pot. Cook, covered, until the water is absorbed (about 20 minutes). Empty the contents of the pot into a bowl.

Preheat oven to 350°F.

Assemble the cholent in the ovenproof pot:

"Lay the bones and meat to the bottom of the pot." Alternate layers of potatoes, barley, and vegetable mix, and beans. Top with a layer of barley and vegetable so that the cholent will stay moist. Pour salt water over all. Add enough clear water to cover the mixture. Cook on stove, covered, to boiling point.

Place in preheated oven. When contents "boil," turn oven down to 275°F. Bake for at least 8 hours.

Turn out upside down into a serving bowl (Miriam). Or dish directly out of the casserole. Serve some meat with every portion. Keep the marrow bones for yourself.

Yield: Serves six as a main course

ZION

$\mathcal{M}$y father, born in Brooklyn, went to Detroit as a young man in 1948. He never meant to stay, exactly, but he had stayed. He never quite changed his colors from east to midwest, never quite acculturated, never was quite at home in Detroit, and neither were we, his children. New York, where I had never lived, was home.

New York was our reference point, our Old Country, our wellspring. Over time, it came to be more, to contain and to embody our aspirations. The possibility of returning to New York my father kept open always. The matter turned in his mind. New York was the golden city to the east. It was the ideal. New York was Zion.

In the diaspora of my childhood, I felt myself to be the outsider. We were renters, in a town of owners. We didn't have a swing set in the back-yard or a cottage on the lake. We weren't synagogue members with a jovial golf-playing dad and a mom in the Sisterhood. We weren't off to suburbs with most other Jews. I didn't celebrate Christmas, I didn't eat milk with meat. I didn't believe that "the policeman is your friend." My father had gone to jail for civil rights, implying the opposite.

My favorite sandwiches—sardines and onions on pumpernickel; cream cheese, olives, and walnuts; chopped liver on *kiml* bread, the crusty cara-way corn rye—were the objects of hilarious derision in the school lunch-room. Kids refused to sit near me, the very ones with Miracle Whip oozing out of their lunch meat and Wonder Bread.

In New York, I thought, I would Belong. New York would solve all my problems. I never wanted to live anywhere but the Jerusalem of my father's youth. The trips home to Brooklyn only sharpened my yearning. These pilgrimages inflamed, rather than satisfied the soul.

Once, twice a year, usually spring but occasionally fall, we would breathlessly ask our teachers for extra schoolwork—sometimes several weeks' schoolwork—to take away to New York. At six o'clock in the morning, we all were awake, roused for an early start. My father spent the fresh hours of day in our driveway trying to pack a challenging volume of luggage into the vast trunk of our Plymouth. Hours of tense excitement would pass, in which my mother might be forced to stridently defend the number of shoes, the variety of outfits, the abundance of garment bags. You had to have raincoats. Transitional weather was unpredictable.

We kids sat on the front steps, eating the salami sandwiches, fruit, and Fig Newtons intended for lunch on the road. We crayoned, read comic books, worked through our math problems, busied ourselves with all the activities that were supposed to occupy children quietly across Michigan, Ohio, Pennsylvania, New Jersey, and into New York State. In the car itself, of course, we would be riotous, crazed.

Finally, as the sun drifted west and the day took on a still, luminous quality, we were summoned to depart. My father drove late into the night at eighty-five miles an hour—there were no speed limits on the turnpikes then—passing oil tankers and freight trucks, to make up the time. We counted tunnels, stopped frequently, nagged fruitlessly to turn off the road for this tourist attraction or that. We were asleep by the time he pulled into Donegal or Tall Timbers, motels in the Pennsylvania mountains. It was a long, two-day trip in those days.

My grandmother still lived in the childhood home, the red-brick two-family house commanding a sun-splashed corner at the top of a long, two-block hill. My father's parents had built the house in the nation's burst of optimism a few years before the Great Depression. There, our grandmother kept up her housework, chatted with neighbors, and worried about our father, her son, who seemed to have little, if any, desire for personal, material success. On the kitchen window sill my grandmother kept an arsenal of pebbles to fire at stray dogs who got into her privet hedge.

The interior seemed to us grand, furnished in carved mahogany wood, marble, and crystal. The dining room chairs were upholstered in garnet-red velvet, and you sat up high on their springs. Gold curtains glowed in the sun parlor, where my parents would sleep on the daybed, after my father once again got the hang of the mysterious, not to say dangerous, mechanism that levered a single width of mattress into more.

My grandmother's room was a tidy jewelbox of kept secrets, which she would reveal in her own good time. In the other bedroom, we children quietly opened closets and drawers on our own, to review the sacred, ancient relics among which we would sleep.

At my grandmother's house we entered my father's childhood.

We explored the Brooklyn streets together, we children and our father. We heard his stories, imagined his days, absorbed the atmosphere. The streets were full of noises, interest: cobblestone still, in places. Once horse-drawn wagons rattled here. Cars on the steep hill stopped at the traffic light, transmissions struggling against gravity. People puffed along with packages. We were outside with our dad. Our mother remained indoors, helping with the housework, and trying to please her mother-in-law.

From the neighborhood children I learned stoop and sidewalk games. We bounced a hard rubber ball to an alphabet play: A my name is Ada and my husband's name is Abe we live in Alabama and we sell . . . Alligators.

There was a park down the street, where my father had played stick-ball and basketball and games of pretend. We had the playground with its hopscotch grid and big steel swings to ourselves on weekdays, until the neighborhood kids came running after school. My father approved of the social life of stoop, street, and park. He opposed the inward-turning anomie of TV in the den, of the backyard swing set. My father's playground offered righteousness and joy.

Behind the playground was a deep, wild park, with abandoned walk-ways and bridges, broken street lamps and unkempt stretches of green. Our dad showed us where heavy rain would turn a passage into a river. He and his friends would build and launch rafts, and play pirates. We climbed up to the vast reservoir, around which my great-grandmother, the magisterial Rivke Blume, had promenaded daily until her death at ninety-three. Beyond were the cemeteries and houses of Queens, also the parkway that had sliced up the neighborhood and added to the pressures on my grandfather's pharmacy, the family business, after the Crash.

The pharmacy was down the boulevard the other way. Around a corner, beneath an overpass, my father showed me his initials, where long ago he had carved them into wet cement. Past was visible. There was the store, owned by someone else now, edged by the parkway no one would bother to cross for a pack of cigarettes, an egg cream, a tin of lozenges. My father stood outside letting memory wash over him. I could not help him but I held his hand.

We visited neighbors who had watched my dad grow up. I took out a borrower's card at the oak-paneled, cavernous, echoing library in which my father had discovered King Arthur, Huck Finn, and Penrod and Sam.

I soaked up his stories of childhood until his childhood seemed more real to me than my own. I knew about the time he and his gang got into a neighbor's vat of sauerkraut and ate until they were sick. That was the last time he ate sauerkraut. I saw the house wherein, invited to view a Christmas tree, my father had tripped on the light cord and upset the whole thing, his pure mortification truly a Jewish memory. He pointed out the apartment house where had lived his aunt, the dear beautiful aunt who, although blind, made a home for a husband and three children, and made ends meet by selling eggs from a basket door to door.

Here in my father's old haunts I had footprints to walk in, ghosts to conjure. I sat on my grandmother's stoop chewing the ends of my hair, sometimes just watching the traffic pass until it was time to go in. In New York I belonged to my father.

One year, Rosh Hashanah, the Jewish New Year, fell right when it should, mid-September. I was the best age, ten, and I owned sharp clothes that fall: shiny checked drop-waisted dresses, one blue-green, one brown, a white button-down blouse, a plaid kilt, matching kneesocks. My raincoat reversed from floral violet to antique gold, and the umbrella was see-through.

This wardrobe hung in my grandmother's closet. We were in New York for the fall holidays, a long three-week stretch. The school year, barely begun, was cheerfully disrupted, and my father, who was not working, saw no great need to hurry back.

The weather was clear azure autumn. Our family never took summer vacations, because July and August were busy months in my dad's trade. So now, under a benevolent sky, we leisured and played. We went to the planetarium. We went to the automat, inserted our coins and received lemon pie. We swam for hours in the rough cold ocean at Coney Island, a beach bereft of lifeguards and summer crowds, as cawing gulls circled overhead. We sated our hunger with franks and fries, strolled the board-walk, drinking in the carnival sadness of the place.

For a handful of dimes we shivered in wind and spray, on the Staten Island ferry, leaving Manhattan and riding back. We pressed up to the rails to gaze at green Liberty, as my mother, along on a rare excursion, declaimed, " 'Give me your tired . . .' "

The new dresses came to my grandmother's table for holiday dinners and Sabbath meals. We called on the great-aunts, the grand-uncles. We saw cousins and children of cousins my father had known as a Brooklyn boy. At the tattered synagogue where he had been a bar mitzvah, the door was unlocked, and a remnant of old people *davened* (prayed) within. My father took me down cellar to the *cheder* room, where the children had studied. Behind the mustiness of the classroom seeped a vile odor of neglected plumbing. Books were scattered on desks and benches and lectern, their brown pages open as if all the Jews had suddenly blown off the face of the earth.

One crisp afternoon, my father took me alone to the Lower East Side. We walked the streets where my grandfather had been an immigrant boy in knee-pants, and by the age of thirteen, man of a family—widowed mother and children six. I saw Hebrew letters on awnings, sidecurls on men, smelled dill pickles in the air. A bright-eyed addled old hag nibbling a matzo cracker gave me her blessing. *Jerusalem.*

We passed from sunlight and traffic through big swinging doors to the dim cool Essex Street Market. A brick shell, high ceiling, and chicken-wire windows surrounded what had once been open-air pushcarts, and retained a raffish double-parked look. The walls echoed the primeval din of trade. Smells reverberated: raw food, dry goods, roach spray, filthy layers of floor.

Here, a cart vending buttons and notions, stockings, gloves, under-wear, hair nets. There, cheese. At a long, refrigerated counter selling kosher meat, my handsome father stopped, as if unintentionally. An aproned woman attended him with interest. He was casual, diffident—cool and smooth as a perma-press raincoat. He chose a package of lean red steak. Farsighted, he examined it at arm's length. His wallet opened.

"You're a lucky girl," said the counter lady to me, appraisingly. "Your father takes you to Essex Market."

That same ineffable week, the week between Rosh Hashanah and Yom Kippur, my father took me to visit his old public school. I wore the white shirt, the plaid kilt, the kneesocks. The principal, a brisk woman with fluffy white hair, seemed to recall my father by name; in his time she had been a newly minted teacher there. She took me up to the sixth grade classroom, and let me sit in for the morning. The pupils asked questions about Detroit.

"Did you see a car get made?" asked a cute boy named Victor. He had black curly hair and pudgy hands, and he was impressed when I said yes.

At recess Victor told everyone I was his girlfriend. That moved me. No one wanted to be my boyfriend in Detroit. In Detroit I was a misfit, an onion roll amongst cupcakes. In Brooklyn, I was among my own kind, yet almost a cupcake myself.

IRISH MARY

"*I* was born in Ireland," she used to say, though not to me. She died long before my time. She was my great-grandmother, known down to the present day among us by this name: Irish Mary. Her real name was Mary Brown. In 1880 or so, she married into my grandfather's family, who were *Litvaks,* Lithuanian Jews. In fact, she herself was a *Litvak.* Her marriage to my great-grandfather united two local families in the district of Kovno, a town not far from Vilna.

The families lived in Shott, a small, obscure Jewish village or *shtetl* attached to Kovno. Shott was never easy to find on a map, even when gazetteers traced out the Jewish Pale of Settlement in partitioned Poland, back in the time of Mary Brown. Now Shott has vanished from the earth, and its principals have turned to earth. Still the claims of Irish Mary will be heard.

"It's a cock and bull story," my mother's cousin Rocky used to say. "She was Irish like I'm Chinese."

Mary, his grandmother, spoke English with the same accent— *Litvishe* Yiddish—as everyone else. Her eldest sons had brought her over to the States from Lithuania, with her husband, my great-grandfather, and the younger children, in 1911 or 1912. She died in Detroit in the 1930s.

"They stopped for a while in England on the way to America, that's all. Mary's brother, Yankele, was living in London for a few years. But Irish?" Cousin Rocky would visit my mother, sit in a big tweed armchair, set his hands on his knees, and laugh.

Still, family lore has it, and I have heard all my life, that Mary Brown's father moved his family from Lithuania to Ireland in the 1860s. Irish Mary was born there. Things did not go well for the Browns, who may or may not have been deported over a usury charge. They returned to Lithuania, and Mary wedded Zalman, my great-grandfather, the son of a fruit farmer in Shott. Jews were not allowed to grow grain in the Pale of Settlement.

Fourteen children over twenty years, beginning in 1882, were their issue. Eight survived.

For years I have hoped the story could be true. As the granddaughter of Polish Jews, whose childhood homes can never be found, I enjoyed placing my young great-grandmother in Dublin or Cork. I see a young girl playing "London Bridge" on the street, see a dewy adolescent with ropes of glossy hair pinned about her head under a cap of Irish lace—learning to keep a kosher kitchen in a land of silver poetry, nationalist yearnings, and mythical sprites. Perhaps she loved Ireland, with the intense investment that the child of immigrants may feel. Perhaps the rare fact of her Irish birth made her truly a daughter of the soil. Not just born there, but Irish.

And if she loved Ireland, how was it to leave under a cloud of injustice or suspicion or shame? How would it have been for her to move from the shadow of the great Irish cathedrals where a Jew was unusual but not the sworn enemy, to see for the last time that particular emerald light? What did she think, arriving at the Lithuanian *shtetl* her parents called home, and then how was it to raise a Yiddish-speaking brood under the threat of arbitrary Cossack violence?

Had she quietly sung lilting Gaelic lullabies to her babies, settling them down at nighttime in a few crowded *shtetl* beds? With her children too busy to notice, did Mary speak English at once on arriving in Detroit, a woman of fifty then? And when she slept, what were the location of Mary's dreams?

Zalman, Mary's husband, was not known to have had any particular occupation. He may have known the shoe-making trade, and he may have been a *Ba'al Tefilah,* a lay prayer leader, which would have made him a rather learned man even among Jewish men of his time and place, who were universally literate and frequently pious. But he was not known for his hard work in the world. He was a good-natured man, one for a song and a story. As father to eight, as husband to Mary, by all accounts, he was not much.

Her daydreams must have been Ireland. She caught herself recalling Ireland's colors and sounds, neighbors' greetings, horses and wagon wheels, sparkling sunrises, carefree childhood. She thought about these things as she washed her husband's socks in a wooden tub, or set her Sabbath challah to rise. At least at first she thought of them, when the children were young and she was young, when the memories still were bright.

• • •

"I remember your great-grandfather," says Cousin Sol, a man nearly ninety with a young man's voice, and a head full of history. "He was my mother's brother. I remember sitting on his lap in my mother's kitchen, near the stove. I was the youngest one. He would stroke his beard and sing to me in a sweet, small voice." And Sol sings gently:

Fli oy fli oy gildene feygele	Fly oh fly oh little golden bird
Iber ale yamen	Over all the seas
Lozt g'risn	Bring this message
Der vayb un di kinderlekh	To my wife and my children
Un mayn tayrn mamen	And to my dear mother . . .

This was more than eighty years ago. Sol closes his cloudy eyes as he sings. Sol was a little boy when his Uncle Zalman made the train trip from Detroit to London, Ontario, for an open-ended visit. This was not unusual for Zalman, who had no job to leave and two adoring older sisters in Ontario to visit, and besides, seems to have preferred almost anything to staying home with Mary, his wife.

We sit at Sol's table late into the evening. It is Friday night, and Sabbath candles are burning.

"Mary Brown's family spoke Yiddish in Ireland," comments Cousin Sol, with authority. "Naturally. They were *Litvaks,* from Shott."

"Family stories?" Sol's wife interrupts in a loud, humorous voice. She is ninety-two years old and practically deaf. "Solly's ma was quite a gal! All the sailors wanted to make it with her on the boat," she shouts, "even if she was pregnant, with a baby nursing at her chest!"

Sol's mother, in fact, the sister of my great-grandfather Zalman, once was engaged to wed Yankele Brown, the brother of Irish Mary. Yankele, grown up by the time the family returned to the Kovno district, had remained (perhaps) in the British Isles. Sol's mother broke off the engagement, and the gossip still tingles more than a century later. It was the 1880s. . . .

"She got to London and found out that Yankele wasn't a kosher Jew anymore." We are all at a family reunion and a cousin from Sol's branch of the clan stands at a microphone. A tape recorder runs. My mother's cousins are taking their turns with the family tales.

"She found out he smoked on the Sabbath. She wouldn't have him after that," asserts the cousin.

My mother pulls herself up with hauteur at this hoary slander. "Do you realize that is the elder brother of my grandmother Mary Brown Glassman of whom you are speaking?" she mutters into the air.

There were Jews in Ireland. It was possible for Joyce's Leopold Bloom to buy a pork kidney on June 16, 1904, and to recall his "poor papa" reading the Passover service from right to left. *("Takes practice, that.")* And Charles Stewart Parnell, Irish Home Rule partisan, born in 1846, was of Jewish descent. So claimed his mother, Delia Tudor.

Irish Mary, I surmise, raised her eight children in Shott for the most part alone. Zalman, my great-grandfather, was not one to stay home. He was said to be a traveler, a man who left his wife and family for long stretches to wander the crust of the earth. From the district of Kovno, Lithuania, he visited the capitals of Russia and Europe, cadging rides on wagons, walking, riding trains, finagling passage on boats . . . who knows how or why.

He didn't work. He sent his sons out to work. There were six of them, and one by one, they were apprenticed to cobblers at a young age. Once, the great rabbis of a famed Vilna yeshiva exclaimed over the brilliance of Lazar, my grandfather, who knew the Hebrew prayer book and more by heart at the age of ten. The examining rabbis offered to house and educate the boy without a *groschen* in payment. His father, Zalman, turned the examiners away.

"I don't have children to study Torah. I have children to support my old age," he told the somber men. And it was a soulless, spiritless religion that my grandfather came to practice in the end.

Mary kept her house with the coins that my hapless grandfather and his brothers earned while learning their craft. And Zalman, the father of these boys, wandered the world. They say he got to China and Japan, to South Africa and Australia, between his visits home to Shott.

In the 1960s, when many of the Old Ones were still alive, my mother tried to get to the bottom of these traveling tales. Our immigrants insisted on their truth—though they had witnessed only the circumstantial facts:

Zalman's long disappearances, Zalman's assertions. According to himself, Zalman Glassman actually went to America three times on his own, and returned to Shott. This was before his eldest sons emigrated, before the sons brought the father to Detroit to live out his restless life.

And what of Mary, stuck home in some sort of small, poor home far from Ireland with eight children to raise while her husband rambled God knows where—to Africa or only to the other side of the mountain, who will ever know—with a pack on his shoulder and a song on his lips about little birds in flight? Did she long for her escape or accept her destiny? Did her husband in fact leave only when Mary threw him out, and return when she relented?

All I know of my great-grandmother comes from what she left in the world, her line of children and grandchildren. There were two daughters as well as six sons, and the daughters turned out determined, strong, and tough. They must have learned this from Mary.

"It's just a cock and bull story. . . ."

I have wondered long enough, I desire facts. I pay a visit to a library and find call letters for the Irish Jews. Opening books, I read. Jews have lived on the Emerald Isle from early times, Spanish Jews escaping the Inquisition, German Jews, communities from England—drawn by Ireland's unusual record of tolerance toward the Jews. . . .

And then I read this: *The present Jewish community and its founders of the 1860s were almost exclusively composed of Lithuanian origin hailing from the districts of Vilna and Kovno.* Here are tales of arrivals, sagas of rival synagogues, politicians urging tolerance. Here are peddlers and housewives, teachers and ladies of charity, throwing down roots in Limerick, Dublin, Belfast, Cork, Londonderry, Ligroin, Dundalk.

It didn't work out for the father of Mary Brown.

. . . a record of tolerance toward Jews, broken only by the rare charge of usury, the rare blood libel. . . .

She didn't hold it against them, this daughter of the soil. "I was born in Ireland," Mary, my great-grandmother, used to say. And so she was.

MIRIAM'S KITCHEN

$\mathcal{M}$iriam wakes very early, and gets up right away.

"I can't stay in bed," she apologizes when I arrive at her house. What she means is she got started without me.

For me, this is early. I sped off from home without shower or breakfast to arrive at this hour. Now I slip out of shoes at the front door, and work my stocking feet, which have never seemed so large and woolly, into an extra pair of Miriam's house slippers. Pink vinyl, little wedge heels. Miriam wears the beige pair. House shoes are the comfortable custom here. It keeps the floor clean.

"She was downstairs by five o'clock," puts in Jacob, as if this were a new, amazing discovery.

I have heard this sentence, with this very inflection, perhaps hundreds of times. Invariably, too, I have been welcomed with this same quiet, gracious gesture, as Jacob takes my jacket to hang in the small, tidy closet, closes the door, returns to his living room chair and the Yiddish papers. Nearly eighty, he is slight, ageless, formally dressed in worn, clean, ironed, unfashionable clothing, shirt and tie. These are my husband's parents, the grandparents of my children.

"If I lie still, I am thinking, and I don't want to think anymore," Miriam says. Her blue eyes plead and challenge, deep in her moist, lined, luminous, beautiful face, the ever hopeful eyes of the child she was when childhood ended in 1939, in Poland. She was twelve years old.

She brushes something off the front of her smock, a loose housedress brightly patterned—her everyday housework attire. Today each hour is accounted for and the outcome is a certain thing. The day has rhythm and coherence, only for the work of these stiff, pearly hands. Miriam stands, waiting.

I am welcome, and I am a disruption. There is no one else to learn the recipes.

"Would you like something? A coffee, a tea?" she asks. "A roll with cheese? A tuna salad?"

These are polite, company offerings. From September to May, Miriam and Jacob eat oatmeal for breakfast. From May to September, cold cereal. Breakfast is a thing to be got through, in the gray dawn.

Now, the empty kitchen sink, burnished and buffed, glows under a bright window, framed with crisp lace curtains and a sill full of dusted houseplants. A precise number of breakfast spoons and saucers are dried and placed away. In the air, a vibrating urgency to get on with the day, along with a faint scent of raw liver.

My temples throb with the memory of coffee, stomach growls.

"Oh, no," I say. "Just fine." I know she cannot stand to wait another second.

"Then we can start with the *leybern*." *Leybern*—livers. *Lukshn mit leybern*: chicken livers with noodles. I am here to learn this, and next Friday, something else. For my husband, and for our children.

It is far too early to think of liver, the thought makes me gag. Then I remember my first taste of this dish. Just home from the hospital with Miriam's first grandchild, I found her in my kitchen, warming her pot on my stove and insisting I come to the table.

"You must get your strength back," she said.

Leave me alone, I had thought, as the steamy, superstitious fragrance of Jewish Poland wafted into the bedroom and behind my eyelids. I wanted to sleep, more than I ever wanted anything.

"You have to," said my husband, ignoring my scowl. "My mother cooked." Clumsy and depressed, I sat down on the chair. Then I lifted the fork, sauce dripping from the noodles.

The richness, the oil, the iron, the cholesterol, the onion, the salt overtook my body like an intravenous drug. Miriam beamed. "It's good," she stated. The baby cried out, and my milk came in. There has never been a dish like this one.

"But you've already done it," I reproach her now, ungrateful daughter-in-law that I am. Miriam always cooks first thing in the morning, in a division of act and appetite that is utterly foreign to me. The cooking must be finished or like all incomplete actions, it is a burden on the heart.

"All I did was clean them," protests Miriam, displaying a small broiler tray arranged with glistening, ruby lumps. I would have liked to see her arthritic, manicured hands working a knife over fat and connective tissue, rinsing, slicing. "I wanted you to see this yellow thing—it is gall. You must clean it away, or it would be bitter."

"Biter vi gal." Jacob, just audible in the distant living room chair, quotes the Yiddish colloquial phrase.

She must have found it hard to contain herself, to have the livers cleaned and ready, and then have to wait, idly. She has already diced a large onion and set it in a bowl, ready to use, just like in a cooking show on TV. Faded old linens cover counters and floors, to catch stray drips or spills. All the pots, utensils, and ingredients we will need are set out on these. After the cooking is over, Miriam will carefully gather up the lengths of cloth, shake them over the back porch rail, launder and put them away.

I tiptoe here, damp paper towel crumpled in my hand, ready to wipe away any offense. When I cook at home, liquids spray through the air, puffs of flour blow and settle, the soles of my shoes turn to mud on the damp floor. I may peel onions over the dirty dishes in the sink or balance a colander on an unwashed coffee pot. While garlic sizzles and beans boil, I race about the kitchen looking for recipe items, or sink to my knees pulling equipment out of cupboards. The smoke alarm sounds. I forgot to use the fan.

In Miriam's kitchen the livers wait in the broiler tray of the toaster oven.

"It cleans by itself," explains Miriam. She has a self-cleaning toaster oven. Even so, for the livers, the toaster oven is lined entirely with foil, even the little glass window in front. "It's not worth it to use the big oven just for this."

Miriam doesn't broil in her stove. "It is too much to clean," she says.

Yet broil she must. In a kosher kitchen, meat must be free of blood. This is a mark of respect to another living creature, a symbol of the regret with which we indulge our carnal natures. Flesh must be salted and soaked, to wash away the life fluid before cooking. Liver, which cannot be soaked and salted like other meats, must be broiled so that the blood runs out.

These chicken livers, cut to bite size, are gently broiled, then drained on paper towels. The toaster oven is wiped out. Spotless.

You see, each appliance and pan in Miriam's kitchen gleams as if it were new. There is no patina of grease. She wouldn't leave a broiler pan soaking overnight. All the hard black lumps, sticky brown spatters inside a big oven, would have to be scraped, scoured, and wiped dry that same day.

Kashrut—being and keeping kosher—is part of it. You clean after one meal, which may be a meat meal, to be ready to prepare the next, which may be dairy. But there is more than ritual observance in Miriam's itch to wipe the slate clean. As a small girl, I think, she wanted most to be good. And so it was done in her mother's house, in a world that is gone forever, except here, in Miriam's kitchen.

Many women of Miriam's generation and background have moved toward broiled fish or chicken. But Miriam stays with her chopping bowl, soup pot, and frying pan, with the old labor-intensive recipes, the rich and salty ways.

"This is healthy," declares Jacob. He has a full head of black hair, and all his own teeth. He still drives to work three days a week, and he eats this food every night. Science will vindicate Miriam, predicts my husband, a man who believes that deep-fried cauliflower is a vegetable.

"Do you have something to write down on?" she asks. Somehow, I never do, here. For years I worked as a magazine reporter. I wore a blue suit, and never was without my spiral notebooks and extra pens. But nothing I have done in the big world beyond is of use or relevance here. In Miriam's kitchen, I must reach into her supply of scratch paper—cut-up cardboard neatly stacked in a box—and the hand-sharpened number 2 pencils preserved from my husband's school days.

Nothing is wasted here, not an object, not a motion, not a bit of paper, certainly not a bit of food. Miriam's father, ill with typhoid, died of starvation in Buchenwald. How could she throw away food, she asks, her hands tightened into fists, when her father died of hunger?

"Write down," commands Miriam. "One large or two small onions." The tiny onion squares sweat, their scent drawn up into the stove fan. Only when the onion is hot and dry does she add oil. "This takes away all the bitterness," she claims. "My mother taught me this."

I remember the carefully dressed little woman, Miriam's mother, bent over her walker. Miriam was lucky to have come through the war with her mother. As a young bride, after the war, she had learned from her mother how to do.

Miriam pours oil, a lot, straight from the jar. It is a luxurious gesture. For a moment we are in a land of peace and plenty. Time stops as we watch the oil flow.

Her mother, she believes, was the real cook. "She knew so many recipes, and not from a recipe either," she has said. Miriam's mother was a creative cook, where Miriam mainly cooks by rote. Even after the last terrible thing happened, a few years ago, when Miriam lost her sense of taste and smell, each dish has been perfect, just enough salt, or sugar, or garlic, or vinegar.

She was with me that day, when a blood vessel burst inside her skull. I was waiting in the car while Miriam went to the bakery, a quick stop en route to a party for my brother's bride. Miriam walked past my car, two pastry boxes in her hands, looking frightened and confused. I ran after her. My sister, a doctor, called the ambulance against Miriam's protests and rode shotgun through the wilds of emergency decision-making. Our co-hostess, the bride's sister, somehow kept the party afloat.

Seven hours' microsurgery of the brain Miriam endured, while Jacob wept and prayed and threw his sixty-five-year smoking habit into the bargain, a vow he kept. Everything came back—miraculous—except taste and smell. Is it ungrateful to bemoan what was withheld, the senses essential to Miriam's understanding of life: that preparation of food is duty and love, while the partaking is pleasure and community? Life was given, but at this price. Still, she bested it, healed to cook again, to create the world again, by memory. This is what survival is.

Can I use less oil, I wonder?

With a plastic spatula, she mixes onions and oil, frying until the onions are just golden. My mouth is watering. Now I could eat the whole panful on toast, with a large cup of coffee. She stirs in the livers, turns up the heat.

"A few minutes, you cook them."

She washes the bowl that held the onions. She wipes it dry, puts it away. There is nothing for my hands to do.

"I have to get a new letter," announces Jacob. He is at the kitchen table. He moves so quietly, sparely, I hadn't noticed him walk in.

In thick black reading glasses, he is pulling onionskin sheets from a yellow envelope. Letters from doctors over the years, attesting to health losses during the war. Now the German government, which pays restitution to my in-laws each month, has offered to increase payments for medical reasons.

Miriam adds a bit of flour to the livers, to thicken the sauce. She spoons in a bit of sugar, in the manner of Polish Jews, who used to put sugar in everything, from fish to bread.

"Now hot water, just to cover it, and you boil them, ten or fifteen minutes."

I write. "Boil 10 to 15 minutes." It doesn't look or sound right. I'm used to cookbooks, and such terms as simmer and sauté.

I look at the first letter, dated 1968, signed by a doctor who too survived Hitler. I have never seen this list of breathing problems, broken nose, depression, nightmares. "The patient," states the careful English of Dr. Steiner, "will never live a normal life."

"Nightmares?" I ask stupidly.

"Both of us," says Miriam. "I wake him up and he wakes me."

Jacob removes his glasses. I have known him for fifteen years, and only now see his crooked nose. One day Jacob paused for breath while digging ditches and laying pipe. In an instant, a rifle's butt came down hard on his face. The place was Chestochowa, a concentration camp in Poland, where Miriam, a girl of seventeen, met Jacob, then twenty-nine.

They were the lucky ones, sent to a work camp, and not to a death camp. Jacob's mother died in Auschwitz, with all his sisters but one.

"The German police," Miriam spits, telling me about Jacob's nose, savagely broken. I am trying to understand the force of that sudden pain, blood in the throat and mouth, what was said, what Jacob said to himself, what place he went away to in his mind, what he left there.

"They beat my mother, too," recounts Miriam. "A Polish girl we knew used to smuggle bread to her in the camp, and they found a loaf. My mother wouldn't tell where she got it." Miriam blows her nose. "Seventy-five lashes she got, on the back." Then, for twelve hours, my husband's grandmother was forced to stand on a thin board balanced over a fast-moving stream, while a soldier stood guard.

"If she would fall or sit down, he was going to shoot her," Miriam says.

I remember the little woman, her hair coifed, gold rings in her ears, bent over her walker, with Miriam in the kitchen.

"They made an example," says Miriam. "She was not the same woman after that."

We are silent. There is nothing to say. Jacob folds the letter. He sets his glasses on the table.

Miriam measures, salts, stirs again. She presses back the past just for a little while. "Now you would make the noodles."

I write down "salt" and "noodles."

"Egg noodles, the medium thick ones. Or mashed potatoes. My mother used to make it this way sometimes, with potatoes. Delicious."

"It smells so so good," I say.

"It is for you," says Miriam. "For you and your family. And now, a cup of tea?"

I will have tea now, with sugar—Miriam's way—and drink it slowly, here in the kitchen, a room so warm, and so full.

LUKSHN MIT LEYBERN
(CHICKEN LIVERS WITH NOODLES)

1 lb. chicken livers
1 large onion, diced
Black pepper
$^1/_4$ cup vegetable oil
$^3/_4$ tbsp. flour

$^3/_4$ tbsp. sugar
$^1/_4$ tsp. salt
Egg noodles (medium width)
Hot water

Clean chicken livers. Slice into generous bite-size pieces. Broil gently until done, then drain on toweling.

Place onion in medium saucepan and sprinkle with black pepper. Cook on low heat until onion pieces sweat.

Add the oil to cover bottom of pan and onion. Mix. Sauté until just golden. Stir in livers. Cook for a few minutes over low heat. Add the flour and sugar and mix together. Cover with hot water and simmer for 10 to 15 minutes over low flame. Add salt to taste. Simmer for a few more minutes. Serve hot on cooked noodles.

Yield: 1 lb. chicken livers serves four, as a main course

YIDDISH

I was named in memory of my great-grandmother. She died of cholera after the First World War. Her death left the *bubbe,* my mother's mother, alone in Warsaw at twelve years old. Her father, away in Canada for many years, remarried swiftly. She believed he would send for her. While waiting she was shuttled from one relative to the next.

There is a hand-colored photograph of the *bubbe* with her mother, a Warsaw studio photograph with shiny, peeling edges. The mother sits on a carved settee. The girl leans at her side, lightly holding a mandolin, an instrument my mother says her mother as a girl could play. In the serious, beautiful face of the girl, the deep eyes are already a bit sad and knowing, as if they see the future. The woman and girl are dressed in their Sabbath best for the photograph. This photograph is all that is left. It must stand for the *bubbe*'s childhood.

My two grandmothers came to the New World by chance and by choice. Each left a mother in a Polish graveyard to join a father and find an uncertain future. They did not flee pogroms, exactly, nor come to seek their fortune. They neither discarded their roots nor flung themselves from terror as would the refugees of midcentury. They left the Old Country, but not for streets of gold. They were betwixt and between; they were girls; they arrived and they married, they made their accommodations, and they cooked the foods they remembered. Motherless, they learned to be mothers.

The *bubbe* waited four long years in Warsaw, and still her father did not send for her. Cousins were leaving Poland now, for Canada. They had an extra ticket she could use, since a child had died, a child named, like the *bubbe,* Malke Feltsman. She had a ticket with her name on it.

Two worlds: one was Yiddish, vanished, familiar. One world was Canada, real and strange. The stepmother did not want her, the father did not insist. She married the *zeyde,* my grandfather, at seventeen, in order to have some place to go. It was a loveless marriage. The babies came; the babies saved her. She must have managed her heart with the work of her hands: cooking, cleaning, charity, what she knew.

How she learned what she knew I cannot fathom. How had she, the unwanted one, learned to gather friends and family into a welcoming, onion-scented kitchen, cooking *kreplekh* or cheese blintzes by the hundreds; simmering pot roasts and dumplings; stirring batters, peeling apples, putting up cucumbers and plums, plucking chickens, slaughtering carp, rolling noodle dough, *kasher*ing meat? All the while washing diapers for six babies, laundering dresses, shirts, sheets, and menstrual rags by hand, ironing—and she never was cross, they say she never scolded or yelled.

"She loved to be among people," my mother explained. The pleasures of solitude, of privacy, eluded the *bubbe's* comprehension. "*Vos mir* privacy? *Ven mir* privacy?" she used to say. She found the concept ridiculous.

She never grew comfortable writing English, although she enjoyed reading *The Toronto Star*. Once in her kitchen I sounded out a mysterious word scratched on paper in Hebrew letters, Yiddish script: it turned out to read "Bananas," the start of a grocery list. After she died, a few letters, mementos, came to our house. There were postcard messages in Yiddish, insignificant news from home, that she had cherished. There were names scribbled on the backs of photos, names that once meant everything to someone, but were become empty, useless, history's anonymous flotsam and jetsam.

"I think she went to Israel," my mother would consider, when I brought a raveled portrait out of the basement, Yiddish scribbled on the back. Another photo, a black-eyed boy: "A cousin, I think, a boy my mother loved."

Her mother left Poland and that black-eyed boy forever, at sixteen. He was a distant cousin, for what other sort of boy was she to know? They wrote back and forth, and he died in the war. It is wrong to look at the words, for these words were meant for her. I cannot read the Yiddish anyway. His name? A vow? A young man's Yiddish, a lost Yiddish, a Yiddish of passion, hope, and possibility? There is no such Yiddish in the world today.

"My mother used to mention him, and weep."

All my life I have wanted Yiddish. It is, for me, the language memory should speak, a language of secrecy, magical and profane. It was a loving, far-off world. It was the *bubbe,* and it was her childhood.

When I was a child, Yiddish hovered, invisible as air, storing moisture and electricity. You opened a door and heard the atmosphere crackle. I captured little of the charge. I hear the guttural music, draw off simple meanings, perceive glints of wit and sorrow. I am deaf, though, to grammar, to nuance, to all the layered compound that builds a language from elemental sand. I have solitary words: I have *bendl* for a little wire to bundle a plastic bag. I know *gopl,* my primal fork, and poor *schlemiel* that has no English to it. This, however, does not help me understand what they went through, those like the *bubbe,* who had no great desire to leave the Old Country, but also had no choice.

There was not one kind of immigrant, but many. From the day of his arrival as a ten-year-old boy, my father's father took the New World to be mastered in English. His tenement building spoke Yiddish; there, too, the pots and the pans spoke Yiddish, but at the kitchen table at night he pored over English. He distinguished himself in English; he preserved his prize composition, published in the *Evening Telegram*, pressed among the photographs my father brought home to Detroit after the Brooklyn house was sold.

In 1913 or thereabouts, in the locker room at City College, my grandfather shed his *tzitzis,* his ritual fringed undershirt, for the last time. There was no place for such a garment in the locker room, or in his new world. Yiddish was a relic, cast off, ultimately, like *tzitzis*. The act left you American—naked, in a sense, but free.

I try to fathom life in the wrong language.

I think of my *bubbe,* living for decades in a city she could never really navigate, in a neighborhood that was not Jewish. She could do so much: one autumn, visiting our house, she nimbly sewed a Halloween costume in an afternoon. I was a pagan witch of her design. We gave her the apples from our Halloween loot, and she made applesauce.

She read, wrote, and spoke Polish and Russian as well as Yiddish. She could say her prayers in Hebrew and could speak to her monolingual grandchildren in a language they understood—but the outside world on this side of the water was a threatening, strange thing. Even with an address, a sheaf of directions, an encouraging hug, my *bubbe* could not find her way to a place she had never been. The world outside was the wrong language.

November

NATIVE GROUND

November

I teeter on some intermediate balancing point. On one side there is kashrut, on the other, citizenship in the regular world. My balancing point is the kosher meat I bring home for cooking, the segregation of milk from meat in one meal, the picky selection from restaurant menus: no bacon, no prosciutto, no pork.

The pivoting plank, unstable, leans to the kosher end. I who loved shellfish have caused their extinction within my house. It happened in stages. I lost the taste for it when pregnant, or when jostled by pollution scares. We began to feel scruples about preparing shrimp at home, when our ecumenical pots would be called on to serve my observant in-laws. My husband requested we desist for their comfort level, and increasingly, I understood, for his.

Our scruples escalated as the children grew. Dining out as a family, I found myself avoiding mollusks, crustaceans, not out of pure conviction, but in the interests of consistency. Eventually, the shifting standards—here shrimp, there none—made me seasick. I began to slip away from the appetite of it, the idea of shrimp and mussels and squid.

I am not sure that I want this. I always have wanted the world. So I teeter, I worry, but I don't turn away. Because it is the tradition of my grandparents and those who went before. Because I'm not sure I can bear to finally cut the string connecting those lives to those of my children. Because I don't want hamburgers with milk shakes at my table.

I am trying to balance the claims of the mind and the soul with the belly's blind, indulgent appetites. I am trying to respect the life of the calf that I eat. I will imbibe of its mother's milk, but at some other meal. Still I do not say I can possibly meet the detail evolved by generations of rabbis. I don't know if I can truly scour myself and begin afresh. I don't know if I really wish to. Purge the ambivalence, the daring U turns, and what is left after all?

Keeping kosher has this value: I daily reaffirm identity, purpose, and rhythm. Separateness is intrinsic to that, separation from the world outside as well as within the meal. Yet I do not enjoy setting myself apart. I fear a statement of difference in a world that needs to see itself as one.

OLD NEIGHBORHOOD

I explored my neighborhood, its shops and alleyways, and came home in the Detroit dusk. Some days I meandered alone. More often I was with, and vaguely responsible for, a younger brother and sister. We were together a lot, my siblings and I, in an evolving subculture of our small family pod. We have jokes, touchstones, that no one else in the world may truly share.

My sister and I were two little girls, our hair in long braids. We window-shopped Six Mile Road. We pedaled bicycles into twilight, jumped rope on driveways, shared a pair of roller skates: She wore the left one, I the right. We rescued a sparrow that had fallen out of its nest, and we took it home. In the alleys behind the stores, we emptied hundreds of packing crates filled with excelsior, and once, shrieking with triumph, unearthed a rosette-painted Mexican ceramic pig.

My brother climbed trees in an empty lot, and watched slot cars race at Drag City. With his best friend, the fatherless Junior, he picked up pocket money. They unpacked car floor mats, helped Junior's uncle sell the *Racing Form* at the track. Junior often fell asleep in school; most nights his grandmother took him along to the movies for the half-price midnight show.

I tried to learn the Cool Jerk, despite rumors that someone had dislocated her back doing this dance and died in the hospital. I learned new rope-jumping rhymes from Renée, who just moved in, from the Projects. I wore two pairs of bobby socks, one over the other, because Renée said that was the style. Why did Renée want to fight?

"Hit me!" she taunted. "Hit me!"

Let's go for a drive.
This was the old neighborhood.
This was the old neighborhood.
This, too. Where you were born.

This was Detroit, the city to which my parents had journeyed from their parents' homes. The city changed, dispersed, but still it was the destination of their youthful dreams. They had a stake in the sidewalks that had welcomed them, and they were committed archeologists of Detroits past. We children living in the here-and-now became their students of the used-to-be.

In Rome, the pedestrian turns a corner to find an ancient monument, with children playing on its sandy, excavated stones. In our everyday life, we would drive somewhere, and there it would be, a recognizable relic of the living past. We experienced past and present simultaneously, and cherished the layers of compressed time.

When my family went for a drive, I looked out the backseat car window. I observed the visible: a Christian Science Reading Room, a gas station. In the front seat, my driving father and lipsticked mother narrated a different tour. Here my *zeyde* had owned a shoe store with his brothers before World War I, before resettling in Toronto. Here he had driven his first and only automobile through a plate-glass window.

"He was satisfied to take the streetcar after that," my mother said.

Here was the Studebaker plant, where the eldest three brothers had worked to bring over the rest of the family from Europe. They saved up for years, and at Ellis Island, one of the little boys was discovered to have a scab on his head, and the whole family was sent back, and the brothers had to start saving again.

We motored back and forth through time; cruised radical, hopeful, younger days. Up there, on the second floor, Mom once had worked as a typist and, with the other office girls, had brought in the union. Here was the meeting hall, now an apostolic church, where my mother first spotted our tall, curly-haired dad at a socialist lecture, and arranged to walk out in front of him, hoping that her stocking seams were straight.

Here, once the Top Hat Bar, my mother accepted my father's proposal of marriage after hearing his opening words, "Do you think—?"

We took long slow drives, discussing dynamics and might-have-beens. We rehearsed the minutiae, lamented the fallen trolley line or dwindled street life. Each building, each block was microcosm, metaphor, a problem to plumb and unravel, and then understand and savor your understanding.

My parents put the kind of energy into seeing and parsing and recollection that others, perhaps, put into building businesses, painting sailboats, improving homes. Weekend and evening rides embarked on as a whim, as if there was nothing else to do in the world.

Thus the first time a boy held my hand in a way that mattered was at a roller rink in the old neighborhood to which my father gravitated one day on such a ride. My sister and I excitedly entered, the only white children there. Dance music poured from rusty speakers, cigarette smoke rose in mushroom puffs to the roof.

I, perhaps eleven maybe twelve, was asked to skate by a slender teenage boy with mustard-colored silk pants and a lavish conk. I was a sidewalk skater, only practical, perhaps a bit of a klutz. He took my right hand in his right hand, slipped his left arm around my waist.

"I'll show you how," he murmured. We dipped and glided about the rink. There was my father on the periphery, looking on, my sister somewhere on roller skates in the laughing party noise.

"Thank you," he said as my heart pounded, and he looked, thrillingly, into my eyes. The thrill was the sudden notion, to learn all at once that one would be desired.

This was the old neighborhood. This was your nursery school. A big fuzzy dog lived here. I taught you the names of the cars: Chevrolet, Studebaker, Plymouth, Ford.

This was the old grid, bubbling with industry, commerce, ambition. I remember the brick houses filled with furniture, paid for in cash. Libraries stood on wide stone steps. Bold new cars paraded up Woodward Avenue, and along Gratiot and out Six Mile Road, a vision of the future that soon became the past.

Detroit roiled like a riptide. Friends moved away. The butcher followed. My mother ordered the meat by telephone then, with many stipulations as to cut, trim, and packaging. The results were unsatisfying. You really must stand there and watch.

Once, Mother, unwrapping her order, angrily knifed excessive fat off a brisket, called the shop to demand a refund. The butcher's puzzled delivery man was dispatched to us from the suburbs a second time. I can still see him at our door, his cap politely doffed, peering through bent eyeglass frames at our white faces.

"I'm here to pick up some fat?" he ventured, as I died of humiliation, absolutely died.

And then, one day, meat deliveries to our neighborhood, the newest old neighborhood, ceased.

· · ·

I left it behind in the summers. I packed a footlocker with sneakers and jeans. Summers I went to camp. I grew lean and mossy, a summer thing of moldy T-shirts and mosquito bites. Only an hour away from Detroit, and run by the city's Department of Parks and Recreation, camp was a refuge from parents, home, neighborhood. Every one of earth's children needed it most.

I was a creature of lake, swamp, and cattails. I slept in my swimsuit, and rowed over the waters, the oars under blistery hands. Out in the boats, sunburnt, dreaming, we heard the whistle blow early and frantic one day.

Two counselors stood on the boat dock waving, shouting, signaling us to come in. Opal and Donna. As we bumped our boats to the mooring posts we heard the crackle of a transistor. It was August 1967.

"They're burning Livernois!" Tears sparkled on Donna's face. Donna was gorgeous as a Motown star, and she straightened her long, black hair on a jumbo-sized tomato juice can.

"The Avenue of Fashion," said Opal, bleak joke. "Avenue of Ashes."

They hustled us into the mess hall as if to a fallout shelter. We gathered together. They didn't know what to do. They tried to get us singing. In the confusion I ran and I sat, then I ran for my sister. I paced, in my mind, the distance from Livernois to my parents, passed all the shops I still remember so clearly: pizza, chop suey, a telephone substation, Brickley's milk. I turned up my street, counting off the good square houses of Butler, Brown, Jonas, Silverman, Koszinski, reaching at last the concrete stoop and front door I knew best.

Was it standing? Was it burning? Were the parents within? What was it all about, anyway? The causes were many, and this the effect: Some new kind of fear that sent everything spinning.

The parents were safe, the house was sound, and life went on in its way. Integration didn't have a chance.

This was the old neighborhood.

STUFFED CABBAGE

One autumn in Brooklyn as we visited for the holidays, I watched my grandmother in her kitchen day after day. It was one of our last visits, toward the end of my grandmother's life. I was in high school. I wrote down nothing, but could not forget the tastes. I can cook these dishes now, by guesswork, heart's leap, memory.

No taste sets off memory for me more than sweet-and-sour, my grandmother's mixture of honey and lemon, sugar and vinegar—opposites that, thrown together, highlight the essence of each. This was a standard flavoring in her cooking, Jewish Carpathian Mountain—*Galitsiyaner*—style.

She made a cabbage borsht or soup that season, sweet-and-sour. It is not complex, this borsht, at least in my rendering. I chop half a cabbage. I simmer it, adding carrot disks, potato cubes, onions, tomatoes, a bay leaf, salt, a dollop of honey, a squeeze of lemon, water. Many is the time I have gone out and searched grocery shelves for "sour salt" citric acid—because I remembered a bottle of it in my grandmother's hand. She stirred to dissolve the citric crystals for that characteristic sour in the soup.

I cook the soup slowly, tasting as it goes. If too sweet, I add sour, if too sour, I add sweet. Some boil this soup with a meat bone; I don't. Sometimes I serve it with sour cream and caraway seeds, though I really don't know why.

My grandmother made sweet-and-sour meatballs, small in size. I watched her mix chopped meat, salt, pepper, pressed garlic, egg, and a bit of matzo meal to bind it. She took a bit of meat mixture and rolled it in a ball, then rolled each meatball in matzo meal. In a large, flat, cast-aluminum frying pan, she fried them in sizzling oil, crunchy brown. She added onions and green peppers to the pan, and a sauce of tomato, sugar, sour salt, salt and pepper. These elements danced, tangos and mazurkas, in the rich, bubbling pan.

She served the meatballs with spaghetti. It was her Brooklyn Jewish Carpathian way with Italo-American cuisine.

That autumn in Brooklyn, my grandmother's sky rained soup. I remember polishing off three consecutive bowls of split pea soup intended for the evening's dinner, as she sat on her tall stool by the stove, stirring the pot. She was amused when I, at the kitchen table, accepted seconds, but I thought I detected a slight consternation when seconds were not quite enough.

There were soft shreds of beef *flanken,* short ribs, suspended in the rich green soup, and tiny transparent flecks of onion and celery, and bits of carrot and parsley. She may have added a potato, grated or diced, if the soup needed thickening.

When we had eaten all the pea soup, she made mushroom barley soup, boiling marrow bones with onions. She added chopped vegetables and barley, and diced mushrooms, and bay. Maybe paprika. Is there someone I can ask? (The first time I tried to make this soup, in a college kitchen, I used a whole bag of barley, not knowing how it would expand. It cooked quicker than I realized, and filled the large communal cauldron, while the bottom scorched black.)

And then that season, as the Brooklyn holidays were drawing to their trumpet close, the fall holidays in procession from the high days of awe to the joyous festival days, as we were about to pack our holiday skirts and suits and polished leather shoes into the trunk of our latest Plymouth and head west again to our secular lives, my grandmother made stuffed cabbage, *geviklte kroyt.* I may have watched her make it. I must have watched her make it. I tasted the meltingly soft cabbage wings enfolding velvety spiced meat and rice under a thin sweet-and-sour tomato sauce studded with raisins, and never forgot it.

My grandmother died when I was fifteen. We had lived in different cities. Eight hundred miles of distance had limited the visits to once or twice a year. There had not been time enough to watch her do, to learn the tricks and methods, although I do remember some things, I am sure I do— the way she peeled apples, seated at the kitchen table, with her thumb on the sharp blade of a short knife, and the peel coming off in one long furl, dropping to a sheet of newspaper spread on the table to catch the mess.

Stuffed-cabbage-making memories are not so clear. So I used trial and error to come to it, to the taste and fragrance, the look and the nuance that I remembered, or thought I did.

As a teenager in our Detroit kitchen, I grated onion and squashed garlic into ground meat, mixed this with cooked rice. I boiled a cabbage head and scalded my hands on it, and then its leaves were either too hard or too soft to properly wrap filling. But I did devise a sauce of tomato juice and black raisins, flavored with every kind of sweet and sour I could think apt: white sugar, brown sugar, honey, vinegar, lemon, sour salt. I tasted after each addition, shook in a tiny hail of salt. I baked the little cabbage rolls in this fluid until the leaves fell apart and turned black on top, and only a thin reddish slip was left in the pan.

In college, once or twice, between everything else and probably just when I should have been studying chemistry or French, I learned to score the bottom of a cabbage bulb with a sharp, short knife, to steam and remove a few leaves at a time, to pare away the hard outside stalk fibers, for easier filling and rolling. College was one long fatiguing struggle for sanity, self confidence, truth. Did that pan of stuffed cabbage symbolize my malady, or the cure?

In my first apartments, trying out adult life, I found savoy cabbage easier to work with. That was when Grandmother's daughter, my aunt, entrusted me with her mother's old pots and pans: an enamel soup cauldron, the cast-aluminum pan, and an electric skillet, in which she used to make chicken fricassee, I am told, with chicken wings and little brown meatballs and a lot of garlic and maybe a hint of spirits, just a hint . . .

Some years ago I showed my daughter, four years old, to securely wrap filling, tuck in the frail petal-ends, arrange the rolls in a glass baking dish. We poured on sauce and stuck in a bay leaf. We tightly smoothed foil over the baking dish.

In the oven, sauce bubbled gently but did not disappear. Meat absorbed flavor. Cabbage sleeves turned tender but remained intact.

My grandmother had been gone for twenty years.

A cousin was coming to dinner. A grandson of my grandmother. He lives in Europe; I had not seen him in years. I had firm, sealed affection for this cousin. As a little girl visiting east, I had tried to shower him with puppy love: He, terrified, dove beneath a table and refused to emerge. I had envied him as well, a boy growing up in New York, surrounded by tall buildings and proximate to my grandmother's home.

The buzzer buzzed. I shouted into the intercom. An elevator rose. A few moments later, my cousin was at the door—tall, balding, handsome, laying aside a tweed jacket. He followed his nose into the kitchen.

"It smells like Grandma's house!" said he at once.

It is not enough. I too want to go away and come back and open a door not expecting and then know, with that sudden rush of certainty, that the dishes I remember have magically returned to earth to remind me of childhood and of boundless love.

This is not to be. I had better cook it myself.

APPLE CAKE

$\mathcal{I}$t is the day before Thanksgiving, and I am with Miriam. She is baking her Thanksgiving dessert, apple cake. Under the influence of America, this cake, which brings in Miriam's Jewish holidays every fall, has extended its reach to the fourth Thursday in November. It has all but wrestled my sunken, self-righteous, nondairy replica of a pumpkin pie off the dining table.

"First we will make the dough," announces Miriam, once my toddler gets busy with his grandfather, Jacob, and I wash my hands. I see she is ready. In her immaculate white sink, on a white rubber rack, rests a large white enamel basin, a *shisl,* the sort of all-purpose thing my grandmothers, too, had in their kitchens.

Balanced calmly on the basin is a metal strainer with a worn plastic handle. Beside the sink, an old tin canister, lined with a plastic bag, is open, revealing a five-pound paper sack of flour precisely fitting within. A soup spoon is upended jauntily in the flour; a glass measuring cup waits nearby, to receive the flour spooned up, to pour the flour through the strainer into the white basin. Escaping puffs of flour can be rinsed down the drain.

There is no flour sifter in Miriam's kitchen. There is no food processor, apple corer, mixing bowl, measuring spoon, basting brush, egg beater, wine coaster, or tomato knife. Miriam, in general, does not acquire kitchen equipment. She has good old kitchen things that adapt to many uses, and the few absolutely necessary specialized gadgets, ones she has used many times. She has the minimum necessary. If a fork will mix batter, why buy a whisk? She knows exactly what she has and what she needs, because Miriam's repertoire is a dependable selection. It is Bach, Brahms, and Beethoven, with a little Chopin, Dvořák, and Irving Berlin added in over the years.

Life, with such constancy to the classics, can be managed. The logistics are predictable, the economics can be planned for. A shopping list must contain onions, parsley, carrots, eggs, flour, matzo meal, potatoes, vanilla sugar, sour cream. If there will be a meat loaf, there must be kasha to go with it, mushrooms, beans, broccoli, a known and time-tested quantity of each, and Miriam knows how many meals will be served thereby. At the market, Miriam can be tempted unexpectedly by fuzzy kiwis or plump avocados, but she knows these will go on a Friday night fruit plate beside the melon she was buying anyway, or replace an egg salad at Saturday lunch.

Keeping kosher, I think, must also be simpler, less of a headache, if one is rendering the same symphonies, sonatas, and songs each year. Keeping kosher is hard in my house, when my cooking style resembles a long, undisciplined riff: madrigal fading to muzak, the Mexican Hat Dance, the overture to *Carmen*, and, for the children, endless variations on "The Cat and the Fiddle." I may want to try a new creamy fish soup, but the right pot is the wrong provenance, perhaps meat and not dairy. If I try the soup somehow, I will have no storage for the leftovers, because my large plastic containers, let's say, are dedicated to meat. Or I may have some aging rice in the fridge that must be used up, and a chicken soup boiling away, but if I think back, I guess I buttered that rice.

My instinct is to improvise, and so far, *kashrut* has checked me, rather than unleashed creativity. Miriam, in contrast, hews to foods complementary to *kashrut* as well as to the rhythms of her life. Will the logic of things place me less and ever less in the kitchen, or will my own rhythms change?

I have eaten apple cake for nearly twenty years, and never seen it made. I should have been a young bride hanging over Miriam's shoulder to see. Well, I was antimatrimonial if not anti-cake, imagining myself in my power years. The upshot is that I am twice the age Miriam was when my husband was as small as my toddler, and I have never made an apple cake.

Miriam spoons and pours. She sifts through the strainer four cups of flour, two teaspoons of baking powder, and a dash of salt. I see the soft sifted white mound in the white enamel basin, and feel a pristine comfort, wonder indeed why everyone doesn't use white basins and recycled candy tins.

In the flour she makes a silken hole with the bottom of her spoon. She opens a jar of sugar, and measures out a cup.

"You put a cup of sugar all around, and in the middle of the hole," says Miriam, working out sugar lumps with her hands. This cake is made with the hands. "Put three eggs in the hole." She cracks the eggs in the kosher way, one at a time into a glass, to make sure there is no blood spot, no visible sign of fertilized life, rendering it unfit to eat. Each egg is poured into the dry ingredients before another egg is cracked into the glass.

The egg yolks and whites drop, and each time Miriam cleans egg white out of the shell with her thumb. "My landlady in Germany taught me to do that. She said, from six eggs, you get one egg." The recognition that egg white clinging to the shell is habitual waste stayed with Miriam. She was a refugee in a small German town, waiting to see if there was going to be a future after hell. Husbanding her egg whites was thrift, a lesson well learned in such hard times. There is a glint of optimism in the gesture, too.

"No, *shepsele*, you eat it," Jacob is heard to say. I glance out to the living room, where my two-year-old, the "little sheep," is eating raisins from a plastic margarine tub, and trying to stuff some into his grandfather's mouth. At home, the hungry lamb has shelves full of toys. Here, he has plastic containers, Jacob's eyeglass case, raisins, and perfect happiness.

"Put a stick of margarine, softened," says Miriam. "I take it out always the night before, so it will be easy."

What could be easier than knowing you will bake tomorrow, and having your ingredients in the house, all prepared? Indeed, were I not here observing, Miriam would have prepared the dough a day before, and would be grating apples for the filling now.

Miriam mixes egg and margarine a bit, in the floury hole, with a fork. "Now, four ounces of oil." She measures, glancing at a rusty brown paper recipe.

I have never seen her measure before, and I say so.

"Of course I measure," Miriam says, with feeling. "With a cake, you have to measure. It has to be exact ingredients, or it doesn't come out."

I am trying to absorb this statement into an entirely different paradigm I have of the way Miriam works. After all, I have not watched her bake much.

"My mother had a glass," Miriam comments. She opens the refrigerator. "She used to cut the margarine, put it in the glass, and fill the glass with oil. I thought to myself, one day I may not have the glass. So one time I measured the oil. It came out to four ounces."

She brings forth a china teacup: fresh orange juice, prepared before I arrived.

"You squeeze a medium orange. It should be about a quarter of a cup. Let's see." She pours the juice into her glass measurer, shaking the gold-rimmed cup to capture the last golden drips. The concave meniscus shimmers at the "2 oz." line—precisely one fourth of a cup. She empties the juice into the well in the flour.

"First, you mix this way," explains Miriam, using the fork to fold flour into liquid. "And then you use hands."

Miriam's delicately gnarled hands work the dough. She scrapes dry bits off the sides of the basin with a plastic spatula blade. "I had a friend in Israel," she recounts. "She used to love a cake I used to make, so I told her, come and watch me prepare it, and you can have it too. So she came to mine house. I showed her to do everything, a cup of this, a cup of this. Then she went home." Miriam mixes, fingers and palms. "The next time I saw her, she said, 'By me it doesn't come out good. Probably you didn't give me the exact recipe.' "

Miriam stops, silent. My stomach tightens in something like panic. I think I am hearing one of those untrusting female stories, an unjust accusation, the end of a friendship. There are people who jealously guard their recipes, I know, even to the point of deception, but my mother-in-law cannot be one of them.

"I went to her house, to see what she is doing there," continues Miriam, to my relief. "I see her throwing things in—flour, eggs, here and there. 'Zita,' I said, 'no. You can't do like that. You have to measure, exactly, the way I showed you.' She saw, it came out good."

I write down "must measure," underline it. I'm a bit like Zita, maybe that is why I rarely bake. But what is this? With a tablespoon, Miriam scoops two quick heaps of flour to the center of the dough, and kneads it in.

"Now you add flour," Miriam remarks casually, testing the texture, "so it doesn't stick when you bake. Not always the same amount—I don't know why."

There is a question to be asked here, but I can't quite formulate it.

"When you bake," states Miriam authoritatively, "cake, or cookies, or anything, you put in the exact amount of flour they say, and then you add more." She lifts the ball of dough, and shakes into the basin two more heaping spoonfuls of flour. "You have to use the exact amount."

"Let me see."

Reluctantly, Miriam gives me a turn kneading the dough, tossing in another spoonful of flour as she relinquishes. I knead. She adds flour. I've lost count. Eight tablespoons?

"Put more," Miriam instructs.

I put. "Have you tried to start with more flour?" I venture.

Another silence. Miriam pinches the dough, dissatisfied.

"You see," she says, with a sigh. "Sometimes you have bigger eggs, a larger orange, so you have to add. Today the eggs were large. Very large."

"I bet we've used another cup of flour," I persist. "At least." I glance at Miriam, and I think I see a smile.

"It's better this way. You work it through," she murmurs.

"And your mother—?" I ask.

"My mother? No, she didn't measure."

"Yakob, *oytser.*" Jacob, treasure. "Bring up the apples in the paper sack on this side by the table downstairs."

"Let me go for them," I say.

"He will go," assures Miriam. He is gone.

My toddler is at the pantry door looking for more raisins, and Miriam beams. "A blessing on your smart little head," she says. I feel the dough, try to memorize this just-right soft resistance.

"Tell them to use smaller eggs," suggests my mother-in-law.

Now Miriam sprinkles flour into a chipped china bowl, sprayed with green blossoms. She transfers the dough to this bowl. She washes the basin, the measuring cup, and dries these things with a green-and-white dishtowel. Jacob closes the basement door behind him, sets down the bag of apples. Miriam takes out a small hand grater, embossed with Hebrew letters—the manufacturer's name.

"You brought this from Israel?" I ask. My husband's family left the Promised Land in 1961, when he was eleven.

"I left everything," says Miriam, with passionate, fresh regret. "This I brought."

I am thinking about the house she loved, with its fruit trees, chickens in the yard, flowering hibiscus, kittens. Her mother's youngest sister, spared at Auschwitz, was raising a family next door. Down the road were friends from the old village. There was dazzling warmth and sunlight, economic hardship, a pioneer life of kerosene lamps and outdoor plumbing, and she was equal to it. For a moment, she thought she was settled, that her raw, tender, practical spirit, wrenched from home, would root in the sandy dust of that disputed place. But her mother and her husband wanted America, they wanted prosperity, and Miriam packed up to begin again.

"I brought the Passover dishes, with the roses. I brought one crate, that's all. One crate like this—" She marks a space with her hands from the floor to her waist. "Bring to America?" She shrugs.

Miriam turns to the sink and washes apples.

"Beautiful apples," I say.

"Macintosh." She admires an apple. Miriam likes the Macintosh in applesauce, too.

"If I could have taken everything I had into that crate, I would have. I had good things, too, from Germany. I spent all my money there, on kitchen gadgets, before we left to Israel."

I do a quick turn in my mind, seeing a young bride in Germany after the war, with nothing to inherit, assembling a sort of trousseau of chopping knives and strainers. A displaced person waiting for her papers, and against all probabilities, filled with plans and hope.

"But to America? I was going to a rich land."

There is a sweet fragrance as Miriam peels the apples. I begin grating, on the little pocked aluminum grater that has seen this corner of civilization through four decades of autumn apple cake. Many of the left gadgets, if there were many, must simply never have been replaced.

"You have five pounds of apples," notes Miriam. "My mother used to use three. That was a smaller pan she used." The same dough? Less dough? Thicker in the pan? Miriam's look says all of these are possible, if I only knew what she meant by "exact."

The shredded apples are turning brown. Should we add lemon? Miriam goes for sweet, not sour: "It turns brown in the oven anyway."

As I grate, Jacob hovers.

"You are taking from me my job," he complains.

"Play with the baby," I tell him.

"This is hard work," says Jacob, referring to the apples.

"Sure it's hard. That's why I have muscles," says Miriam. "He always *raybs*—grates—the apples, except when he's not home."

"*Abba!*" summons the baby, with the address he has heard me use for my husband's father. *Abba* is Hebrew for father. *Ema,* mother, is what I call Miriam.

"I used to think a person was either a cook or a baker, but not both," I reflect. "Until I met you."

"My mother was both," says Miriam. "I don't even know half what she knew. The things she cooked in Poland." Once, she recalled for me a sweet pastry, made with beets, never to be tasted again. Now Miriam tries to describe another confection, this made with green pears, preserved in something she calls *chellik,* some sort of substance used in construction. "Builders use it," she repeats, failing at the English word. No, no, not brick, not clay. Lime, maybe? I make a note to find a Polish dictionary.

"In this *chellik* it would stay a few days. Then she did something with it, cooked it with sugar? I don't know." There is no one to ask. Far away in time, she, a little girl then, loved a pear dessert, and it is unrecoverable.

Miriam greases a dark blue speckled enamel baking pan with margarine. She drains the grated apples in a colander, squeezing handfuls of apple to separate the unneeded juice. Nothing is wasted: the strained juice she tips into a little two-handled cup for the *shepsele.*

Now for the filling. Miriam mixes sugar with the apple. Into a bowl of warm tap water, she shakes raisins—"three quarters of a box." She stirs the raisins for a moment, bundles them in paper towel, squeezes out the liquid, and adds the raisins to the apple. With a soup spoon, she measures out three tablespoons of matzo meal, adds cinnamon, ground cloves, "a quarter of a teaspoon, no more, else it would be bitter."

Miriam rolls out bits of dough into various quadrilaterals, examining the thickness of each.

"I'm always afraid there wouldn't be enough," she admits, pressing and patting the pieces of dough into a lining for the pan, and leaving a third for the top crust. The bottom crust extends slightly over the edge of the pan. She spreads the apple filling evenly.

"More," I hear my toddler say. I turn. He is finishing the box of raisins, while my father-in-law laughs silently.

"*Abba,* it's enough already."

"*Es shadt nisht,*" scolds Jacob. It doesn't hurt.

"It's enough raisins, Yakob," echoes Miriam. "I have cookies."

I'm used to cookies here. But then Miriam opens a large plastic bin, and I gasp: cookies shaped into dozens of turkeys, pilgrims, pilgrim hats, and pumpkins. The pilgrims have chocolate chip buttons, mouths, and eyes. "When did you do it?" I ask, but I already know—today, five o'clock in the morning, the latest.

It is Miriam's American statement: If apple cake has made Thanksgiving Jewish, these cookies, something new, represent a late, sugary embrace of the New World. Maybe having grandchildren allowed that to be. My tot's little hand closes on a pilgrim, and he bites off the head in a heedless instant.

"It's good, *oytser*?" she asks him, radiant. "Yes, it is. It is good."

"This takes patience," remarks Jacob, who must have watched the rolling and stamping, the careful placement of chocolate chips.

"For the children I have patience, plenty."

"Just for the children patience, for the husband, nothing." There is a bit of a smile.

"He's never without his cookies, so don't say a word."

My husband's father, at eighty, still works. Two days a week now, he leaves the house at six a.m., drives through the Bronx, over the George Washington Bridge, and into New Jersey, where he opens a curtain-and-bedspread factory for its owner and commences his foreman shift. He drives through all sorts of weather, not quite comfortable on the road, having learned to drive only in his late forties. And every day, as she has for decades and decades, Miriam packs him lunch, which always includes home-baked cake or cookies—usually the cookies Jacob prefers: plain, thin, crisp, brown, vanilla-flavored ingots extruded with little ridges from a special attachment of Miriam's electric grinding machine.

The oven is warming. The stovetop gleams, covered with silver foil to protect the burners against grease. It is so pleasant here. Miriam rolls out pieces of dough, laying them over the apple filling, neat patchwork for the top of a cake.

"I will have enough, more than enough," she muses. "I always panic. It would be all right."

"May I help?"

"Let me do this, it has to look—good."

I take no offense, watching a virtuoso separate lumps of dough, flatten each on her floured board, roll out, and examine each in silence, calculating how much she still needs.

"I did let myself go, it's too thick," Miriam suddenly exclaims. "Now I will not have enough." The self-reproach is reflexive—there is enough, more than enough, and Miriam can drop a ball of cake dough into a freezer bag with eight or ten other small spheres. I will take home this extra dough, leftover bits from every cake or cookie. A few days past Thanksgiving, when the turkey is all gone, I will press these lumps together, combine them, roll it all out for a pie crust, and make a pumpkin pie, with cream.

The patches of dough are worked together. The seams are smoothed. Miriam folds the doughy sides over the top crust to make a neat hem that won't burn. She pours oil over the cake, ordinary vegetable oil, and spreads it with her hands, a lot of oil, as I feel my customary shock at how much. Then she shakes sugar and cinnamon over the cake until the unbaked dough appears dark brown. How much oil? How much cinnamon? An exact amount, no doubt, but one that has not yet been writ.

With a sharp knife Miriam cuts lines into the cake, two-inch squares through the top dough. This way, the crisp top crust will remain intact on each two-inch piece when the cake is served. Then she bakes it. I eat a pilgrim hat, and then a pumpkin, dotted with chocolate. The kitchen fills with the smell of autumn and rectitude.

APPLE CAKE

For the crust:

4 cups all-purpose flour
2 tsp. baking powder
Dash of salt
1 cup sugar
3 unbeaten eggs

$^1/_4$ cup softened margarine
4 oz. vegetable oil
Juice of one medium orange,
   about 2 oz.

For the filling:

5 lb. Macintosh apples
10 to 12 oz. dark raisins
1 cup sugar
3 tbsp. matzo meal

$^1/_4$ tsp. ground cloves
$^1/_2$ tsp. cinnamon
$^1/_4$ cup vegetable oil

Preheat oven to 350°F. Grease an 11-×-16-×-2$^1/_2$-inch baking pan with margarine.

Sift flour, baking powder, and salt together. Make a well in the flour. Put half the sugar in the well, and sprinkle the rest around it. In the well, add the eggs and the margarine. Mix. Add the oil and orange juice. Use a fork to gradually mix the flour into the ingredients in the well. Then mix with your hands. Knead gently. Add flour a little at a time if the mixture is too soft or sticky. Set aside on a lightly floured surface.

Peel, core, and grate the apples. Drain in a colander. Save the juice for other use, if desired. Pour warm water over the raisins. Squeeze out the liquid in toweling.

To the apples, add raisins, sugar, matzo meal, ground cloves, and cinnamon. Mix.

Set aside one third of the dough. Roll out the other two thirds in several pieces to cover the pan bottom and to come up just over the sides of the pan. Put the pieces together in the greased pan.

Spread the apple filling over the crust evenly.

Roll out the remaining one third of the dough thinly to form a thinner top crust. Roll it out in strips of even thinness and pat them together on top of the cake. The filling should be completely covered with crust dough. Fold the edges of the bottom crust neatly over the top.

Pour oil over the top of the cake. Spread with hands. Shake sugar and cinnamon, to taste, over the oiled crust. Score top crust dough into serving-size pieces. Bake in preheated oven for 90 minutes. Cool before cutting it.

December

INHERITANCE

December

Let me just see if I can do it. I mean we've been moving in that direction. We're on the way to getting there. Our ingredients are kosher, our intentions are kosher. The wooden bowls and spoons are separate, those very porous implements of wood.

I'll divide up my dishes. I have a lot of dishes. I'll say blue are dairy and white are for meat. We'll have a trial run.

I'll need a few sponges, a pot, a pan. No big deal. I remember enough from the olden days. Miriam will tell me the rest.

Gradualism is the answer. This is going to be easy. We're practically there, more than halfway there. Sixty percent kosher, I'd say.

WEDDING RING

I went out shopping for a wedding ring. I gave myself one bright August day to find it. What I had in mind was nothing unique or spectacular, just a circlet of rose gold, gold strengthened with copper, a common alloy years ago. The band would be simple and unbroken, as is traditional. It would be rolled, not flat, its surface a bit domed all around.

That rolled and soothing shape long spoke "wedding ring" to me. My parents wear such bands, yellow gold. My mother, in fact, wears two. Since her mother died, she has worn her mother's ring as well as her own. The soft glint of gold on my mother's right hand reminds her daily of the person she loved best in all the world.

My mother-in-law, Miriam, my father-in-law, Jacob, wear the same sort of ring, a fine patina of lifelong service etched on the gleaming bands. These orbit their right ring fingers, as was the custom in Europe after the war when they were wed.

I couldn't find the ring I wanted. On my lunch hour I drew up to the spangled counters of Fifth Avenue. Attendants listened, recognized the style I sketched. Yes, they nodded. Certainly, given many many many many weeks, the rings—one for bride, one for groom—could be measured, ordered, cast, finished, boxed in velvet, and received. I didn't have that much time. I hadn't much time at all. We had left the rings for August, a month before the wedding. We had a summer for the planning, and there were so many other things to do.

Six years of noncommittal affection, different zip codes, separate bank accounts, confusing signals between the principals, were behind us. We outlived my ideological opposition to marriage, my fears and uncertainties. We survived six years of deep and troubled sighs from Miriam, the puzzled mother-in-law-to-be, who at nineteen years of age had known her own mind and was clear about what mattered and had married Jacob without the least misgiving or doubt. We two postwar ambivalents finally had plighted our troth.

In honor of our pledge, my parents, visiting New York, went to dinner at the home of Miriam and Jacob and Miriam's tiny, silver-haired mother. Around the delicate glasses of schnapps, everyone beamed. Miriam offered gefilte fish. She and her mother had made it the old-fashioned way. Carefully, they had filled the fish skins and skulls with the ground, chopped, flavored fish flesh, then gently poached these intricate sea offerings in sweet fish broth. My mother was startled, moved, to meet this construction again.

"Would you like the fish head?" Miriam respectfully asked of my mother.

To my surprise, my mother answered, "Yes."

Miriam had an Old Country story to tell from her childhood: Two Jewish men, one of them known to her family, but strangers to one another. Both were ranking officers in the Polish army. Both were posing as gentiles, Christians. One evening, chance brought the two men to an officers' banquet. They eyed one another across the table, each suspecting a shared secret. When the waiter came around with a salver of fish, one *incognito* discreetly requested a head. The other did the same.

"So they found each other," said Miriam. "Jews in Poland liked the head of the fish at that time. Gentiles usually did not."

We appreciated the story, the fish, and one another. Miriam went on serving the dinner she and her mother prepared with such effort, pride, pleasure, and to such effect: the slow-roasted beef-bean-and-potato stew, cholent, the sweet carrot-and-honey *tsimes,* the red cabbage salad, the simmered fruit. My parents exclaimed, in reminiscent wonder. How well they remembered those long-ago, home-flavored ways. I fancied myself cynical, but I had stars in my eyes, thrilled anew to be one big delicious family.

However, strategic matters were in the air; gefilte fish was the least of it. This was May. We would wed in September.

"*Oy,*" said Miriam happily. "There would be a lot to do."

My parents looked at her, not quite comprehending. For them, between that moment of contentment in the fine quality of their future in-laws, and some future moment when I actually would be married, stretched a murky gulf into which they had cast small thought. They brought neither map, nor preconceptions, nor expectations, nor demands.

Miriam had. Miriam wanted a big, festive wedding. She yearned for an occasion, a *simcha,* an abandoned few hours of gaiety and plenty and unhampered celebration for the marriage of her only son.

For Miriam and Jacob, life, essential daily life, is not about the pursuit of pleasure. Much of life, indeed, has brought them grief. Yes, there was *nakhes,* pleasure, along the way, mostly when their children were young. They have welcomed security, community, the achievements of those they love. In everyday life, though, they do not seek pleasure for its own sake, do not splurge in restaurants, do not take lavish vacations, do not indulge in shopping sprees. They do not indulge themselves in any way— not out of self-denial, but rather out of modest habits, a sense of proportion, and self-sufficiency, which I admire.

Against this backdrop, my husband's parents believe in the concept of the *simcha*. A baby naming, a graduation, a bar mitzvah—such things deserve a party, and the party is worth working for, saving for, putting many eggs in one basket for. When the rare great occasion of life rolls in, my husband's parents rise up to meet it, clapping and singing. The contrast with everyday life, perhaps, elevates the joy.

Miriam had waited a long time for her joyful moment. That May Sabbath eve, as we Detroiters ate Miriam's fish, her son was going on thirty-four years old. This age, to Miriam, was an advanced one—particularly in view of our long involvement, or as she always said, engagement.

By then, Miriam had watched cousins and sisters-in-law and friends marry off their children, and watched the children acquire homes and babies, the good things in life, the source of meaningful *nakhes*. Evening gowns were bought for these weddings. Satin shoes were dyed to match. The best jewelry was carefully removed from quilted cases tucked within the safety deposit box in the bank. Again and again had Miriam brushed Jacob's tuxedo and ironed his white pleated shirt and seen to it that Jacob washed the car.

She had not begrudged the many generous checks written out in her careful hand and tucked within apposite greeting cards, to help all the newlyweds furnish their new wedded lives. Year after year, she carried home floral centerpieces, sort of a consolation prize.

By the time our two houses handseled over fish, I had attended some of these weddings, introduced prematurely as the "fiancée." I daubed my eyelids with kohl and carried a beaded evening purse. I had encountered the smorgasbord, the lavishly filling hors d'oeuvres buffet and cocktail bar previously unknown to me, which in the New York schema opens a big traditional affair. I ate chopped liver, nibbled chicken wings, sipped gin.

In sanctuaries adorned with countless fresh flowers, I watched each twining twosome meet in nervous formal finery beneath the wedding canopy, the *khupa,* symbol of the home that they would share. Dignified rabbis slipped rings on forefingers of brides and, optionally, grooms. This position on the hand was ceremonial only; the ancients believed the forefinger's blood flowed directly from the heart.

I had eaten the four-course meal with three alternative entrées served by bow-tied waiters, danced between courses to a six-piece orchestra, smiled for photographers making the rounds of twenty tables, and exclaimed at the profusion of sweets at the Viennese Table, especially when there was apple strudel, my favorite.

Naturally, I enjoyed a *simcha.* However, for me? I already regretted not having eloped. I wanted a small wedding, and a long trip. Italy. France.

"A hall or a *shul?* Saturday night? Sunday? We don't have much time," said the practical Miriam. "For a wedding, they are planning a whole year before."

Had my family ever planned anything a year in advance? No, nor thrown a big party. My brother's bar mitzvah was a hasty affair. My father, mourning his mother, who had died within the year, couldn't face major festivity then. Izzy, a Hebrew school dropout, studied his *Haftorah,* his section from the Prophets, at home on the dining room table, with a little old bearded rabbi delighted with my brother's quick mind.

My brother was called to the Torah in the rabbi's little *shul,* a struggling down-at-heels Orthodox synagogue in a neighborhood that had once been Jewish. It was the only synagogue we could find that would let him fulfill the *mitzvah,* the commandment, without membership. My parents gave money, but did not want to join a *shul.*

The congregants were happy to have us. They were aged and few in number, and it had been years since a bar mitzvah had been marked in their midst. I sat, with my mother and Cheryl, my sister, behind the *mekhitza,* the Orthodox dividing wall that kept women from praying beside men, and—so it seemed to my resentful teenage self—kept the Torah from female pollution. My brother had a cold that morning, but he chanted melodiously. My father made him swallow a raw egg after breakfast to clear his voice, as had been required of him some thirty-five years before.

Afterward, a few friends and relatives came to our house for cold cuts, whiskey, and cake. We were proud of Izzy, who had accepted adult obligation. This was one way, it was our way, and it was a perfectly valid *simcha*. However, the experience gave us no insight into handling the wedding currently at hand.

"A *shul* is nice. A hall is nice, also," my mother remarked. "A hotel can be nice, too."

"I really don't want—" I began.

"We were married in my mother's house, in Brooklyn, in the living room," my father offered. "We came in from Detroit on a Thursday, I think. Maybe it was a Wednesday."

"It was a Thursday," my mother confirmed.

"Mother served a meal afterward, in the house."

"Sure, that's how we did it years ago, in Europe." Miriam was momentarily nonplussed. "But today, you make a party." Her voice grew passionate, firm. "With a smorgasbord, with dancing. Seventy-five, one hundred couples, it's usual today. Even in Israel, they are making the big parties now. Even bigger."

"The smorgasbord is the best part," commented my intended. "Especially those little hot dogs."

"I don't want little hot dogs," I said.

"How many couples are you thinking?" Jacob asked.

"Well, let's see," calculated my mother. "There's the two of us, and Isaac, and Cheryl." She turned to my dad. "And your sisters, their husbands. Your cousin Edwyn would probably bring a friend. Is he still seeing that redhead?"

"We're up to fourteen definite yesses," noted the man I was going to marry. "Counting my parents, the bride and the groom."

"My uncle Leybl had one hundred and thirty couples for his daughter Ruthie's wedding," enunciated Miriam, a bit bleakly. "It was a beautiful *simcha*."

Jacob donned his thick-framed reading glasses. From his chair at the end of the table, he reached for a Jewish calendar, which, in this organized household, is always to be found in the same place. With his forefinger, he pushed the empty pages of summer away.

"September is not so easy," Jacob mused. Indeed, this page was spattered with red dates. The Hebrew month of Tishrei, roughly corresponding with September, is crowded with one *yom tov*, or holiday, after another. And Tishrei holds the big ones: Rosh Hashanah, Yom Kippur, Sukkot, Shemini Atzeret, Simchas Torah. These are days when marriages are not allowed. What with one thing and another, we had two open Sundays and a single Saturday night.

Miriam's mother spoke up for the first time. The table fell silent in deference to wisdom and age.

"A wedding costs *gelt,*" she said.

"Let me make the engagement party," Miriam offered. Her hands itched to begin.

Thinking of these things today I want to weep. At twenty-nine, I was too old to have parents plan my wedding, and I was too young to understand what was at stake for Miriam.

"I don't want an engagement party," I said.

"Buy rings" was an item scratched near the bottom of a long churning list of tasks that civilization and custom impose on the decision to wed. Early on, the vows of love are personal, private, but a marriage is social. The event belongs to the families, to the community, to the world, not to the bride and groom. I see this now. My mind flailed against it then. That hot New York summer before my wedding, I struggled, arranging details one by one like tiny sequins. Each sequin met requirements, few of them mine. Yet I hoped in the end to assemble something, some wedding garment that would fit my skin.

All right! we would have a wedding! O.K.! Sixty couples! The smallest possible wedding acceptable to Miriam, the largest I could imagine. The parents all were generous, copiously so, offering what looked to me like a down payment on a co-op or graduate school tuition, to be blown in one day. It killed me. Still, I would try to please everyone.

The avalanche began. A leads to B, then to C and beyond. Out-of-town guests need hotels and meals. Sundays are cheaper—but the life partner I thought I knew suddenly championed Saturday night—big and festive, late and fun. Dinner, and dancing. A dance floor, a band.

If I had to do it, and I had to, I decided to throw a party my way. Not for me the package deal, the one-size-fits-all wedding program that would have been the easy way out. I rejected the standard prescripts, the well-trod paths that greater minds than mine, often in command of larger budgets, had fixed on to solve eternal problems. No, I wore out shoe leather on the road less taken, pricing spaces and *shuls,* hotels and halls, skylines and views—this was New York, after all—finding a printer, interviewing florists, renting dishes, hiring cars, auditioning musicians, engaging a rabbi, locating a parking lot for guests, designing a ceremony, ordering wine.

I flitted from one catering encounter to another. I was fixed, unfortunately fixed, on beautiful food, consistent with the excesses of a particular fashion moment in fickle New York. I had been guest at too many fabulous expense-account cocktail parties, dinners, teas, and luncheons footed in the end by unwitting taxpayers eating baloney sandwiches and clipping coupons from coast to coast.

I blush to think of the scorn I heaped on "entrée, choice of two." The ethereal foods of the Roaring Eighties sounded their siren call: pasta tossed with shrimp and dill; bite-sized quiche lorraine; *uni,* the custardy Japanese sea urchin eaten raw.

We would stand together, my groom and I, under the wedding *khupa,* a canopy formed from a prayer shawl woven of holy, lustrous wool. And then eat *uni?*

"A wedding must be kosher," Miriam said.

No shrimp, no lorraine. No shellfish, no pork. No cold lobster salad, no rumaki, no pastries from bakeries that might (one had never inquired) make pie crusts flaky by adding lard. No Thai noodles dosed with invisible dried shrimp powder. No clam broth Bloody Mary. No *uni.*

And too: no meat mixed with dairy. Obvious? Nothing sauced with a bit of cream if a bit of meat, downtable, was served. No butter frosting on the wedding cake an hour after beef. Not pâté, but chopped liver. No leg of lamb; only kosher cuts of meat. Pitfalls were everywhere. I swallowed hard and tried to focus on the main thing, marriage. I did want to get married, didn't I?

I didn't want meat, anyway.

I turned my thoughts to sea bass and salmon, brie and butter tarts. I spun a web of creamy fantasy: caviar and crème fraiche, mozzarella and tomato, baked goat cheese, ricotta cheese cake, watercress sandwiches on fresh brioche. But wait—is mozzarella kosher?

"*Milkhiks* (dairy) at a *simcha?*" Miriam wrinkled her nose in disdain.

Steak? Salad? Strudel? I didn't really understand. I had forgotten, or I had never known. Avoiding *treyf* was not enough. Not even kosher meat cooked in any old pots would be good enough. Something objective was required, a recognizable standard. Supervision. Rules. A kosher caterer with a kosher kitchen. Kosher wine. Kosher bread. Kosher salt.

I was falling, spinning. I was down the rabbit hole.

With everything we had to do, we left the rings for last.

"Hello, I need a caterer for a wedding."

"Your party is too small."

"Your party is too big."

"September is booked, darling."

"I can't do New York on your budget."

"I can't do dinner on your budget."

"September was booked a year ago."

"Knives will cost extra."

"I'll pick up a ring after we're married," decided the throb of my heart.

I had delusions. The simpatico catering hydra I sought—nouvelle kosher, artsy, not too ethnic, glamorous, friendly—was not to be found at a digestible price. In a high-rise office furnished in stainless steel, a taut husband-and-wife party team showed us slides, extolled simplicity's virtues: funereal platters of hard-boiled eggs, triangles of yellow cheese, sliced pound cake. In a red-and-mirrors catering hall, the man *would not* budge from his standard plan. Mandatory smorgasbord: bottom line.

Through steamy kitchen catacombs winding beneath a great hotel, I clattered at breakneck pace, in heels, suit, and briefcase. I ran alongside a bearded, paunchy, white-coated *mashgiakh,* the guarantor of *kashrut,* on the move before a wedding. While running and checking and looking and shouting and pointing, he reached out to steam tables, trolley carts, hot plates, snatching *maykhls*—tidbits—out of their pans for me to taste as I tried to keep up with him. One salty little frankfurter, one mini knish, a chopped liver puff, a chopped liver triangle, a chopped liver won ton, a greasy little meatball. Where were God's vegetables? Where was the vinegar, lemon, the toothy crunch of life?

Oh, how they promised. They promised kosher sushi, they promised cream cakes concocted of nondairy cream. I fell in love with the promises of one young chef, but, after begging for a taste, found the cuisine dusty, dry, and plain. I hit bottom in a soaring loft with a view of the Brooklyn Bridge, when the owner said he could do kosher, then followed this phrase with an anti-Semitic slur.

THOUSANDS OF WEDDING RINGS! So the sign proclaimed. It hung over a long, crooked counter set down the middle of a vast trading bay, one of the giant jewelry markets in New York's diamond district. I had been prowling 47th Street at lunchtime for a week, trying to find my simple rose-gold band. A simple task had become a challenge. Everything about a wedding took too many tries, too much angst. Life is too short. And the jewelers were folding up shop for August vacation.

I moved on tired feet, squinting into the glass. How can there be so many wedding rings in one small world? Carved, jeweled, wire-like, ostentatious, heavy, uncomfortable-looking, gleaming, open-work, ornate, particolored, multimetaled. My mind was overloaded, blown, blitzed. Hot carving stations, cold carving stations, white wine, red wine, out-of-towners' dinner, lilies, roses, Aunt Lily, Aunt Rose, reservations, carnations, alterations, invitations, engraved versus printed, white satin shoes—*Bloomingdale's?*

"Let me show you these," said the helpful young woman, lifting a black velvet card, but I couldn't look at any more displays. On her hand was a delicate ring.

"Oh, this? Our goldsmith upstairs made it for me."

It wasn't my simple circlet, but I liked it. Green gold, alloyed with zinc, a bit of a swirled shape to the metal, a glint of rose gold in the swirl. It fit me. It suited my hand. In a blue plush box, I carried it away.

Two days before the wedding, Miriam came to me.

"I had an uncle, my father's youngest brother," she began. "He died in the war."

I was madly circling and checking entries on lists that would never be done. My dress was ready, my veil was ready, my nails were oval and smooth. The *sheva brokhes,* seven matrimonial blessings, were typed out and assigned to seven readers. Would this prove chaotic, or would it actually work?

"As a young man, this uncle left our village. He wanted to live in a big city. My grandfather used to say, 'Mother's *lukshn mit yokh*—her noodles with soup—weren't good enough for him.' "

"Yes, *Ema?*" I said. I had begun calling her "mother" in the Hebrew way, to mark our imminent kinship. I felt a bit absent, however. My mind was racing. Would this work? Would that? Sabbath ends late in September, and our rabbi could not leave Brooklyn until after sundown. It might be nine thirty, or even later, before he arrived via F train. We would serve wine, a few appetizers, while our guests waited. Would everyone just get drunk, drinking wine on an empty stomach? And what was I supposed to do meanwhile? Hide in a corner? *Shmooze?*

The logic of smorgasbord hit me, but it was too late.

"He went to a jeweler in Warsaw, offering to work for nothing to learn jewelry making. He was very good at it," Miriam continued. "He brought jewelry to the family on his visits home."

Extra hose, evening coat, lipstick. Car booked for eight p.m.

"After the war started we buried some in my grandparents' ice cellar, where they kept the beer kegs for their business. We took out a board covering a step and buried the jewelry inside. After the war my cousin went back and dug it up. Later I got a few things."

"Ema?" I ask, for Miriam is taking a plastic bag from her purse, and handing it to me.

Wedding rings. A dozen, all sizes. Thin circlets, rose gold, gently domed. One fit me perfectly. Another slipped easily on the hand of my groom.

"I want you to have a ring from these rings," said Miriam.

This explains why both my hands wear wedding rings today.

In the end I found a restaurant owner who catered parties on the side. He *kashered* the pots and ovens, ordered kosher wine and dishes and knives and meat. He cooked the deep, good, delicious veals and salmons and mushrooms and peppers of the Romania of his Jewish youth. He baked a butterless chocolate wedding cake perfumed with brandy. I must admit he also broke promises, but these I cannot divulge, or risk unblocking anxieties still too great for my breast to bear.

I could not escape the feeling when all was said and done and fifty-five couples had witnessed our marriage and sung *Mazel tov!* and there was an indelible splotch of apricot strudel across the front of my white silk dress, that we had reinvented the wheel. Sequin by painstaking sequin, I think we fashioned a recognizable thing. A Jewish wedding, if not by the book. A joyous thing.

At my next *simcha,* though, God willing, we will serve chopped liver.

SUITCASE

$\mathcal{I}$t was a caramel-colored, hard-sided suitcase with snapping locks, a leather handle, and the motto OSHKOSH on an oval brass plate. Inside it had golden-brown satin linings, two soft secret pockets, and satin tie ribbons. It was a small suitcase, neat and clean-looking, and it was Dad's little suit-case, one of the few belongings so specifically named and claimed in the communal life of my childhood.

I loved that suitcase. I knew, or perhaps imagined, that my father had bought it to move to Detroit in 1948. It fit the image I had of him as a young man, before my mother married him, and, I imagined, roped him into frustrating, limiting, domesticity—slim and spare, ascetic and refined, classy, but not showy. It represented travel, change, risk. One day I, too, would pack up and leave.

That was fantasy. What was real was the family, the house, and the basement. The basement, filled with belongings, made leaving unlikely. Our family's history was down there, its mysteries were down there. What was down there, in fact, was often revealed in someone's bored moment just looking. Once a thousand dollars in silver certificates, stored in an unmarked envelope, casually turned up in a shopping bag.

I wanted to live in the basement. Not in the clutter of the main "rec" room, paneled in knotty pine and upholstered in green vinyl by the land-lord, who had lived in the house when new—but in a small room in the rear of the basement. This the landlord had fixed up as a bedroom for two young sons, before moving his family on to grander quarters. There were built-in bunks of knotty pine, and shiplike closets and drawers. But my father was resistant to clear out what was called "Dad's little room," resis-tant too, I believed, to losing physical—was it control?—over a growing child away from the family. My mother feared that the basement was cold.

In one closet was a plaid mackinaw jacket that would fit my father but that I had never seen him wear. Years later I found a photograph of him in the jacket on a New York street. One bunk was filled with drafting paper, seven-foot-long rolls of smooth white stock, heavy buff paper, and brown stock, stencils and drawing implements, drafting machines and tool boxes.

These were his working tools as he went about the job shops of automotive Detroit, and here they rested during months of unemployment, for his trade was seasonal.

The second bunk held the family's luggage. A large navy pasteboard valise with a gray lining, a heavy vinyl garment bag, something with my grandmother's Queen Elizabeth ship decals on it—I did know there was a wider world out there—and that little brown suitcase. I would open it, smell it, carry it, hide a postcard in it. I wanted my whole life to be as classic, as neat, as golden brown and satin smooth as that suitcase. I wanted to live in it.

When I started taking trips in high school, I took Dad's suitcase. It went with me as a teenager, to New York to visit my aunt, and to Cleveland to visit a girl met in summer camp. I took it to college, and to my first apartments. In my twenties, I stored scarves and jewelry within. I displayed it. On a bentwood chair it became an end table.

Then I got married and it sat under the bed for five years, holding nothing but my wedding veil and a pair of lace gloves. With the next move I became ruthless. I had begun to worry about becoming a hoarder, a prisoner of things. The basement of my childhood rose to haunt me after dark.

I began throwing out. Gone: an iridescent Mexican shawl brought back to Canada in the 1950s, smelling slightly of mildew. Gone: a stained and frayed apron handsewn by a great-aunt. Gone: my high school yearbook, a file of college papers, a stack of real wooden cigar boxes. And I put it out too, in front of the service elevator, the little tan suitcase, now with a broken lock, a dent in its side, a torn lining. Time to streamline, to go spare and classy. What the suitcase represented, I thought.

Several moves later, installed in a house with not only a basement but also an attic, my daughter turned five. For three weeks I turned the house upside down, inside out, looking for it, the perfect little suitcase for doll clothes, with all that history beside. Finally it hit me. I remembered. I had lost it, wasted it, while filled with the blind passion of destroying the past and moving on. Until that day, and I sat down limply, sick at the pit of my stomach, in my own basement empty and bare.

When I looked around I saw storage space.

RIBBON

*T*he grandmothers were not wealthy women. Because their husbands had worked hard, paid so and so many dollars each month toward the mortgages of their own homes, because of veterans' benefits and Social Security, and because my parents helped, as widows they never wanted. Then too they kept their wants to what they could afford. They had good serviceable clothing that lasted from year to year and they were moderate with their long-distance telephone calls. Restaurant meals, vacations, carryout dinners, entertainment, magazine subscriptions, dry cleaning, fashion, and so on they never inserted into their budget of needs. Never could, so never did.

As I child I could not know that such discretionary spending would swell in my life and threaten to overcome my own lazy financial health. I visited my grandmothers' gleaming homes where handmade food awaited on every shelf, and treasures of the ages were secreted in dresser drawers, and I felt rich.

For my parents, the great thing was that their mothers did not want. My parents could expect no substantial *yerisha*—inheritance—and this was in no sense a disappointment. My parents were children of immigrants, making their own way in the world. After the grandmothers died, the houses were sold, the expenses paid. The small yield of money was divided among my parents, their siblings, and the grandchildren. Our share went into the Detroit Bank and Trust toward college. The money changed nothing in our lives.

But there were objects, evocative and sentimental, never mentioned in a will or bequest that devolved to us and that brought the grandparents and particularly the grandmothers into our every days. After a stroke felled my mother's mother, and she was buried in the undeserving ground, some of her possessions came to live in our house. The *bubbe* had always a good eye for furnishings, and she had gathered into her home a collection of *tsatskes*—knickknacks—and heavy furniture from secondhand stores. In time, these budget purchases acquired objective monetary value. Indeed, it was with the greatest of pleasure in her last years that she would visit antique shops with my mother, examine a price tag, and remark with a bit of a laugh, "I have one just like that in my basement."

Thirty years later my daughter digs out clean socks from a tall dresser, reddish oak, topped with a pivoting beveled mirror, that the *bubbe* once waxed and polished. She dresses her long hair, in play, with the *bubbe*'s rhinestone comb.

My two-year-old boy hides thimbles and dice in the drawer of the *bubbe*'s fruitwood cigarette table, a light thing he drags from room to room. We mash potatoes with her red-handled potato masher, while back in Detroit my mother chops liver with her mother's chopper, half-moon wood handle fit to a half-moon blade.

The dark oak dining table, sideboard, and the dish cabinet, which the *bubbe* called a *shenkl,* are in style again as they never quite were in the crowded dining room behind the store of my *zeyde,* as my mother taught us to call her dad. Back in style too are the Depression glass bowls, and the Bakelite hairpin box, and the Victorian alphabet plate, and the tall oak plant stand. One day taste will catch up to the shoe irons and awls from the *zeyde*'s store, packed up in my parents' basement. His ebony clock, its upside-down numeral two for a five, will still be hanging on my parents' wall, its brass regulator beating defenseless time.

A few years after the *zeyde*'s clock went up on our wall, my father's mother took her last breath in a New York hospital. My father blamed the hospital and still follows its every bit of innuendo and bad news in the midwest edition of *The New York Times.* The following summer he went to Brooklyn to sort through and sell the house his parents had built and filled. He took with him my brother, then nearly thirteen. How it must have been, the restive adolescent and the grieving dad, waking up in the boyhood house and commencing another day of recollection and unwanted decision.

When summer was done, someone else owned the house that had been the closest thing we all had to ancestral home. Then they, the two of them, rumbled west in a U-Haul truck loaded up to the roof with artifacts of the heart. Thereafter Detroit would be home for all of us.

To Detroit came a carved mahogany sofa upholstered with coffee brocade and stuffed with goose down, and a chair to match. In the trailer was the marble-topped server, from the grand Spanish-style dining room set, wrapped in a coppery satin quilt. My father unpacked the crystal fruit basket, the three-shelf bookcase and the books it had shelved. There was a rolled-up Belgian carpet in trellised maroon and a brooch of green cut glass.

He brought home shoeboxes full of photographs, some still from Europe, some from the early Brooklyn years, and some the shiny Kodak snapshots sent from Detroit as a bridge to long-distance grandchildren. He brought an expired memorial certificate, listing fifteen years of *yahrzeit* dates, Hebrew anniversaries of his father's death.

He retrieved a stack of handkerchiefs embroidered with X's and swirls and forget-me-nots by his blue-eyed mother, and reproductions of famous paintings that had been matted and hung by his sisters. One of these was Rousseau's *The Sleeping Gypsy*, in which a lion visits the woman camped on the ground in the moonlight. I had slept under this strangely disturbing and peaceful print on every visit east for fifteen years. The woman's skin is black and her raiment is biblical and a lute lies by her side. Now this picture hangs in my parents' house, on the wall near the *bubbe*'s *shenkl* and just to the side of the ticking wall clock.

He brought his father's prayer books and chess set and memorandum book and his mother's Passover dishes and silver, and a crate of everyday kitchen things so intrinsic to his mother's days that with them my father could not bear to part. He brought my grandmother's Passover soup pot, and I took it with me to my first apartment and all subsequent dwellings, and in my years of risotto and scampi and mulligatawny could never bear to cook in it other than a kosher chicken soup.

So there was a *yerisha,* a bequest, after all. These things were part of it, and they continue, they carry on. My father took his dad's toolboxes from the cellar, massive wooden crates with brown hinges and rusty locks, filled with augers and wrenches and levels and planes. He took metal canisters that had once stocked his father's store, tins and wooden boxes and stone crocks and glass jars. He packed up a twenty-five-year-old bottle of blue-berry cordial, his father's home brew. We opened it for my brother's bar mitzvah.

He was confused and upset in the sorting, at times I believe he did not know what he was doing, mourning his mother and father and clearing out their home of fifty years, and he took things that it made no sense to take. He packed his mother's rimless eyeglasses, a white enamel basin, a maple kitchen chair, his old desk and wardrobe, the meat grinder out of the kitchen, the solid furniture he grew up with, wrong for our house and worthless to anyone else.

My father brought home a black cashmere coat, acquired at B. Altman in the 1950s, and I have worn it for more than twenty years myself—in college with jeans, on New Year's Eve in Manhattan. It is still in style, short and full, shawl-collared; it has never been out of style. That's service in a garment. That is style. It's a small thing, but still a gift of a kind, to know how to buy such a coat, and such knowledge my grandmother had.

He brought home two hats she had made—she was a milliner—a black plush hat with a turned-down brim, and a brown felt cloche trimmed with a sprig of brown tulle. We wore those hats, my sister and I. He took a packet of letters, tied with a pale ribbon, and expressed regret as my sister and I passed them between ourselves, reading letters of courtship and youth, when she, still Chaya and not yet Irene, was trying out many an English name on the Lower East Side of New York.

"She kept her papers one to one in a certain order all the years," he mused. He didn't feel right somehow when the ribbon fell to the floor and the sheaf of letters opened.

There were letters written to her by my grandfather, who had decided "Irene" was the name of choice. He would humor her: the envelopes were addressed variously—Miss Ida Kusher, Ludlow Street; Miss Charlotte Kusher, Ludlow Street—but the letters all began one way: Dear Irene . . .

Perhaps we saved more than other people, and threw out less. We were folk who told the stories and held on to the objects, until the objects embodied the stories. Thus the distant past, the immigrant past, is for me as close as yesterday, as close as the things on the shelf, as close as the shelf itself.

A few years ago, a three-year-old girl played with a box of ribbons in my house, her great-grandmother's ribbons, millinery supplies. Her great-aunt had kept them all these years, and presented the box as a birthday gift. Satins and real velvet and grosgrain, in colors that no longer exist or are only hinted at in photographs of lost decades: a blue somewhere between slate and sky, Viennese chocolate brown, Empire State Building navy blue (I mean a career girl's navy suit at a certain moment in American life), also pink-beige, and lavender.

This, too, was part of the *yerisha*.

As a child visiting Brooklyn, I also played with my grandmother's ribbons. There was a long curl of narrow satin, blue on one side, pink on the reverse, its edges beautifully picoted. The two-toned ribbon once had looped through the dining room chandelier, decorating my aunt's Sweet

Sixteen party in 1937. This my aunt recalled over tea in the 1990s, how her mother had done what she could to dress up her home for a party on a Depression budget. She painted the radiators herself, fresh silver paint, and polished the floor by hand and festooned the chandelier with ribbon. Then, when the tea had been poured and the cake served, and the last guest politely shown to the door, my grandmother carefully spooled up the ribbon again, pink and baby blue, for a lifetime of genteel reuse. Thus she became, in my eyes, rich.

Some years ago my sister and I strolled through a museum together to view an exhibit on American Jewish life. We don't always agree, my sister and I. We diverge, our different understandings of life bristle like steel wool, and from our closeness comes hot friction. But in the Jewish Museum that day, my sister grabbed my hand, and we laughed and cried and we didn't let go until we were back on icy Fifth Avenue.

We were a museum. The young curators had studied and researched and collected to reconstruct an authentic immigrant household from the century's childhood. They should have just called us up. There was our *yerisha:* the *bubbe*'s wooden-handled chopper and chopping bowl, still in use in our mother's kitchen; the enamel *vanele,* or basin, in which we bathe our babies when visiting Detroit. The spice canisters, the meat grinder, the wood-covered saltbox filled with coarse salt. My grandmother's carved sofa and matching chair, and her candlesticks. The maple kitchen chair and the rimless spectacles. The *zeyde*'s Regulator clock.

As for themselves, the grandmothers chose what to keep. They had little nostalgia, no sentiment for hardship. They were the immigrants, self-taught and self-made. They left much behind, could not dwell in the past. They created their lives anew.

We are different. We treasure their gear, divining meaning beyond material use, bearing it across a continent in a U-Haul truck. They approximated and knew their shortcuts for what they were; we raise their guesswork on pedestals.

We cup in our hands a satin ribbon, and it tethers us to our past.

MANDELBROT

*I*t means almond bread. It is a crisp and crumbly twice-baked nut cookie. There are many versions. This is Miriam's *mandelbrot*.

"It's not my recipe," says Miriam. "My mother had the same recipe, almost, but I can't find it. This is Sonia's mother's recipe."

"I don't remember chocolate chips in *mandelbrot*," I say. Miriam's is made with chocolate chips. I remember *mandelbrot* from the dim recesses of the past, packed in a shoebox and carried in a grandmother's shopping bag. I am looking at Sonia's mother's recipe, copied in Miriam's ornate, vertical script on a loose-leaf page. I don't see chocolate chips in the list of ingredients, either.

"I put them in for the children!" sings Miriam. "And now I will not take them out."

"This last batch tasted of cinnamon," I remark, scanning the page again: No cinnamon.

"I tried a different recipe. I found one with cinnamon, and my mother used to put cinnamon. Did you like it?"

"Well, yes—" I say. I remember *mandelbrot* a bit different, not quite as sweet as Miriam's. It was marvelous. Miriam's is marvelous. Whole boxes of almond-fragrant chocolate-chip–studded crisp oval slices neatly packed disappear in a trice.

"Sonia's mother used to make *kreski*— crumb cake. It was out of this world. But she doesn't have the recipe. I asked her for it," says Miriam. "I was heartbroken."

I have never had crumb cake. I, too, am heartbroken.

"Nu?" says Miriam. "Take the recipe."

This is Miriam's *mandelbrot*.

MANDELBROT

$3^{1}/_{2}$ cups all-purpose flour
2 tbsp. baking powder
Pinch of salt
$^{1}/_{2}$ tsp. cinnamon
$^{1}/_{4}$ tsp. cloves
1 cup finely chopped walnuts
$^{1}/_{2}$ cup chopped almonds

$1^{1}/_{4}$ cups sugar
4 eggs
1 tsp. vanilla extract
1 tsp. almond extract
6 oz. vegetable oil
10 oz. semi-sweet chocolate chips
(optional)

Preheat oven to 350°F.

Sift flour, baking powder, salt, cinnamon, and cloves into a mixing bowl (a *shisl*). Add the walnuts, almonds, and sugar. Mix. Make a well in the flour mixture. To the well, add the eggs. Capture all the egg white from the shell with your thumb. Add vanilla extract, almond extract, and oil. Mix first with a fork, then with your hands. Add chocolate chips, if desired.

Chill the dough for at least six hours, preferably overnight. Remove from the fridge and divide into four parts. On a floured board, roll each section into a snake-shaped loaf 18 inches long. Place "snakes" onto pans greased with margarine. Flatten dough loaves until $^{1}/_{2}$-inch thick. Bake at 350°F., for 20 to 25 minutes. Remove from oven and let cool. Lift loaves off pans carefully. (Miriam uses two spatulas.) Set on a clean surface (the rolling board is fine).

Wipe the baking pans. Remove any particles or crumbs, but don't grease again. Slice the loaves $^{3}/_{4}$-inch thick, at an angle. Arrange slices flat on the pans. Bake again at 375°F., for 15 to 20 minutes until light brown.

CHRISTMAS GOOSE

*A*fter my grandmother died, and the Brooklyn house had been emptied and sold, my father's family no longer gathered for Passover. Brooklyn was scattered—the needlepoint chair went to one grown child, the gold-rimmed Passover dishes to another—and without my grandmother to hold things together, its Jewish essence also dispersed. We were fond but evolving, choosing different roads. Our reliable reunion became Christmas. We met each year at Aunt Selina's Christmas party.

My aunt had been making Christmas all along for her husband, his family, and their two sons. Uncle Charles was Presbyterian by birth, non-practicing. He had Methodists and Catholics and a couple of hidden Jews in his family tree. It was an American religion; he believed in the life of the mind and the Fourth of July. Aunt Selina made atheist Christmas, red, white, and green. She invited us all to share it, the December after my grandmother died.

My parents, brother, sister, and I drove through the midday cold into the rolling old mountains beyond the city, our suitcases, duffels, and teenage hormones serried like jigsaw pieces into the family car. We found our way up the mountain road banked with snow. We counted mailboxes. We made the hard turn into the long driveway. Under the black lace arch of bare branches above, our tires crunched ice-crusted gravel. It was our first Christmas. I was sixteen years old.

Flat-roofed, welcoming, the house appeared in its wintry clearing, sheltered by shapely green pines in a row. The trees had been planted year by year; they stair-stepped in height like children of sequential age. Each had begun as a tinsel-tipped Christmas tree, alive, here in the one country house our family had attained.

Indoors stood the newest small evergreen aroot in its nursery tub. Selina dressed her tree with a bit of tinsel and her handmade ornaments, whimsical sleds and poppets and tiny brown bears fashioned from pipe cleaners and colored felt. Selina sewed, baked, and gardened; she had a career and two well-run houses. Spectacular nest builder she, whose

Hebrew name, Tzipora, means "bird"—bespeaking the skillful nest as well as the winged flight from home.

I was nervous and exited; I was a Christmas virgin. Uncle Charles offered me eggnog with rum like a grown-up. I met his brothers, their wives and sons. The brass Christmas angel spun and chimed when a candle was lit beneath it. Family friends buzzed about, drinking cocktails. My great-uncle and great-aunt were here, transplanted it seemed from the Passover table, yet perfectly at ease. These were our New Yorkers, with whom I had associated The Tradition.

Aunt Selina had little gifts for all of us, and we hadn't brought anything but a house gift, since we didn't know from Christmas. The other aunt, Millie, was in on the secret, too. My father's two sisters had been exchanging Christmas gifts for years while we were home lighting the menorah, our Hanukkah candelabra, and eating my mother's crunchy *latkes,* Hanukkah potato pancakes fried in oil. Aunt Millie brought me a handprinted tunic from Europe, where she and her family were living in those years. I donned it over my turtleneck sweater right then.

Someone took a head count of Christians and Jews, a diversion my father disliked. Maybe he thought it took away from the secular spirit of the thing. My brother and Cousin Jeremy began drinking beer, a twelve-year-old's adorable joke. I couldn't lock the bathroom door and feared lest one of the boy cousins should walk in. We had chopped liver, made with mayonnaise, not schmaltz, as an hors d'oeuvre, and clam dip on celery, and then it was Christmas dinner.

Aunt Selina set out her buffet. We passed before the platters in a merry appreciative line, choosing sweet-and-sour red cabbage with raisins, wild rice, sliced cucumbers in dill vinegar, buttery string beans almondine, whipped chestnut, sweet potato, scalloped potato, roast goose, baked ham.

Yes, ham. There it was, pink, brown-sugared, smoked pig, a whole ham next to the crisp carved goose. Ham, it seemed, was the annual contribution of Selina's dearest friend, a brilliant intellectual, also of Jewish birth. (A few years later, hoping to become a brilliant intellectual, I would serve myself a first slice of ham. After the eggnog with chopped liver and clam dip, this last barricade of particularism too must fall. Kosher was long ago and far away by then, beside the point and even a bit embarrassing, as was even Hanukkah itself.)

This first Christmas I skipped the ham, and helped myself to the goose. Roast goose was a conversation piece that year. Aunt Millie's mother-in-law had reached back into her Frankfurt childhood and said to Selina, "And will you serve the Christmas goose?" Selina had picked up the gauntlet.

Somehow, for years, I mixed up the story. I thought that my grandmother had posed the question before she died. I even imagined her asking this, wearing a good suit, a gold brooch, seated on her brocade sofa upholstered in plump goose down. I pictured her hands folded in her lap, her face a study. Irene, my grandmother, had spent her teen years in middle-class Germany. She was not thrilled about Christmas, true. But she would have known about Christmas goose.

In the light of Christmas candles, adults sipped their amber and garnet drinks. We ate the marvelous dinner, goose, ham, and all. There was intoxicating laughter and affectionate argument and there was more than a little in it of the red velvet Brooklyn Passovers together. My brother and Jeremy, having moved on to wine, were outside now, rolling in snow by moonlight.

Dessert arrived, Selina's cakes and country club pies. The mince, I remembered from Dickens, might be concocted with suet, rich and thoroughly *treyf*—unkosher—under hard sauce and whipped cream, and the crust was probably lard. I scraped every bit off my plate. My brother was back, saying something like "help" in a whisper, and I was too deeply happy to attend. He threw up on me and the new tunic. What a party it was.

What did it matter the religious roots of Christmas, and whether Christmas or Pesach brought us together each year? As the years went on, I saw Christmas becoming nondenominational, as American as Thanksgiving, less Christian indeed than pagan. I could relate to pagan: We all want the sun to come back, we all want our mead and joint and sweet candlelight. At that moment, and for many years after, no holiday could have been more authentic for the family we were, the people we had become.

Goose was on the menu every year after that, and most years, when I could be there, I was. Selina's story of Christmas, often retold, was my first Christmas, the First Christmas Goose. Provoked or inspired, but anyway (figuratively) goosed, she had purchased two birds from a country butcher. On the kitchen counter they lay.

"Then what?" recalled my aunt, professing that she had no idea of the thing. Cookbooks were opened, recipes compared. Telephones dialed and rang. Women consulted: Selina and sister and sister's mother-in-law and a German friend married to a Jew, a gaggle of women honking and ruffling over how to cook a Christmas goose.

The secret, it turned out, was all in the fat. Aunt Selina told me this. I was not there, but understood it thus: A roasting tableau. Handsome women in aprons, cheeks ruddy from the oven's heat, as cabbage boiled sweet-and-sour on the stovetop and potatoes awaited scalloping with butter and cream. You had to prick the birds all over so the skin crisped and the fat ran out clear. And then you poured, poured, poured off the rendered fat so the fat would not burn.

"In Europe, you know, the goose fat was prized," Selina told me. "It would be saved and used for cooking throughout the year."

This had a strange, familiar sound to me, something like the distant sizzle of nineteenth-century cutlets and potatoes, perhaps even *latkes,* before the words "cholesterol" and "polyunsaturated" entered Jewish vocabularies.

One Christmas Day she held up a mason jar for me to see.

"I saved the goose fat," Aunt Selina said proudly.

It showed yellow and thick in the mason glass, and it startled me. This was definitely familiar. When I was a girl, my mother and grandmothers had regularly made schmaltz. It was a thing of the past with us now, although exactly when the schmaltz era ended I could not say. At one time, a jar filled with pure, rendered chicken fat, a frill of waxed paper under the lid, was a fixture in the refrigerators I knew best, ready to mix into chopped liver or to have for frying or to spread hot on matzos at Passover time.

I thought about my grandmother, Selina's mother, steaming large, square matzo crackers in a long-handled wire rack over a boiling kettle, brushing the damp warm matzos with hot schmaltz and sprinkling it all with coarse kosher salt. I thought about Selina saving the fat from her Christmas goose. I marveled at all that goes on in a single life.

When I moved to New York on my own, Christmas tree vendors appeared on the streets in December. I breathed the fir fragrance with rapture. I scavenged loose pine boughs from the pavement to tie with red ribbons and scatter to effect on the mantelpiece in my room.

That year I invited my boyfriend to New York at Christmas. There was eggnog in the tiny fridge, pâté on a plate. I wore a red silk blouse. I lit a tall green candle. His eyes found the ribbons and boughs.

"What is that?" he asked, and not very sweetly.

"Winter solstice," I said, taken aback. "Nothing, love. Nonsectarian—"

I don't think I ever finished, for he, this son of concentration camp survivors, this boyfriend raised in Israel on tales of martyrs to the faith, this man that I would one day marry, firmly insisted that this particular trimming must go.

The Hanukkah story has in it a strong anti-assimilationist thread. The brothers Maccabee led their guerrillas against the full-scale assault on Hebrew worship and learning that had begun with attractive, harmless inroads of Greek language, culture, and sport. If you celebrate the Jewish festival with any thought, you can't also celebrate Christmas. Frenzied December, ubiquitous Christmas, must then be resisted, at least in one's mind, at least in one's very own home.

Such reflections were all in my future then, as I reluctantly tossed out the evergreen spray. I was proud to think of my family bending and blending and being themselves as they also became something new. Selina, as far as I was concerned, had made Christmas a proto-Jewish holiday, rich in feeling, continuity, intelligent talk, and bottomless food.

But time was running out on us, the second generation. Our ecumenical center could not hold. In a few years there would be children with no memory of my grandmother's Passover to balance Selina's Christmas. We would have to create new Jewish memories for them, or find the text of their later longings to be scalloped potatoes, tinsel, and ham.

Still, the next day, December 25, driving to the country—my boyfriend at the wheel, a case of wine in the back seat, and a sack of witty knickknacks tied up in gilt—Oh, it was pleasant to anticipate Christmas and the introductions that were to be. Christmas was perfect at the country house, as the storm door closed behind us, leaving immigrant uncertainties out in the slush.

Uncle Charles offered drinks. Talk gathered the men, including mine. I drifted to the stove, where my aunt stood in a red silk blouse and an apron, warming raisins and cabbage on a flame so low.

"When will you let someone help you?" I asked, mock stern, wineglass in hand.

"When you grow up and take over," Selina parried at once. I was only a little offended. I was working my way through my twenties, quite done, I thought, with the protracted adolescence my generation seemed to share. I could begin to imagine a house and a kitchen and being the one to invite.

But no one took over Christmas. Selina, finally, gave it up: "Too much" this year, "too much" the next, and it had been prodigious, the work. I ached, wanting to give back something for all the years of our enjoyment. It was wonderful, and I miss it. But by the time I grew up, I couldn't do Christmas. I do Hanukkah, with potato *latkes*. I build a sukkah booth in the fall. I do Passover, and I invite. Charles and Selina always come.

First I did it all for the children. Now I do it for myself.

As Passover nears, I open a file folder labeled "Jewish Holidays," hoping for a miracle of organization, of simplicity. Out slips a sheaf of paper, Selina's handwriting, and there they are: the Christmas recipes. Red cabbage, potatoes, the buttery beans, the roasted goose "to be served with a whole ham," as she notes, just in case I were to forget.

I am filled with nostalgia, and I sit down, leafing through the recipes, remembering times in my life that will never come again. When the telephone rings, it is my mother-in-law, Miriam, calling to plan Pesach, Passover. On a whim I ask her if she ever ate a goose.

"Sure," she answers, as if I were witless, "in Poland, in winter. Roasted. The Hanukkah goose."

Hanukkah goose, of course, with sweet-and-sour cabbage and potato *latkes* for Hanukkah on the side. And then she tells me something else.

When the goose came from Radom, a town near her village, Miriam's mother would clean her stove. She scoured, she scrubbed, she burned it hot, as though for spring cleaning. From a hidden place, she would take out a Passover pot, and her Passover jars, and roast the goose in what she had converted into a Passover kitchen for a day.

She would prick the goose all over until the fat ran clear, and pour off the valuable fat into jars, boiling and sealing to keep it until winter's end. And this special prize, the savory goose schmaltz, would be ready to open, and kosher for Pesach, when Passover came around.

"We would *shmear* it hot on steamed matzos," Miriam recalls.

A luscious bit of my rightful past: Selina's Christmas goose.

SWEET-AND-SOUR CABBAGE

1 red cabbage (5 lbs.)
1/2 cup margarine or olive oil
Salt and pepper
1 tsp. nutmeg
3 tbsp. white vinegar

3 tbsp. brown sugar
1/2 cup white raisins
1/2 cup dried currants
2 cups peeled apples, small dice

Cut away core of cabbage. Shred crudely.

Heat fat in large saucepan. Add cabbage. Sprinkle with salt, pepper, and nutmeg.

Add vinegar, brown sugar, raisins, currants, and apples. Cover, bring to a boil, cook about 10 minutes, stirring a bit. Cook, covered, 1 1/2 hours, stirring occasionally.

If desired, add more nutmeg and brown sugar to taste.

WINTER HOLIDAY GOOSE

11 lb. or more goose, to serve 6
to 8 (3 geese for 25 people)
Lemon juice

Salt
White pepper
Garlic powder

Preheat oven to 400°F.

(Allow 4 hours of cooking time; 3 hours or so if day before; 1 hour to reheat.)

An hour or so before cooking time, take fat out of cavity. Reserve.

Cut off wing tips. Wash goose with cold water and lemon juice.

Sprinkle inside and out with salt, white pepper, a touch of garlic powder.

Put goose on rack in heavy pan, breast up.

Place loose fat taken out of cavity on the breast.

Add about 1/4 inch cold water to pan to prevent burning.

Start with 400°F. oven. Turn down to 350°F. after 45 minutes. (Or, start with 450°F. and turn down to 350°F. as soon as bird is in.)

Baste every 10 minutes for first 45 minutes. (Thereafter baste a few times.)

Prick the bird occasionally once it has started cooking.

1 1/4 hours from start, when breast is brown, lift out rack with bird.

Tilt pan to pour clear fat into container (see note on p. 108). Leave juice in pan.

Turn bird over (wearing rubber gloves). Return to oven.

After 2 1/2 hours from start, again take all fat out of pan.

Empty juice from cavity into pan.

Place bird breast up again.

Let juice brown in pan (half an hour?), adding a little water from time to time.

Gravy

3 hours from start, add giblet gravy to pan (see recipe, p. 108): keep adding water as needed. If done the day before: After juice has browned a bit, add it to the gravy saucepan to finish, instead of finishing gravy in roasting pan.

At end, brush salt water on goose to make skin crisp.
Remove gravy from pan. Wash pan and line with foil.
Return goose on rack to pan. Place in lowered oven to keep warm.

GIBLET GRAVY

Best done the day before because it's tedious. Also, cooling facilitates removing fat. Reserve liver for chopped liver.

Neck and remaining giblets	*6 tbsp. flour*
6 tbsp. oil	*$^1/_2$ cup red wine*
4 tbsp. minced shallots (or 1	*$^1/_2$ cup beef broth*
chopped onion)	*$2^1/_2$ cups beef broth*

Break or chop neck to fit in heavy saucepan. Brown neck and giblets in the oil with the shallots. Stir in flour and cook lightly until light brown. Remove from heat and stir in wine and half cup beef broth until smooth. Return to heat. Add remaining broth slowly, stirring as you do so.

Selina's note on goose fat:

Nice to save fat, clear of meat juices (good for frying potatoes or sautéing chicken livers).

Hence, take care fat doesn't brown: Add a little water to stop the browning if it starts to sizzle.

As you take clear fat out of the roasting pan, pour into a saucepan to cool. (Don't worry if some drippings are in it; they'll settle to the bottom as the fat cools.)

Then pour into small plastic containers. Can be frozen.

MIRIAM'S POTATO LATKES

For every 5 lb. Idaho potatoes, you will need:

¹/₂ tsp. ascorbic acid powder, or 1
*   to 2 vitamin C tablets,*
*   crushed (to keep potato white)*
1 egg

3 tbsp. flour or matzo meal
Salt to taste
Oil for frying
Small piece of bread

Grate potatoes on a hand grater into a large bowl. Grated texture should be wet but not completely mush. Mix with citric acid powder to keep the potato white.

Transfer grated potato into a fine mesh strainer. Drain water from potato into a bowl—about 5 minutes.

Pour off the water. There will be thick, sticky potato starch left in the bottom of the bowl.

Spoon up the starch and mix it with the drained, grated potato.

Add slightly beaten egg, flour or matzo meal, and salt.

Fry spoonfuls of batter in ³/₄ inch of oil in a large frying pan until brown and crisp; turn. Oil should be very hot when you spoon in potato mixture. (A small piece of bread in the pan will collect the small bits and keep them from burning.)

Drain latkes on paper towel.

Good with applesauce, sour cream, or (Miriam's way) sugar.

January

OBLIGATION

January

Does anyone draw a January list without a diet or exercise goal, without aspiring to self-perfection? As the secular calendar turns, I, too, plan on fitness, on household organization, on wisely budgeted resources and time. Most calendar years begin tired or hung-over or a bit physically overindulged. These conditions are incentives to forswear excess and attempt a fresh, more disciplined, routine. In contrast to the old, flawed me, I will create a person whose achievements engender pride, whose willpower will be evident from without and can be judged by all who care to notice.

My thoughts in autumn, the start of the ancient lunar year, tend differently. After a week of introspection and a day of fasting, I am more worried about the pitfalls of envy or gossip or indifference than about a few excess pounds. Of my success or failure in that sphere, no one at the gym will know.

Beginning the autumn new year, I do not turn my mind to willpower, but to the acceptance of obligations. It is not a matter of resolutions, but of opening one's eyes to the same old requirements that were there all along. They are always there, notice them or not, accept them or not. Choose them or not, they are inevitable, yours. The rabbis of old, I have read, believed that even outright renunciation doesn't change your internal essence. Lapse, turn hostile, disconnect, convert, be named pope, what have you—you are still inescapably of the people.

It is January. So, sculpt a shapely muscle.

Grandmother's religion waits.

PARIS

I almost slept with a boy in Paris, but then I didn't. I went to Paris for love and internationalism and beauty and art and urbane radicalism and all those essentials that make France itself. Imagining ahead of time, I thought I might fall in love and stay in France forever.

But I didn't find love. I found Maurice, a retired humanities professor who had escaped from German-occupied Warsaw with his brother as a boy of thirteen. The two Jewish boys found work washing dishes, and taught themselves French. Maurice now was divorced. His wife, a Catholic woman, had left him. He needed someone to help him keep house. I was the unlikely hire.

Before I met Maurice I bought a French grammar and studied it on the Metro. I carried a sketchbook with me. I was nineteen. I slept in a youth hostel. I hoped for love. I picked up my mail at American Express.

There was a letter waiting for me at American Express from my mother: *Are you lying in a gutter dead or what? Your father's hair is turning gray.* I had not been the best correspondent during those months in Europe, after dropping out of college to avoid flunking out. I wrote back: *Paris shimmers with a strange light. Don't worry about me. I still have some money and I am studying art.*

I was in fact attending studio classes at a venerable art academy with no authority to do so. I brought my own newsprint and pencils and stood at a spare easel in the back of an atelier while a wan, languid youth with a birthmark on his thigh posed on a stepladder. I was impressed with the free availability of cultural education. Soon, however, an official of the school chased me down a long marble hallway yelling French threats and curses. I escaped out the portal.

For a week or so, I took my pencils to the Louvre each day. I made sketches of the Winged Victory and, pretending to be French, sold them to tourists. I can't remember how I got my student pass to the museums of France or my tickets for the student cafeterias. At one of the student cafeterias I ate rabbit, *lapin,* for the first time. I thought it was chicken until I tasted it. I instantly knew what it was. It tasted like a long-eared, large-toothed rodent, and the drumstick was not a chicken bone. No ruminating stomach; no cloven hoof—the old kosher constraints. Well. It was clear, perhaps, that my bohemianism only went so far.

At the cafeteria I met a young man, Tunisian, a compact, muscular man with beautiful teeth. He took me to a Tunisian food stall and bought me a fried tuna sandwich and a tiny cup of sweet black coffee. I think it was he who first planted the idea in my head that my calling was cinema studies. Our third, potentially decisive rendezvous never took place. Then I met a Nigerian, tall and handsome, and he understood physics as well as the political history of cinema.

I didn't find love there, either.

As far as it concerned me, there was no sex in Paris.

The Nigerian did lead me to school. His suburban university campus was an appealing hotbed of left-wing politics and alternative studies. The university's administration had developed it after the student strike of 1968, as a place to put radicals and inconvenient countercultural types and third-world students.

Here, earnestly listening to lectures on film theory, I encountered a Marxist contingent, disciples of an American who would later move his Committees to the wild far right. They were highly organized, articulate. I had no desire to join in.

I was interested, though, in the disciples. We sat down over coffee and cigarettes. It dawned on me that they were all Jews, occupying that old emotional nexus in which I too was raised. Subordinating oneself to a cause, raising oneself by trying to make the world better, loving one's fellow man in principle and hating men's foibles in practice, throwing a theoretical construct around history and a moral net around the world, and of course the endless arguments over interpreting texts and events—it all seemed very familiar, very Jewish. My father, always a partisan of dialectical reasoning, had once hoped for the millennium, the coming of a rational society, the way pious Jews hoped for the Messiah.

Leading this group was David, a stiff-haired, tall man in a black leather jacket, attractive in an unsmiling way, an American national with flawless French and a crusade against marijuana. There was a Parisian fellow, comfortably drawn in wire-rimmed glasses, red beard, and never without a stack of leaflets, who told me his grandfather had been in the *Bund,* the Yiddish socialist league, as had mine. A slight long-haired young woman kept company with him. She was Cuban-born of parents fleeing Hitler.

The boat had not been allowed to enter New York harbor, and went to Havana instead.

I did not get involved. I didn't want to be an outsider, an observer, a crusader for a better world, a Jewish radical in France. I wanted to ride the back of a *moto* behind a boy who read *Cahiers du Cinéma* and visited his grandfather's vineyard in August. I wanted to eat *lapin* without flinching.

Every turn in Paris, though, brought me back to my Jewish past.

I was running out of traveler's checks, and I didn't want to go home. I needed a job. In Scotland, I had worked as a barmaid in a hotel, securing wages and meals and more glasses of whiskey in lieu of cash tips than was strictly beneficial. In London, I lived in a rooming house, trading chores for my digs. Now I wrote out an ad, in labored French, seeking job with room and board. I taped it to a wall in the college. Since I was living in a youth hostel that threw out its guests each morning, I had no phone number to leave: *Si vous avez une place, laissez votre nombre de téléphone, s'il vous plaît. Je vous téléphonerai. Merci.*

Miraculously, when I checked a few days later, there was a *nombre*. But when I called Maurice, it seemed that another American girl had seen my sign first, called him, and gotten the job that morning. Maurice was too kindhearted or passive to turn her down or refuse me, so he hired us both.

Phoebe, a dancer from Chicago, in Paris to study mime, got the room. I had to sleep on a couch in Maurice's living room.

I felt a strong maternal protectiveness toward Maurice, who sat in his dressing gown and slippers at a desk piled high with encyclopedias and notepads. He had retired from a job teaching history, and was up to his neck in a scholarly project of his own devising, a unified theory of western civilization incorporating all fields of human knowledge and endeavor. He envisioned a dozen large volumes. It was hopeless, unfinishable. His house smelled of coffee and stale laundry and unwashed dishes and cats.

Phoebe, a serious student of mime, took care of the cats each morning. She had studio classes from 8:30 until 6. She would strike extreme, androgynous, stylized poses in front of Maurice's dresser mirror, and she turned up her nose at narrative pantomime. She thought it too vulgar; her studio master maintained that it pandered to the crowd.

In the evenings, Phoebe had an active social life in the nascent world of Parisian radical feminism. Once she took me to a lecture on menstrual extraction, which was going to free women from one more biological burden. We sat in the auditorium, with Phoebe evaluating the female *derrières* passing by. *Je préfère les femmes,* she told me. Her checks came regularly in envelopes addressed to "Phyllis," signed by her dad.

After Phoebe emptied the cat box each morning and left, I took care of Maurice's housework. I was aggrieved at Phoebe for shirking, and I used to complain to Maurice. I wanted the spare room, and I wanted Phoebe out. Phoebe and I squabbled. Maurice would not make waves, especially after he learned that Phoebe, too, was a Jew with no place to go.

"*Jamais, jamais,* never again," I would hear him mutter at times in frustration. "Never again will I live with two *jeune femmes, absolument non, jamais.*" But I loved Maurice and his messy life. I gathered the coffee cups from around the apartment, and washed the grease off his dishes. I swept out the kitchen and watered the plants. I laundered his linen in a little spin washer beside the kitchen sink, and I folded the dry clothes and put them away. Organizing his dresser drawers, I was slightly alarmed to discover a package of condoms. He wasn't a father figure exactly, but avuncular anyway. Were they intended for Phoebe, or for me?

I received my formal education in French at the local market. Maurice sent me out most days with a list—breads and lettuce, pâté, butter. Phoebe's staple, *fromage de campagne* ("I finally found cottage cheese in Paris!"), was usually on the list. Maurice would coach me on the grammar before I left the house, then I would wander among the fragrant stalls with a dictionary and phrase book for an hour or two.

I worked up the nerve to ask for each baguette. I studied the French self-assurance on display, but never got the hang of it. This trait, easy assurance, was everywhere in Paris. The chic market shopper, her basket heaped with anemones, had it. So had the *vendeuse* selling fish. No matter what they're wearing, no matter what they are doing, in Paris—it's intimidating. I made my face into a mask and rehearsed.

"My brother and I escaped through the border," Maurice told me one night. Something about a fence and hiding at night in the kitchen in which they worked. He blew his nose on a handkerchief I would now have to wash. His eyes were watery. The brother had died. Except for his married, childless son, Maurice was all alone.

"We got jobs, and went to school. But we studied *grammaire,* and why is it that you, and Phoebe, *deux jeunes femmes très intelligentes,* sound like illiterates? You must study more!"

"J'essaierai plus forte," I said earnestly, "I will try harder, Maurice." Phoebe just laughed silently and went to her room. Gesturing dramatically, she pulled the door to.

Once Maurice threw me for a loop by adding *2 côtelettes de porc* to the list—and asked me to cook them. I stood at the butcher stall under an entire dead pig and many sausages made from the pig's friends and relations, and I uttered my order with as much casualness as I could muster. I slipped the parcel into my string bag, and I paid. *Merci, madame,* said the butcher, with a gratified nod. "Good day!" Well, well, I was in at last. But did I want to be?

Back in Maurice's kitchen I confronted the pale pork flesh. I had eaten pâté, and it might have been pork liver, I had tasted crisp bacon and lean smoked ham, but this was different. Under my bare gaze were two raw pork chops. I felt that a suppressed condition, *Jew,* was flooding my bloodstream, and blood was beating against my temples. I had to cook this pig for a fellow Jew.

What I did was this. I took a cast-iron skillet and heated it. I seared the chops. I browned them with diced garlic and chopped onion, a lot of onion and garlic, in a bit of oil. I cooked the hell out of them, with every kind of seasoning I could think of. I cooked them under the lid and without the lid. I cooked them for a long time until every bit of fat was rendered or turned to carbon. Yes, I did cook pork chops like a Jewish grandmother, and served them with mashed potatoes and fried onions as you would a nice veal cutlet. Maurice, Jew that he was or once had been, was pleased with the result.

Phoebe thought it was disgusting. *"Je suis végétarienne,"* she said in her clunky accent, reaching for her cottage cheese. All the while my parents thought I was irresponsibly comporting myself, lost to drugs and free love in the capital of love.

Maurice was sick. He had *une grippe,* likely contracted from *un courant d'air,* an errant draft. He buttoned on a wool sweater and placed a hot water bottle in the small of his back as he sat down at his impossible desk, using up a whole stack of clean handkerchiefs. I took it into my head to make chicken soup. *Pauvre homme sans femme,* thought I, a thorough failure as a bohemian.

I knew how to make soup. There at the local market each day were the plump and juicy fowls of France that made you think of a grandmother in an apron. The City of Paris seemed to own an agrarian grandmother, a collective memory of the ancestral farm. I would buy onion, leek, carrot, and a big, fat hen.

"Avez-vous racine de persil?" I asked the produce vendor, hoping "parsley" and "root" would compute in French. Parsley root was my mother's signature addition to chicken soup, and I loved to eat a chunk of it right in the broth, along with a juicy, whole, boiled onion and the other vegetables cooked to flavor the soup. This was not very French. My French cookbooks insist the chef discard the broth vegetables and steam new ones for *présentation.*

"Racine de persil? Non, je ne l'ai pas."

"Racine de persil?" A shrug of the shoulder, a vigorous shake of the head.

"Mais, pourquoi pas? Vous avez le persil . . ."

"There is in Paris but one sole location to secure the root of parsley," I learned at last. A greengrocer had found me out. "In the Marais, *le quartier Juif.*"

And so I went on the Metro, changing trains—carrying wallet, passport, comb, onions, and carrots in a grimy string bag—to reach the Jewish Quarter, on a mission for parsley root. The Yiddish-speaking denizens knew the neighborhood as the *Pletzl,* which also is the name of a large, flat, onion roll. I found the parsley root with ease. While I was there, I might as well buy the chicken, I thought.

I don't own a picture of myself in Paris. No one in my life today knew me there. I don't know if I was cute or plain. I would like for a moment to glimpse myself, in the blue-and-white summer dress I had worn for traveling in May—a dress cloaked, as it was now bleak November, with a too-small gray wool coat kindly passed down to me by Maurice's daughter-in-law. I wore pink plastic glasses from the British National Health, to replace the gold-rimmed disks I had lost sculling down some river in England, when my craft capsized. My legs were shod in black over-the-knee buccaneer boots with platform soles and chunky heels.

I was nineteen years old, my flesh was taut and firm, and I owned neither lipstick nor brassiere. It was my moment. And there I was, considering signs in the Pletzl until I came to *Bucherie Kasher.*

Now, why was it that my market French, serviceable in Maurice's *banlieu,* was incomprehensible to the skinny, inhospitable man behind the counter here? Under his two long earlocks and a skullcap, he refused to make eye contact, the secret of my communication success in a foreign land. I'm sure, now, that I was wrong and strange in every possible way in this seed pod of isolated Orthodoxy.

Poulet, poulet, I insisted. Chicken. For soup. *Pour le potage.* Kosher. *Kasher.*

I tried a mixture of French and Detroit Yiddish, but I couldn't conjure the Yiddish word for chicken. Maybe I never knew it.

"A 'groyse' *poulet,* a big chicken, *s'il vous plaît.*"

"*Comment?*"

Where I came from, Detroit, the kosher butchers were affable in manner, easygoing in shape, muscular of arm. When I went out shopping there, I enjoyed giving my mother's meat order, asking advice, buying a bit more than necessary. Those suburban Jewish butchers wore plaid sport shirts under their white aprons and lab coats, and their large Buicks were docked behind their stores. They were sensual, they brought to mind carnal desire. They were men you could love and marry.

What I carried home in the end on the Metro in my string bag, was the boniest, scrawniest dead bird in Paris, and I had paid the highest price. I took it home. I turned the key in Maurice's door. I took off my boots and washed my hands. I plucked feathers, cut flesh, scraped offal. The butcher hadn't included the giblets. No liver to broil while you're cooking the soup. And how can you make chicken soup without the neck and gizzard, the *gorgl,* the *pupikl*?

How good it smelled—onion and leek, carrot and parsley root. Maurice kept sneaking into the kitchen as I stirred. While the broth boiled, I made tea. On a creative whim, I steeped sliced lemons with sugar right there in the teapot with the darjeeling leaves. *C'est très bizarre,* the lemon inside the teapot *déjà,* noted poor Maurice. He sipped his strange tea and corrected my limping grammar. Never mind. He was sick, poor thing.

The broth turned out weak and pale, tasting slightly of parsley root. It would be hard to replicate the sheer disappointment Maurice felt at the first spoonful. Maurice who had anticipated chicken soup throughout my day of shopping, travel, cooking. Maurice, severed from childhood, who had lived as an assimilated refugee all the years. I had failed in my odd urge to cure his *grippe* with a rich, strengthening bowl of Jewish soup.

"I expected a really *forte forte* broth, a rich, strengthening bowl," he said, sadly, with a miserable sneeze. There was nothing for me to say. I was too young, perhaps, too vague and uncommitted, to make a really good chicken soup.

Phoebe and I moved out the same day. The studio master, that *bâtard,* said her hips were too big for mime, and Phoebe returned to Chicago in tears. I went on to Rome. Half an hour off the train, I wandered into a bakery. There was a *mezuzah* on the doorpost and an El Al travel poster on the wall.

There was no sex in Italy, either.

TOO BUSY

$\mathcal{F}$or years, I was busy, too busy for the kitchen. I ate muffins at my desk, sandwiches in coffee shops, business lunch food, pushcart street food, canapés with white wine, Chinese noodles packed in cardboard containers. I clipped restaurant reviews and planned evenings out. Yes, I put together a meal, here and there: I folded an omelet over a melting bit of cheese, or tried that week's newspaper recipe. A grocery list from that distant time: orange juice, coffee, pears, brie, peanuts, English muffins, foil (to warm up carry-out leftovers), baking soda (to deodorize the fridge).

"I love to cook," is what I might have said, daintily tearing salad leaves for two to go with the roast chicken I brought home from a carry-out shop. I added cookbooks to my collection. But now I know that I did not know much then. For it is a far different thing when children arrive in one's life.

Even a small baby somehow moves life into the kitchen. You're home more, and you're hungry. Perhaps you are nursing, ravenous for barley or meat loaf, preconsciously desperate for calories to turn into rosy baby ounces. Or, while boiling water for formula bottles, you might as well make a cup of tea, and then you're rooting around for something to go with it, something you can stand and eat with your fingers, such as cookies, chicken wings, or asparagus vinaigrette. You have visitors, and they bring cake. You eat some to be social, then you eat the rest after they've left. Suddenly, there are always dishes in the sink.

And often, you are alone with the baby. Your days seem an endless cycle of feed, diaper, wash, walk and rock the baby, soothe the wailing, monitor the breathing, damp the hiccups, pray over the rash, shampoo the cradle cap, study the baby manuals, wash the baby clothes, write thank-you notes, try to nap, try to brush your teeth, try to take a shower. Punctuation is needed for the long stretched hours. You begin to think about—actual mealtimes.

Then the baby starts on jars of mush. Although your pediatrician has said these jars are fine, you feel strange impulses. You find yourself scrubbing potatoes, baking and mashing them, boiling eggs and dicing a bit into a little spoon, feeding yourself and feeding the baby. . . . You are pregnant again, with a wicked need for liver and onions. Where in the neighborhood, or even in the world, are you going to pick up liver and onions? The next thing you know, you're broiling and sautéing, slicing, buying scouring powder for the broiler pan, and calling your mother for her recipe. The grocery list is lengthening.

When my first baby was eight months old, and I had gone back to work, I used to come home from the office and swing her up into a backpack carrier. We would move about the kitchen, chatting and cooing, as I fixed dinner. Relaxation for me, soothing body contact for her. Growing too big for my back, my child would stand on a chair to watch, stir, snack, mash, and, with a thoughtful look, massage the ingredients into the counter.

For us, it was one way to become a family, this fixing of meals that grew more and more routine. And cooking took on other values. Here was an activity to do with children, who need to learn where food comes from. I reasoned that kitchen work, food-making, was something a child could see her mother doing, something more tangible than disappearing out the door in a puff of makeup, earrings, and pocketbook. It was tangible for me, as well, an antidote to the conceptual big-world tasks that governed much of my life outside.

I was finding a regular way in the kitchen as I was finding my way as a mother—fertile ground for dormant Jewish roots. One day, with two children now, I pulled out a big wooden chopping bowl, meaning to crush walnuts for cookies, cookies made with butter. That bowl, used with a hand chopper, had been passed on to me by my mother. It had chopped a lot of liver. I looked at the darkened, smooth unfinished wood, and I was aware of that liver, I felt the juices, the hot broiled organs from cows, calves, and chickens, chopped with pungent onions and fluffy boiled eggs, salt and pepper, a particular savor and texture that had soaked deep into the wood and become part of it.

I had already opened the bag of walnuts, ready to pour, but I stopped. I wasn't going to chop walnuts in that bowl and add it to sweet, buttery, cookie dough. The ancient prohibition against mixing meat and dairy, fitfully slumbering at the fringe of my mind, sat up and would not be ignored. Smiling at myself, and this unexpected fastidiousness, I wrapped the walnuts in a dishtowel, and tapped at them with a hammer, to the great hilarity of the children. They were, as was I, oblivious to the dominos about to fall.

• • •

Wooden spoons were next. Wood is particularly porous; it can't be cleaned in the kosher sense. A wooden board used often for cheese was set aside for cheese only—no big deal, I had another one for cutting bread or green peppers. Then wooden-handled serrated steak knives looked at hard cheese and recoiled.

A few pots and pans assumed shades of nuance by association. After I burned chili con carne in it, a treasured enamel casserole was shelved mentally in a new place. I cleaned it. I mixed a paste of baking soda and water, and with this marinated the black-crusted pot for two days. I scrubbed the enamel. It was clean, by any usual standard. But it wasn't for creamy things again, it wasn't to slowly coat green beans with olive oil and Parmesan cheese over a low flame, to boil potatoes to mash with hot milk and butter. The pot assumed limits. This was less a decision than a kind of knowledge, an irrational, not particularly welcome, but irresistible knowledge.

I had no intention of changing my life. I didn't want a kosher kitchen; I didn't even want a Jewish life. I watched my mother-in-law live by the Jewish calendar, and the exigencies of the rhythm troubled me.

For Miriam, the week curved toward Sabbath, each day a referenced journey to that goal. Always, she worked, and worked hard. She did piece-work—mending, crocheting—for money, but between and around the cycle of Sabbaths. For years in New York, she owned a business, selling dresses and sweaters from a store in the basement. Whatever the work, whatever the week, by sundown on Friday, Sabbath was ready. The dawn of Labor Day, as the rest of humanity barbecued, picnicked, and walked the beach, meant for Miriam a mustering of forces for the fall holidays: ordering meat for Rosh Hashanah, grating apples for cake, choosing New Year's cards, and addressing them in the careful, ornate script she learned in a Polish village school before her childhood caved in. Spring brought Passover cleaning, anxious checklists, lining shelves, changing dishes. Each day, each lunar month, moved her closer to another holiday, festival, observance, each with its custom, preparation, food.

You have to be aware, always; some third eye is always alert. Memorial candles for the dead are lit at prescribed times of the year. A week in advance, Miriam has the candles on her shopping list. The first January thaw sees her trudging into the Russian stores, to check whether there will be bags of raw poppy seeds for Purim, seeds she can grind and pummel, simmer with vanilla and sugar, enfold with a snow of whipped egg whites to fill little three-cornered cakes. The spinning seasons, bringing sunsets early or late, order different times each week for lighting Sabbath candles.

Miriam is alert to these changing deadlines, and her year is a seamless thing. On Friday nights in summer, there are leisurely dinners on the porch of her country bungalow, and dishes are dry and on their papered shelves long before the Catskill dusk settles. Then it is cold, wet November, with a countdown of Sunday visits, Monday laundry, Tuesday doctors, Wednesday shopping and baking, Thursday cleaning, Friday cooking, until she strikes her match to light candles at 4:24 p.m., or 4:37, and all is ready: soup, and meat, kasha—buckwheat groats—with beans, baked carrots, poached fruits, almond cookies, and the salads for Saturday lunch. These are awesome responsibilities, and Miriam's life is lived in reference to what must be done to meet them.

I didn't want this awareness, this absolute, unchanging priority of duty to calendar, kitchen, home. I sensed that other exigencies would dim, and I didn't want them to. A new movie might beckon one week, a vacation could be taken next month, a work deadline loomed, friends were in town, bills needed to be paid, I think I'll go shopping, and so on.

For me, the Jewish calendar was only a pale, distant, alternative universe, its occasional bright star some optional activity I might choose. I wanted to create life day by day. Even with Miriam insisting on visits for *yom tov*—the holiday at hand—and plying us with the appropriate foods, many observances remained just beyond my awareness for years. Living in New York, I would see men in suits and skullcaps, elegant women in hats, families walking against traffic, as I rushed here and there, and I would think—Lag B'Omer? Shavuos? Yes, maybe it is the time of year, a spring festival few recall . . . then the thought would drift away.

"I don't want to be kosher," I remarked to my husband as I stirred shrimp into risotto one night—risotto made with chicken broth, butter, and Parmesan cheese. Friends were coming for dinner, friends whose roots were Egyptian, Slavic, and Kentucky Anglo-Saxon. Friends who would invite us too, for meals of osso bucco nestled up against four-cheese pasta.

"O.K.," said my husband. "Just don't remind me we're not."

But it's when you begin to think of your kitchen as unkosher, however defiantly, that the roller-coaster ride begins.

• • •

We began in a small, symbolic way. Meat and dairy foods would not be visibly mixed in one meal, and pork was banned. Some of our "separate" meals, I know, were a bit far-fetched. No need to parse that so-flaky pie crust brought home for Thanksgiving, and there might have been meat stock in the take-home minestrone we sprinkled with Parmesan cheese. But I was cooking more, and I could determine what went into a lot of the food.

All I cared about was the symbolism, anyhow. I found objections—aesthetic, perhaps—to feeding my new, pristine babies meatballs and milk. Our baby-sitter was throwing together a meal now and then, and we needed to set out a few gentle rules. I didn't worry about spiritual pollution, only about building a floor under my children. A basic floor that would hold them as they grew and went their way. They should know about meat and dairy, before cheeseburgers and pepperoni pizza appeared on their radar screens, just as I had. They should feel a slight *frisson,* a moment of discomfort, that would link them to pious ancestors who suffered for their faith.

"Give them juice to drink with their chicken," I would remind Anne-Marie, our Austrian nanny, as I flew out the door to work. "Save the milk for naptime."

It wasn't about dishes, or law, or a way of life. It was only a way of feeling. Without any particular sense of obligation, I felt Jewish, I felt a valuable if occasional differentness, and I wanted to pass that on. I wanted my children to eat stuffed cabbage, then yearn for strudel, not ice cream or flan. It was the least way I could honor the grandmothers.

For a while, I was happy simply separating milk and meat on our kitchen table at home. But the simple center could not hold.

One day, our family grew out of the New York apartment, and moved to a house in the suburbs. New York City, for me, had been the center of Jewish feeling and seeming. In that redolent urban atmosphere, I never felt compelled to commit to formal religious practice. The city was layered with immigrant history, attitudes, choices. Everyone in New York, wherever the roots of the family tree, seemed to have a Lou, or Pearl, or Tillie, or Max on a branch. The last Viennese emigrés sipped coffee at the next table. The Greek diners served blintzes. The synagogue ran a homeless shelter: I could support its good deeds with cash or time, and someday choose to attend a service—or not.

When we to moved to a suburb, I could no longer draw identity from landscape, milieu. Fast food loomed larger. I located rye bread, but no longer heard bakery Yiddish. If we wanted to dress up the children for Purim, we would have to join a *shul*. Like my immigrant grandparents who had left the *shtetl,* I couldn't make the same assumptions out here in America. The atmosphere was secular, leaning to Christian. I would have to take a stand: this I began to see. Shunning cheeseburgers was not enough.

I took my little step, and eventually, the world quivered. This is what the rabbis understood, embellishing the simple dietary concepts with numbing layers of regulations. For as much as Judaism is a worshipful religion, it is even more thoroughly a practical one, a guide for living that touches every aspect of physical and social life. As far back as anyone can know, the kid-milk ban was seen to have wider implications. And the rabbis thought about the practical implications in intense detail.

Way back in the misty annals of the past, if you prepared meat in a wooden bowl, you couldn't be sure to scrub out every trace of meat. Rabbi, what to do? Hmm, better have a separate bowl for milk. If you cut your bread with the knife used to cut a chunk of cheese, cheese crumbs might cling to the next slice of bread, and then, this bread must not be eaten with meat. So you need a special bread knife, neither meat nor dairy, but *pareve,* neutral. You need another knife for meat, three knives in all, knives enough to carve your food and thence your life into a tri-part geography.

Even in simple times and places, Jews must have needed relatively complicated kitchens. Today, in a world of food processors, home cappuc-cino makers, and general excess, I have seen kitchens kosher by virtue of two refrigerators, two sinks, two dishwashers, paper plates, and Passover in Florida.

The Torah, the written law, what non-Jews call the Old Testament, is simple and clear, unadorned: "Thou shalt not seethe a kid in its mother's milk," said God. Baby goat stewed in goat's milk is no longer the touch-point delicacy it must have been in biblical times. Still, it is no great stretch to extend the ban to veal with cream sauce, roast beef with milk shakes. It is one of the ironies that in America the Reuben sandwich, corned beef with melted Swiss, is considered the prototypical Jewish-style meal.

"God speaks to us simply," I told my daughter, when she began raising questions. "People complicate things."

Bringing God into it was a bit of hypocrisy on my part. I was already changing enough to let my child have God, though, and I was increasingly devious about hiding from her the orthodox atheism that had been part of my earliest spiritual training.

Divinely given or not, the prohibition began to speak to me. If you are going to slaughter an animal for food, respect it. Never forget that it lived and breathed, a mammal like yourself. Here is a way of reminding, respecting—eat the animal separate from the milk. Thus the tradition comes to terms with human appetite, but demands consciousness. And I had come of age in vegetarian times.

Some kitchen things don't have to be duplicated. Glass is considered *pareve* itself, like an egg, a nut, a vegetable. Anything glass just needs a good scrubbing; its surface can be inspected, and it is considered nonporous. Other materials can change their allegiance. Metal utensils, submerged in boiling water, are neutralized. Thus silverware can be made kosher, or switched from dairy to meat. In my *bubbe*'s kitchen, if a dairy fork found its way into the meat things, as must happen when you have six children eating and helping with the dish washing, she would bury the offending item in the back yard for two muddy days.

The tyranny of all this can seem brutal. Certainly, the goal is perfection. Impossible perfection, to my mind, as messy reality vies with surgically sterile rules. Like the rabbis who fashioned the oral law, the rabbis who uphold and oversee *kashrut* are mostly men, men, men, a species that will never be housewives. They, by and large, don't have to figure out which sponge to use on a toddler's spilled milk while mixing a meat loaf for dinner—or how to pack cream cheese for one child's lunch and turkey for another, half-asleep at six a.m. They are not the ones who have to remember that a blue plastic tub is dairy, that the striped dishtowel dried a meat pot, that the slotted spoon with the black handle . . .

They don't have to juggle a day's dirty dishes. Pretty much, they're not doing the cooking.

Have I consented to my own oppression? I wasn't going to do more than the basics, that window-dressing nod to tradition. But some sort of internal logic took hold, despite my nonintentions, and then I was moving, slowly, haphazardly in a direction after all. "I'm not kosher," I called out weakly into the wind. "But then, I'm not *treyf* . . ."

My mind churned. I washed meat out of a pot; would the same sponge wash tomorrow's buttery colander? I used a spatula for grilled cheese, the good one I also needed for roast chicken, and dreamed up an elaborate cleansing ritual for the satisfaction of no one but myself. I looked with trepidation at a drawer full of handy plastic containers—I ran them through the dishwasher, but I could still smell the faint echoes of other meals.

Ghost and haunts were roaming my kitchen. Inanimate vessels were becoming their contents, the essence of the living spirits that had become food on a plate. It was a kind of transubstantiation. Plates looked at me and demanded a reckoning. A baby-sitter's ham sandwich, wrapped in plastic, blew up in the microwave, and the ham smell never went away. I bought a new microwave. Appliances died. Can openers vanished.

Eventually, I crossed some sort of line, and then I, although faint-hearted and uncommitted, found perfectionist tendencies within myself hitherto unsuspected. I ran a trial, splitting my eclectic dishes into quasi-sets of blue and white. Within days, I cringed at borrowing a blue bowl for chicken soup, hesitated at stacking the single dish drainer with both white and blue dishes, contemplated buying a second set of chopsticks. For the first time, my mind couldn't scour the plates at a restaurant. I ate pasta and salad tasting an archeology of other foods.

Kashrut, I believe, gave Jesus his great opening. He ate with the common people in their homes, when other learned teachers wouldn't. Poor folk might not have had enough wooden bowls, ceramic vessels, and cooking implements to adhere perfectly to dietary laws. They might not have enough knowledge or resources to make their kitchens kosher enough for the standards of a truly learned man. Jesus swallowed his own squeamishness, perhaps, sat down and broke bread. You can get to heaven without all of this, he taught. I can see the appeal.

But oddly enough, and at the same time, trying to be kosher confronts one with the ultimate impossibility of perfection. Finally you have to live with your accommodations, the limits of being human. As with a calculus problem, the solution may draw close to an imaginary line, but never quite get there. At least, I'm sure I never will.

CHOCOLATE CAKE

$\mathcal{T}$o celebrate my daughter's second birthday party I sent many invitations. I invited her playmates from Riverside Park, urban urchins dressed in French baby clothes. I invited my friends, friends I had barely seen during two years of startled parenthood. I invited my sister and brother, my husband's parents, and also my husband's cousins, with their school-aged kids. The cousins' kids seemed impossibly old; their presence reproached my husband and me for starting late.

I invited my parents, who came from Detroit. I invited Aunt Selina and Uncle Charles, with whom my parents were staying.

At the center of all this was an excited two-year-old in a red and white dress bought for the occasion by Miriam. I invited the guests to a New York apartment designed for one person or possibly two. I removed most of the living room furniture and effects to the bedroom. As new parents, we rearranged constantly.

A few days before the party my aunt telephoned.

"Shall I make a chocolate cake, dear?"

She had in mind my grandmother's cake, chocolate sour-cream cake, with chocolate fudge frosting, and yes I said yes oh yes.

Miriam and Jacob arrived hours early bearing a vat of Miriam's mushroom-egg salad, wondering how they could help. Nothing to give them to do. I was moving at the speed of light. I had the near-total rearrangement of my apartment in mind and there was no time to explain Jacob looked at the newspaper. Miriam scoured the sink. I poured wine for myself and put on coffee and set out cheese and Miriam's mushroom-egg salad. Just before show time, my husband took our very excited two-year-old for a stroller ride.

Then my parents arrived with Aunt Selina, bearing a cardboard box. Greetings and kisses all around. Miriam watched keenly as I untied their parcel, a proper bakery box tied with two-color string. The white cardboard flaps fell away from a large round chocolate cake. Across the dark brown frosting read the legend HAPPY BIRTHDAY! in red, my daughter's name, and a curly numeral 2 in a heart.

The lettering was my father's. He had decorated the cake with a tube of red icing in Selina's kitchen early that day. The red letters were spidery, a bit shaky. I looked at that cake, the product of so much care, and at the lettering.

I thought, with a pang of love, *My father is getting old*.

There was an indefinable look on Miriam's face. She is a baker, my mother-in-law, a fine one, and also a woman who communicates love in the alchemy of flour, sugar, shortening, and egg made edible sweet.

"It's my grandmother's recipe," I explained. Selina had baked this cake for our visits to New York as kids, and she had baked it for the birthdays of her now long-grown sons. My father remembered the cake from his youth, rising high and rich in a tin bundt pan. His sister, modernist and adaptive, made two round layers and joined them with chocolate fudge.

Growing up, my sister was our baker. She had collected my grandmother's recipe, and she baked it sometimes when we were still living at home. Aunt Selina, a great organizer, had typed up the recipe with carbons on her Olivetti and sent it to us: "Irene's chocolate cake—1930s?" In our Detroit kitchen, we took it unfrosted, straight from our Detroit Jewel stove, barely cooled, shiny and slick from the sour cream, butter, and egg. It was dense and not too sweet and in color almost black. Grandma's cake.

"It is a beautiful cake," murmured Miriam. There was something in her voice. I looked at her, curious. There was a look to her face I never before had seen. Something thrilling ran through me, something like what witnesses recall in the presence of greatness: determined purpose larger than life.

She had waited long, long, for a grandchild. At the moment, there was one precious baby, a granddaughter two years old.

No one else but she, Miriam, was to bake the birthday cake.

The great crowd gathered. Toddlers found toys, adults discovered the wine. The mothers of new babies sat in the bedroom, nursing, changing, and chatting amidst magazines, cushions, chairs, and TV. The cousins' children, raised in the suburbs, improvised soccer in the hallway, and only one neighbor complained. My husband arrived off the elevator with the birthday girl in her stroller, fast asleep. The cake was to die for and we all said so. Selina was gratified; I was proud.

Miriam never asked for my grandmother's recipe. There was a year of what I presume was concentrated thought, and possibly lab trials shared with Jacob. If it was so, we were unaware. Our year was sweetened by the bakings Miriam has always spoilt us with—butter cake, *mandelbrot,* cheesecake, apple cake, luscious pineapple chocolate-chip cake topped with meringue, pound cake striped with cocoa and prune, vanilla cookies, poppyseed strip. . . .

My daughter, more painfully beautiful day by day, was turning three.

"Let me bring the cake," said Miriam. And she brought: a sour-cream chocolate cake of her own devising, frosted with chocolate fudge. Baked in a bundt pan, even.

Three children now, three birthdays each year, and never a birthday has passed since then without "Grandma's" chocolate cake.

GRANDMA'S CHOCOLATE SOUR-CREAM CAKE—1930s?

$^1/_4$ lb. sweet butter
$2^1/_2$ oz. unsweetened chocolate
1 egg
1 cup sugar
1 cup sour cream

$1^1/_4$ cup cake flour, sifted
$^1/_4$ tsp. baking soda
or $1^1/_4$ cups plain flour & $1^1/_4$
  tsp. baking powder, sifted

Set oven at 350°F. Grease pan well.

Melt butter and chocolate over low flame.

Beat egg; add sugar and beat; add sour cream and beat.

Sift flour and baking soda together and *mix. Do not beat.*

Add melted butter and chocolate. *Mix.*

Bake at 350°F., if one tube pan, for at least 45 minutes; if two small layers, 325°F. for 30 minutes.

Cool 10 inutes in pan on rack.

Turn out and cool 10 minutes more on rack before frosting.

Chocolate Fudge Frosting

$3^1/_2$ oz. unsweetened baker's
  chocolate
3 tbsp. sweet butter
3 cups sifted confectioner's sugar

$^1/_4$ tsp. salt
7 tbsp. milk ($^1/_4$ cup)
1 tsp. vanilla
Dash of instant coffee

Melt chocolate and butter over hot water or very low flame.

Blend remaining ingredients and add hot chocolate mixture. (A rotary beater is best. It gets thicker.)

Let stand in coolish place. Stir until right consistency. Thickens as it stands. Can be chilled in fridge for quicker firming.

CHARITY

During the Depression, my mother's mother, Malke, cooked food for the poor. She was poor herself, but charity was an imperative. A tall homeless man called Long John slept on the sofa in the kitchen from time to time. Malke gave him ten cents to wash the kitchen floor. My mother recalls him scrubbing the linoleum with a soapy rag and a windmill swipe of his long right arm. As the sages taught, you can always find someone worse off than yourself.

During the Depression, the butcher gave Malke a break on the price of meat: ten cents a pound, charity. Thus she fed her husband, six children, relatives visiting for the Sabbath, the poor and the sick, Long John who was not Jewish, and other strays.

The *zeyde,* my mother's father, was a disappointed man. He had loved another woman once, educated, wealthy. Her father had forbidden her marriage to a poor and lowly shoemaker. The woman never married, and later went mad, dying in an insane asylum. The *zeyde,* after some years, moved to a different city, and married Malke, a desperate motherless girl with no place of her own. He never struck her, never raised his voice to her. But her fragile spirit wilted in a drought of love. So she did this:

She divided her great pots of soup, and sent soup out to the poor.

During the Depression the *zeyde* gave credit to his customers when they could not pay for repairs to their shoes. Much of the credit was never repaid. Lines of worry raked his face, but charity was a good deed, a *mitzvah,* an unquestioned imperative.

Some customers, buffeted by wild fortune, disappeared altogether, abandoning their shoes. These were the shoes my mother and her sisters and brothers wore on their feet. Often these shoes were too short and too tight. The bones of my mother's feet are squeezed and stunted as a maiden's bound feet in Old China. She blames this on the way they grew in a hard time of too little charity.

During the Depression the unemployed men of that Scotch-Irish neighborhood where my mother grew up gathered before the potbellied stove in the shoe repair store. They would talk socialism into the night.

The *zeyde* must have seemed wealthy to them, having as he did a store and a stove.

"Malke, bring coffee," the *zeyde* would call to the rooms behind the store, and she did.

Socialism had his sympathy. As a bound boy in Lithuania, he had joined the *Bund,* the Jewish socialist workers' party. Now it was the Depression: Righteous anger simmered in the streets; workers' rights were headlines in the Yiddish newspapers. He believed a man of toil should share in the wealth of the world. This was a man's right, and not charity.

Always, he was a man of ideas, and a man of hard destiny. In the First World War, the *zeyde,* a naturalized American citizen, announced himself a conscientious objector. He was drafted anyway and shipped to the European front in the medical corps. He was in Belleau Woods without a gas mask when the Germans used mustard gas for the first time.

During the Depression, the *zeyde,* a brilliant brooding man, lapsed into bitterness and a lifelong feud with God when he realized that this was all there was going to be. When in the synagogue for the rare occasion, he knew the Hebrew service by heart, could find the very Torah line after hearing a dozen words. All this he had learned before the age of ten, when his father commuted his studies and bound him with his brothers to a cobbler's bench.

"Malke, please, potato pancakes." It could be midnight, as cousins played cards in the kitchen, and my mother's mother would put on her apron, would peel, grate, mix, fry, and serve. She loved to serve guests, and serving the husband was an imperative. She would rarely go to bed before her husband. My mother ached for her mother. Still, my mother loved her father, as children will do.

During the Depression, a black limousine pulled up in front of the shoe repair shop. Inside was a chauffeur and the *zeyde*'s cousin, also a shoemaker. The cousin's daughter was married to an important bootlegging gangster across the border. When she came home for a visit, diamonds dressed her hands, and her hair, dyed red, was a perfect match to her fox fur coat.

The *zeyde* was invited for a ride. After a time, the chauffeur hit the brakes. Begging the shoemakers' pardons, he blindfolded their eyes. The blinds were removed at a country estate, the camp resort kept by the gangster's gang. The cousins were escorted to lounge chairs in the sun, were served tall iced drinks, and were spoken to with polite respect. The *zeyde,* who disapproved of law-breaking, still always recalled the respect.

Two Jewish shoemakers, who once had been bound boys in Lithuania, thus were served cocktails amongst the green trees, by respectful gangsters on the lam for cold-blooded murder. My grandfather, who had yearned for Torah, Jewish learning, then for love, then for a better world, was chauffeured in a blindfold on a country outing, and this was a strange moment, perhaps even a high point in his life.

Having been blindfolded, he could never say where he had been. The gangsters did him a favor, but not out of charity.

The *zeyde* stood apart from the bootlegging in the family. He was an upright man who obeyed the laws of men, though he sometimes believed them unjust, and of God, though he was angry at God.

Yet, family was family. During the Depression, the struggling shoemaker loaned money to relatives toward their mortgages and bills, and this was not always repaid. Once, a relative from across the border appeared at the store in the dead of night. In the kitchen behind the store, Malke shook the sleep from her eyes and lit a fire under a kettle for tea. The *zeyde* stood, stern and silent, and the children crept down the stairs from the bedrooms above. My mother, a little girl, saw the visitor draw a gun from his pocket and place it on the kitchen table.

"Malke," said the visitor into the breathless room. "I've got to lay low for a while." And she, my *bubbe,* fed him his meals and laundered his linen with her frightened and shaking hands until he deemed it wise and safe to move along. You couldn't turn out family. That was an imperative, too.

During the Depression, my mother wore a cotton dress and a sweater and coat to school in the winter. She had no gloves and she had no boots. Her mother, lacking blankets at night, heaped coats on the sleeping children. She did what she could do. This is what my mother knows of comfort: the distillation of those mythic, shadowed days. In my childhood, too, nothing was more comforting than a woolen coat, half dreamed of, draped heavy over my blanket in a January night.

BAKED APPLES

*S*he came to us by air that time, in a navy blue suit and a pink ruffled blouse and a trim daytime hat. She flew from Brooklyn for a six-week visit to Detroit.

My father prepared for his mother's arrival by cleaning his large blue Plymouth. He vacuumed it out and washed it with a bucket of suds and rinsed it with the garden hose. The Plymouth was generous of seat and of shining chrome and firm steel. There were no seat belts then. When I sat in the front passenger seat, my father would fling his right arm in front of me if he suddenly had to stop short.

I rode in the front seat to the airport when we went to pick up my grandmother. My mother stayed home, getting ready. All three children went in the car. We parked and we went in the terminal, small and wide open: we stood at the door and watched my grandmother cross the breezy tarmac, beaming and dignified.

We gathered her into a hug, we sticky children. We retrieved her luggage, the large tan valises, the garment bag festooned with passage stickers from her voyages to Europe. My father hoisted the baggage and we pulled away in the clean blue car.

My grandmother, visiting, slept in my brother's bedroom. His dresser drawers were cleared out for her things. My mother made room in the closet. Izzy's toys were tucked away or put down in the basement. My brother came into our room to sleep with us, his sisters. We pushed the beds together and he slept in the middle, the cuddly little brother we adored. The beds were on casters; by morning, they sometimes slid apart, and Izzy was down on the floor.

"Edward, when are you going to buy a house?" I heard my grandmother say. The house was inadequate, small and rented. She wanted to see the proof of Success in her brilliant, educated, only son's life. My father's recalcitrance gave her "aggravation," a word that I, as a young child, assumed to be Yiddish.

"I don't want to buy a house, Ma," said my father. He was tormented by the memory of 1929, which had made his father a slave to the

Brooklyn mortgage, and he feared another crash. Also, he resisted middle-class self-definition as homeowner. He made good money, but his life was a journey of commitment, thought, and reason; material desires had no part to play.

I was less pure. *Listen to your mother,* I used to think, as loudly as I could. I wanted a room of my own.

In my grandmother's presence, the household, always busy and bustling, rocked. Meal preparation went up a notch in intensity—a notch or two at least. Friday night dinners gained substance and formality; *Shabbas* was *Shabbas.* There was more washing, ironing, mending, cleaning. Cooking and housekeeping now took two women full time. The house was in a "tumult," the word my sister thought was Yiddish. We children basked in the fussy glow. We loved my grandmother's visits.

On this particular visit, my father happened to mention that he liked baked apples.

My grandmother cored half a dozen Northern Spy apples, but not quite all the way through, and set them in a shallow, round, glass pan. She filled the core holes with raisins and a *kvetsh,* a squeeze, of lemon juice. She sprinkled the apples with cinnamon and sugar, sliced on some margarine bits. She poured half an inch of water in the pan. She put them in a hot oven, and let them bake.

The house smelled of apples and cinnamon. The pan cooled on top of the stove. The skins were firm and shapely, and the apple within was supple and soft to the spoon, to the teeth. The raisins were a chewy, concentrated counterpoint. We all liked baked apples. My father enjoyed the dessert most of all.

The next day, arriving home from school, I saw my mother at the oven. She removed a large rectangular baking dish full of plump, steaming apples, their skins split and caramelized. My father praised the baked apples at dinner, and had another in the evening, perhaps while watching the TV and reading a book. He never did fewer than three things at once.

We had baked apples for breakfast. Home from school, I saw two long trays of baked apples cooling on the basement steps. My grandmother's work. Baked apples for snack, baked apples for dinner.

There were chickens no doubt, and soups, and roasts, none of which I remember. There may have been veal cutlets or potatoes or whitefish baked with onions. By the end of the week, this I know: there were pans and plates of baked apples, apples atop the refrigerator, on the mantel in the living room, on the side door landing, on the milk chute shelves. It was breakfast, dessert, side dish, and snack. My father was eating six a day and there was no end in sight.

"Please, Ma, dear. I can't. No more baked apples for a while."

It was hard for her, perhaps. Her son was so far away. She worried about his life. A tray of baked apples just wasn't enough. Even a bushel, even an orchard. A galaxy of apples, scented with cinnamon, flavored with lemon, would have been inadequate, too.

I watched and I learned. There is tumult, there is aggravation. There is love. For a mother, there is no such thing as excess.

February

OBSERVANCE

February

We're not there. We're miles from kosher. I sorted my dishes, pots, and implements for a trial run, assigned drawers and cupboards. Some of these items can't properly be kashered, or bear associations that taint them. Throw them in the drawer and pretend. Pretend I will use that barbecue fork to stir pasta with meat sauce from now on, because I've committed the pasta stirrer for dairy. Pretend the cheese grater never grated Parmesan.

Must I live without real Parmesan?

Don't have enough things. Washing up is a nightmare. Pareve things should be washed separately. Dishwasher half-full of the wrong kind. Meat and dairy sponges stacked together. Quick dinner leaves dairy plates; sink is full of previous meal's meat dishes. Silverware jumbled together in the dish drainer. Spatulas and graters in the wrong drawers, contaminated, pulled out by someone and used the wrong way.

Do I have to stand there clearing the decks after each meal? Washing, drying, putting away, supervising, being preoccupied? Does this force me into a little sphere, the kitchen?

I'm only interested in the symbolism, so what if things get mixed up? I sort them out . . . but it's not the same anymore, the object carries a projected burden, projected by me, if not by actual molecules.

CHICKEN SOUP

*T*he *bubbe*'s kitchen was full of food. Meats bubbled in the oven, kettles hissed on top of the stove. There were cakes on a shelf, covered dishes in the icebox, cookies atop the icebox, bowls of fruit, pans behind cupboard doors. In the summer kitchen, an unheated room through the back, pickles and jars and cans and potatoes posed in readiness. All this plenty my *bubbe*, djinn-like, would ceaselessly, unstintingly, bring forth.

This was no built-in kitchen. There was furniture here and there. It was settled, worn, and jolly. Behind the table a sofa, soft and deep, did for sitting, dining, or sleeping. She had dressed the naked porcelain sink with a homemade calico skirt.

"There are no discrete meals here, just one continuous meal." Thus, with mock gloom, Mother's youngest brother, twenty years younger than she and the last child still living at home, would confront another enormous plateful, following a recent cup of digestive tea. He was a *langer luksh,* thin and tall as spaghetti, in a family neither tall nor slight, and his surprising metabolism provided a mission for my mother's mother in her years of less to do.

We grandchildren loved the *bubbe*'s kitchen, and we loved the *bubbe*'s home. The front of the house was a store, through which we ran to get to the living rooms behind and above. The store had been my grandfather's shoe repair shop. After he died, the space was let to a barber. I was five when the *zeyde* died, and I still recall his thick eyebrows, the smell of leather, the spin of the buffing wheel. Once he lifted me up to the counter, where I watched him seal my sneaker sole with a dripping brush of rubber glue.

When her father died, I found my mother weeping in her apron on the front steps of our house. She didn't go to the funeral. My mother had left her Toronto home for Detroit, and she could not return. She was a foreigner with a left-wing husband in the 1950s. She was advised that had she crossed the border, she might be permanently detained on the other side.

For fifteen years, until she won her citizenship, she missed the kitchen reunions. Without my mother, my family journeyed there, to bask in the heat of the *bubbe*'s food and the light of her treasures. She had lace at the windows, mirrors on the wall, collars of sequined netting to snap on a plain black dress, combs of tortoise for her long black hair, with its one silver strand.

My sister and I used to watch, transfixed, as she combed out the hair, which reached past her hip, then with dancing fingers plaited its length and coiled the braid into a bun atop her head, fastened with a single hairpin. We imitated her adorable accent, a bit wickedly perhaps. We begged her for Yiddish curses and put-downs, and we exploded with laughter when she obliged: "You should grow like an onion, with your head in the ground."

My mother missed all this, and missed her father's funeral.

My mother made these sacrifices out of necessity, out of an immigrant's love for America, and out of a sense of justice. Her father had been a naturalized citizen and a decorated U.S. soldier before moving to Canada. In Toronto, a U.S. consul had confiscated his papers, claiming he had stayed away too long. My mother hung her father's medals on the wall for a while, but seeing them made her weep. She wanted the derivative citizenship she believed her due—and his—and she had the strength to wait.

She loved her mother, but she had left. Canada for her was bereft of opportunity, a place pinched and poor. In Toronto, the Depression persisted, while relatives prospered in Detroit.

"America *far ir is beser*," agreed the *bubbe*. For "her," my mother, America was "better"—this was indisputable and firm.

Menial job upon job had layered my mother's longing years. At age ten she went out to work after school and summers and weekends. She sold hats; she watched babies. For hours a week she took care of a dry goods store; the owner would don hat and gloves and go to a show, or out for the afternoon, and give my mother a dollar a week or, sometimes, a pair of stockings. She worked for a corsetmaker, ironing corsets. The boned garments had been repaired and must be returned unrumpled. Under her small hands the stench of old sweat rose with hot steam in the corsetmaker's back room.

"Unbearable," she told me.

An excellent student, she hoped for academic high school, for college. The grade school headmaster himself pled her case at the cobbler's bench.

"A girl doesn't need an education," said her father, a man beset by his own bitter demons, a man who esteemed learning, a father who loved his daughter's bright mind, but even so. He had not wanted to be a poor shoemaker; he had aspired to scholarship once, but that was what life did. There was nothing my mother could say, nothing her mother, Malke, could do.

She went to technical school instead and studied commercial art. She won the school art prize, but could not find an illustrator's job; she believed the doors were closed to Jews. She took a course in typing and shorthand, worked in factories, worked in offices. She waited for her beaux behind the sign SHOE REPAIR, but none of them seemed to hold her future.

At last she packed her suitcase, straightened her stocking seams, bought a train ticket, and left. In Detroit, she took a room. She sent home wages. She lived on chocolate bars, which she believed were rich in iron and other essential nutrients. She did what she had to do.

What is a woman? What is a woman supposed to be? My *bubbe*'s life in the kitchen was a life of hard work, but in a wind-tossed life, this small domain was hers at least. Doing for others afforded her the nearest happiness she would know, enriching her recipients thereby. There were elements in this to take away. And there was that soup.

But there was more to life than soup.

My mother lived with a problematic legacy. On one side, her mother's fears and generosity and confidence in her, and also that soup. On the other, her father's esteem for learning, his frustration, his dashing of her dreams. Nothing was going to be easy.

"Why don't you just go downtown to the college and see if they'll let you in?" said my father, for the fortieth time.

"They won't," said my mother, certain of the inferiority of her credentials, the uselessness of the thing.

The registrar waved her in. We children were in school when she started college at last. And then soon after, I think, she must have forgiven her father. She remembered walking with him to the art museum on Sundays, his hands clasped behind his back. She remembered listening to *kol nidre,* the prayer of sorrowful repentance, with him one Yom Kippur eve. She took his own dashed dreams as an explanation, and she forgave her father. More than this: she honored him.

She honored him in her studies, I think she did. She went downtown on the bus and brought back books of Russian history, the Russian language. She read Chekhov and Tolstoy, and in the back of her mind she placed her father, whose roots, as a longing little boy, once grew in Slavic soil. The loamy Cyrillic alphabet, the violent sweep of Slavic history, represented a kind of native earth. Later, she told me she wanted to know what it was in the culture, the language, the land, that had made its people so hate the Jews in the particular ways her father had known.

For a decade, my mother studied, enrolling in a class or two at a time. She spread her books and folders across the dining room table at night. She wrote out term papers in longhand, then snapped out clean fast onionskin pages and carbon copies on her black office Remington. She was a crack typist.

At exam time, she repaired to the basement with cups of coffee for serious memory work. Amidst a clutter of storage and playthings, she sat with her Russian flash cards. She assigned us the task of word drills; we three children all learned to read Russian. We learned that a mother could have a determined, separate life.

Like most women, my mother had the running of the house in her head. Someone must. My father, handy as he was, would not have known when to air pillows or buy children socks and you can't live on salami and eggs.

Somehow, it all got done.

There were hot dinners most nights but Saturday, when we ate bagels, tuna, egg salad, and cheese. The bathroom was clean. The bed linens were cool and smooth. In spring, my mother brought lilac boughs in from the yard. She washed the floors on Fridays, brown tile in the vestibule, blue linoleum in the kitchen and on the basement stairs. And when I was in high school, she earned a Phi Beta Kappa key.

Yes, sometimes of a morning, rushing to get ready for school, I sought my clothes in the dryer drum. Ironing was abandoned. If we couldn't mend, we safety-pinned. We cleaned our shoes and hung up our clothes, and if we didn't, tomorrow they would be scuffed and rumpled. Laundry was a family activity: we folded in the living room while watching TV, making tidy stacks of underwear and shirts, rolling socks into hard, neat balls.

As we grew older, we children, arriving home, would start dinner. I never remember Mother or Father faulting our experiments: clumsy cheese omelets, overcooked fish, burned pots, or even the egg shells stuck to the ceiling one time I put half a dozen on to boil then repaired to my room to read. My mother herself had been such a girl, lost in a book with a dustcloth in her hand. We were all of us essential to the economics of family life.

There was no definite, scientific methodology for chores. As children we were free to organize, create, theorize. We rearranged furniture at will. We washed the piano keys, pretending the crashing chords were celestial. My father vacuumed: Mother hated the whine of a vacuum cleaner, as do I.

Possibly it wasn't as easy as it looked.

My mother had a standard, solid repertoire of foods and was little interested in expanding it. Rarely would she consult one of the two cookbooks in our home, *The Settlement House* or *Grossinger's*—and then only to remind herself that, for instance, *kneydlekh,* matzo balls, might have ginger, but never to follow exact quantities or methods. She cooked the quick versions of Malke's cuisine, ad hoc. She mixed the basics, added a bit of this and that, until taste reflected remembrance. If it needed a measuring cup, forget it. She went for the essence, the feeling, the soul.

She had loved her mother's exacting attentions. She enjoyed the perfection of nurturing traditions that meant day and night doing for. Secure within that perfection, she picked and she chose. She cooked in a frying pan, she stirred with a fork. She put steaks or chops in the broiler. She opened a tin, or a freezer pack. Then she opened her books and studied. Chekhov.

Ah, but week in, week out, except during exams, my mother made chicken soup. She used a whole pullet, cut up, and sometimes an extra few pieces besides. She *davened* over that chicken, cleaning it, rinsing under icy tap water and plucking each tiny pinfeather and scraping bits of fat and cartilage and goo off the strange, inevitable giblets—the neck, *gorgl,* the gizzard, *pupikl,* the heart.

In my youngest years, when I came home from school on a Thursday, our refrigerator was occupied by large, yellow chicken feet. The butcher still supplied these amputated extremities then, and the soupmakers swore by them. The chickens also came with unfertilized eggs inside, the now contraband *ayelekh,* pale, tender, yolklike, prehistoric. My mother would carefully remove these unlaid spheres from their hens, to slip carefully later into the simmering soup.

Into the pot on Friday went the soup makings, the chicken, the giblets, whole onions, and salt. To a Friday fragrance of Murphy's Oil soap and floorwax, silver polish and Pledge, the pot boiled, and as the pot boiled, my mother skimmed the soup. Standing and skimming off foam and fat, with her apron on, and a long-handled spoon, until the broth boiled clean.

Into the pot went that which she chose to continue. Into the pot went sentiment, homeland and yearning, the ten commandments, and the right to decide yourself what you want to do. Into the pot went nubbins of carrots, stalks of celery, parsley and parsley root, wisps of dill, sometimes a parsnip, pepper. In the days of *ayelekh,* in went the *ayelekh,* last.

In a saucepan she boiled noodles or rice or *kneydlekh,* matzo balls, in season. We were called in to taste and evaluate, to shake in more salt, if needed. When evening fell, she filled our bowls with steaming chicken, onions, carrots, celery, parsnip, rice, and broth. It warmed our bellies, and moisture beaded our brows. My mother lit Sabbath candles, reciting a prayer in English I am not sure she did not believe.

Sometimes we ate two or three plates of soup, and that was dinner.

REVISIONISM

"*I*'m writing about the way you kept the flame alive," I say to my mother.

"I wasn't trying to keep a flame alive," she says to me.

I look at the page in my hand, and wonder.

"You children had to eat something, and I did what I knew how to do."

A PEBBLE

On visits to New York, we went to the cemetery.

My father would drive over the Verrazano Bridge, recalling out loud the buses, ferries, and other conveyances that once served to transport the large extended family to Staten Island, where their departed were interred. It was quite an excursion in the 1920s and '30s—a day in the country, of sorts. They brought picnic hampers of cold meat. My grandfather photographed these occasions.

Invariably, my grandmother would have to interrupt the narrative: "Edward, why don't you stop and ask someone?" For Dad would be lost, driving in a reverie of circles, figure eights, and U turns.

At last we would locate the graveyard, my grandfather's headstone. Simply carved, the name, the dates of birth and death: dear father, beloved husband. Half the stone was blank, awaiting my grandmother's name. Two great-grandfathers, a great-grandmother, a few great-aunts, grand-uncles, were buried nearby, but that was all. These were the immigrants, they had left the history of their families behind in Bremen, Lodz, Stanislowa, and it was now obliterated, the synagogues razed, the gravesites desecrated.

My father tidied up around the family plots. He plucked bits of trash and dead branches from the evergreen shrub growing over my grandfather's remains. My sister and brother and I gathered pebbles. On our grandfather's stone we lined them up, each a greeting to the world beyond. Our father taught us this.

From her pocketbook my grandmother drew a black skullcap and a pamphlet containing memorial prayers. My father set the *yarmulke* atop his large, curly head. He began to read the Hebrew words.

In Brooklyn my grandmother cleaved to her rituals. Back in Detroit, my father would say, "Just have me cremated," a thing forbidden in Jewish law. He said cemeteries were so much superstitious nonsense, a delusion about the finality of death. Yet those visits with my father to his father's grave were among the tenderest times I recall.

It is good to have a place to leave a pebble, for the living if not for the dead.

CAKE

*M*iriam bakes every week, according to a fine internal clockwork. We never grow bored with the results. Lucky me, rarely resorting to store-bought sweets over these fifteen years and more. Visiting their grandmother, my children open cupboards, never disappointed. They find the plain, brown, crisp cookies, the vanilla-scented ones. They descend on the *mandelbrot*, twice-baked sedimentary walnut-almond-and-chocolate-chip bars. Lucky children: No schoolbox lunch is complete without a bit of Grandma's baking.

I used to see my grandmothers once or twice a year, that's all. These happy visits punctuated the fluid time of childhood, but stood outside our ordinary life. Miriam and Jacob have a different role in the days of their grandchildren. They are integral weft to everyday time.

Indeed, it is their managed rotation of the calendar that paces our life. There is always a Friday night supper if we want to share it, a midweek delivery of *klops*—meat loaf—and *farfel*—onion-fried pasta, or maybe turkey and split pea soup, if we, busy with who knows what, request help in getting from here to Friday. Saturday we know Jacob is at synagogue, praying for us all by morning, then walking home for his midday repast and rest.

There are Sunday visits to our house, and summer visits to their country cottage in season, July Fourth weekend to Labor Day. They prepare for the holidays, winter, spring, fall, with predictable measured grace, and the marking of these is always perfect. The memorial candles burn when they should.

Miriam never forgets a birthday. Grandnieces, second cousins, a fifty-year-old nephew, all still receive a punctual annual card in the mail, inscribed in Miriam's careful hand.

Twice a year, Miriam and Jacob mark the destruction of Miriam's Polish village. The survivors assemble downtown in March for speeches and stories and prayer. Each fall, they gather at the cemetery at the monument they raised years ago, to mourn the long, bleak list of names inscribed thereon, and to seek such comfort as may be had from one another, the familiar accents, the aging faces. When they are gone, my husband and I should take their place, but will we?

I was twelve years old when the war broke out. Our village was bombed September 2, 1939. There was a military base and airstrip and train station there in our town, so the Germans made it a target.

There was a ninety-seven-year-old Polish doctor in town. His great-granddaughter used to come to his big house for vacation. She had long blond braids. I used to play with her. She was killed by a bomb. I recognized the braids hanging down when they carried her away.

My father said we have to get away. The whole family left, my parents, my aunts with their children, my Aunt Sesha, the uncles, my grandparents, the other grandmother. We left at night. We took nothing but mattresses and bedding piled high on a wagon. I was up there with the younger children. But we stopped for a woman with a baby three days old, and my father said, Miriam, you have to come down and give place to that woman. I was asleep already. I had to come down and walk behind the wagon with my father. We were going to a town forty kilometers away, where we knew somebody. It took two, three, four days, nights—who remembers?

When I was sleeping on top of the wagon, one of my shoes fell off. When I came down to walk, I had to walk with one shoe.

The first night we slept in Rikki, in the shul, on the floor. The people we were with wanted to stay there longer. My mother said no, this is too close to the ammunition bunkers. So we went on. A few days later we hard that Rikki was bombed. One family we knew, with seven children, was there. One died there in the shul, one lost a leg—fregn nisht—don't ask. A whole family was torn apart.

We got to that man we knew, a business partner of my aunt, who had a place for us. We were all living together there, three families to one room.

We were there until September 12 or 17, I don't remember when the Germans came in. We hid my father and my grandfather, but the other men they took away. They held them a few weeks, starved them, beat them, shot some of them, and then released the others. They were sleeping outside. The rains started then, people got sick. Some died of sickness. Some they shot.

Then we went home. My grandfather had a horse and wagon. After
a few kilometers, the Germans stopped us. They took away our horse,
and cut my grandfather's beard. This was just to insult him. A religious
Jew doesn't cut his beard.

Miriam bakes. Her greatest pleasure is the grandchildren's birthday
cakes. She mixes chocolate chips in with the chocolate batter, and frosts
the high round tube-shaped cakes with chocolate fudge. She writes their
names on top with homemade mocha buttercream, and daubs on buttercream daisies, decorating them with colored candies.

The year ebbs and flows. Miriam's cakes work, form, swell, and sub-
side, and the universe is good to us: another cake already on horizon's rim.

For fifteen years I have known this cycle of generous baking, this
pineapple chocolate-chip cake topped with meringue (my husband's
favorite), this butter cake with its thin cocoa stripe through the center, this
prune-flavored chocolate marble cake, this *mohn* strip, a thin sheet of yeast
dough wrapped about handground poppy seed filling.

Miriam bakes on a grand scale, 12-inch bundts, 15-inch sheet pans.
The smaller moiety of a typical cake is reserved for self and husband,
their visitors and Saturday night card game. The larger segment is bound
for the grandchildren's house, sometimes traveling thence in my dusty
station wagon, after a dinner at Miriam's house. Other times, Jacob
and Miriam pack up their foil-wrapped treasures, fresh and warm,
arrange themselves into their crumb-free sedan, and carefully navigate
the twenty-minute route to us, always parking in the same spot in front
of our house.

We came home after one month. Our house was cleaned out. The
Poles had taken everything. In the cellar, nothing was left. My mother
used to stand a whole summer over the stove cooking whatever fruits and
vegetables there were. She had jellies, preserves there, you can't imagine.
Nothing. She had wines from France, vermouths from Italy. They took
everything.

They only didn't take our radio. We heard that the Germans had
come three times while we were away to collect our radio. All the Jews
had to give up their radios to the Germans at that time. Probably the
Poles thought they would get in trouble for looting it, so they left it.

We knew the Nazis would come back for that radio. So my father
took it down in the cellar. He hammered it into tiny little pieces, put

them in a sock and the whole thing into the garbage. When the Germans
came for it we told them nothing was left in the house when we returned.

"My grandmother used always to make these cookies," Miriam says.
"Whenever I went to her house she had them. Then my mother made
them, and her sister, Sesha."

Miriam's daughter used to call the crisp brown omnipresent cookies
"doggy biscuits." The memory of that always makes Miriam smile, just for
a minute, until her heart snags on the rusty hook of her daughter's death
twenty years ago.

She makes them in batches of dozens and dozens, and packs them
neatly like brown dominos into a large square tin. She spoon-blends the
batter smooth, then kneads it breadlike. She pushes the dough through an
electric grinder, and holds her hand flat under the pastry attachment to
catch the running ribbon of ridged cookie dough. At four fingers' width,
she cuts off her segment and gentles it flat on a baking sheet, lifting her
hand in time to catch the next bit. Catch, cut, gentle, fall, lift, catch, cut,
gentle, fall, lift, dozens and dozens.

"This is not work," teases Jacob. "The machine is making them by
itself."

"You are right," Miriam retorts. "I don't have to do anything." When
Sesha's grandchildren first visited from Israel, we opened a box of
Miriam's biscuits, and they stared. "I didn't know they had such things in
America," the ten-year-old blurted out, and Miriam laughed.

We knew something about Germany before the bombing started,
because a lot of Polish Jews living in Germany were sent back to Poland
from 1935 on. We didn't know how bad it was going to be.

We couldn't get out anyway. We could only go to Russia. A lot of
young people went there. My uncle went there, to Pinsk, when we got
back to our village, October 1939. He came back for his sisters, my
mother and my aunts, but no one wanted to go. We didn't want to leave
what we had. We weren't Communists. So he went back by himself.

When the Germans went into Pinsk in 1941, my uncle went with
the partisans. They sent him to school in Moscow. He became a para-
chutist in the Russian army. Later they took the Poles out from the Rus-
sian army and made a Polish army to fight the Germans. My uncle was
in that.

• • •

*We lived a few months in our restaurant. My mother was blonde
and blue-eyed, she looked like a non-Jew, so she pretended she was
Polish. She changed the name in front to a Polish name, started to cook
pork, and took in a Polish partner. Jews weren't supposed to own a business anymore. Someone told on us. The gendarme came in and saw my
mother's youngest sister, Sesha, working there, with her black hair, and
arrested her. My mother escaped out the back door, and later ransomed
Sesha out of prison. The Germans took the restaurant away.*

*After this we went to live in the ghetto. Me, my parents, and my
aunt in one room. The Poles took whole houses from families and went to
live in them, and in return gave one room for the family to live.*

*The ghetto was in the worst part of town. It was too crowded. We
had so much sickness, typhus. Jews were coming from everywhere. They
brought people there from little towns nearby. They brought a transport
from Vienna in 1941, two thousand Jews from Czechoslovakia in '42,
and two or three thousand from Slovakia in '42.*

*There was one Jew who helped the Germans. He was not from our
village. He had no heart for our people. Then the Germans took him
away.*

The mixer stands ready, a towel under its metal stand to muffle vibra-
tion and noise.

"This is a good appliance if you bake a lot," Miriam says. She offers to
give me one. I tell her I don't bake much, something of an overstatement.

In a spotless white basin set in the sink, Miriam sifts flour with salt and
baking soda through a strainer, then stirs three packets of vanilla sugar into
the fine white powder.

I ask about the vanilla sugar, a flavored sugar sold in small packets in a
little Jewish store nearby. The packets are marked "artificially flavored,"
which makes me uneasy. In Poland, vanilla sugar was flavored with the
real thing. Still, it is good, assures Miriam.

"Don't worry," Miriam says.

She knocks six eggs, one at a time, into a clear glass, then slides them
into the mixer bowl. She adds softened butter and sugar, and flicks the
switch. The beaters spin, working the yellow mass in its rotating bowl
thick and smooth. While beaters spin and bowl turns, she adds buttermilk,

then sour cream, then the white floury powder is dumped in all at once like a load of beach sand.

She measures with teacups and coffee cups out of the dish cupboard, soup spoons and teaspoons from her silverware drawer. She monitors the roiling batter, and when all the lumps and dry spots are gone, she stops the machine. Using a rubber spatula and a clean forefinger, Miriam cleans the beater's blades.

Half the batter goes into a greased enamel pan, and Miriam hesitates.

"May I put chocolate in the middle?" she asks.

"My mother didn't let me," Miriam says. "She didn't like it. 'Make it the way I showed you,' she used to tell me."

She shakes cocoa, just enough to cover the batter, fine as coal dust, then carefully spoons over it the remaining cake batter. Setting the pan in the sink, she evens the top with the spatula and a butter knife.

"Absolutely even, or it doesn't come out good," says Miriam.

"Now we make the *krishkis,* the crumbs," she says. "Would you like to try?"

I watch her cutting butter and margarine into tiny chunks, with a knife. I take up the knife and try. Thinking of choppers and food processors, or even of two-knife technique, I must have sighed.

"You have no patience? No? This is how you make it!" Miriam exclaims. She spoons flour, sugar, and vanilla sugar on the diced shortening, and I work the mix with buttery hands.

"Now I will teach you a trick my mother didn't know," she says, a bit conspiratorially. Her mother was the real baker, she always tells me. Here is the trick: Make a solution of warm water and sugar, and spread it atop the cake batter in the pan in the sink, so the crumbs will stick. She sprinkles and spreads the crumbs, then wipes the edges of the pan clean with a paper towel.

And so to the oven, and so, butter cake.

"This I like," comments Jacob from his distant living room chair.

> *In the beginning of the war my father worked in the Judenrat, the Jewish council, in the office, distributing food cards. They were supposed to be only for our village, but Jews came from everywhere, and if someone was hungry, he gave. Even he took from our rations to give to someone who needed. He was such a good man.*
>
> *One day he came home and said, Something bit the back of my*

*neck. He took off his coat and scarf, and we saw a louse there. He
said a very dirty man had come from Warsaw. It wasn't his fault he
was dirty. He had been traveling for days. He was hungry, and had
come to the office for food, and my father said he had gotten the louse
from that man.*

*He said, We must count ten days from now, and if I get sick, we
will know it is typhus. We counted, and on the tenth day he got sick.*

*There was one pharmacist in town, a Polish man. He was a friend of
my father. I risked my life to go to him for medicine. Two, three times a
week, I took off my armband and went. If the Germans would have seen
me they would have shot me.*

*I told the pharmacist I couldn't pay, I had no money. He said,
"Miriam, take it and go."*

*The pharmacist's wife was a thief, though. My mother gave her a big
trunk of linens, blankets, clothing to keep during the war. When the man
died, my father said, "Don't waste your time going back for it, she will
never give it to you." He was right. After the war I went there, and
asked her if she still had something of those things. She said she was
afraid to keep our things, and sent it away, and didn't know what happened to it.*

*But there was an assistant in the pharmacy, a Polish girl, whose vil-
lage was near the German border. The Germans first going into Poland
had done to the people there like they did to the Jews, so she felt our
pain. She whispered to me that everything was still there in the house.
On my way out I saw in the hall a sewing machine, and draped on it
was my winter coat. So when I walked by, I reached my hand back and
took it.*

It was a mckhaye *(godsend) because it was very cold that winter,
and I would have had no coat.*

"I got this recipe from my sister-in-law," says Miriam. "My son likes
it, yes?"

She is making the beautiful pineapple chocolate-chip cake, a lemony
cake layer baked with a topping of semisweet chocolate, crushed pineapple, and meringue. Six egg yolks and the juice of half a lemon go into
the cake batter, and the egg whites get stiffly whipped with sugar to form
what Miriam calls a "snow."

She spreads the batter, distributes the fruit and the chocolate. With wet hands she spreads the meringue, then scallops an intricate pattern in it with a rubber spatula tip.

"Bake it on a high rack and watch it," she says. "Don't let it get too dark."

We went to work. The Germans built a work camp at the airfield, another by the station, another in the village. They wanted to rebuild the airfield and military base they had bombed. They needed shoemakers, tailors—whoever could do something.

I went to work at the airfield and came back home every night. I was fifteen years old, it was 1942. I worked in the farm there, planting and picking. Potatoes. Before the war it was an agricultural school. The Germans took it over, growing vegetables for the soldiers' kitchen.

In the beginning they paid, very little, but something. Sometimes you could bring home bread. Then they required people to work, and didn't pay. They took people away to work and shot them. One day they took all the fur coats. If you didn't give up your fur coat, they would shoot you. One day they said no more butter on the ration cards, just bread. Then they said half the amount of bread. Every day there was something. People escaped from Warsaw, they had terrible hunger there, some came to our ghetto. Some were shot there.

My auntie's boy, seven years old, he was shot. My Cousin Elke, nineteen years old, shot. My Cousin Malke was fifteen, too, she got a job laying track. It was very hard work. She was beaten every day, then they took her away to Treblinka.

To live, we bargained for food. We sold our jewelry to buy potatoes and bread, bread and potatoes.

At fifteen, I was no more a child.

Cake is not all Miriam can do, figuring to delight those she loves. There are other desserts. There are noodle puddings and dumplings filled with blueberries or cheese. There are sweet pancakes—*bubelekh*—and potato pancakes dressed in sour cream and sugar. She has an endless repertoire of fruit concoctions, and she calls them all *kompot*. This generic admits the gently simmered chunks of fresh peaches, cherries, and plums we are offered for dessert in country summers, and also the stewed rhubarb and strawberry, as well as the autumn applesauce. A fresh fruit salad, blueberry-dotted, sprinkled with sweet red wine, is Miriam's "living compote," her *kompot chai*.

In early spring, Passover time, Miriam sends me to health food shops, gourmet markets. She spares no expense to procure only the best, the plumpest dried fruits to be had for *Pesach kompot*: currents and sweet prunes, dried peaches, cranberries, apples, apricots. She cooks these with sugar and sometimes lemon juice until the fruit softens and the syrup thickens like honey, and she serves the confection in an etched glass dish.

May 6, 1942, was an Aussiedlung, the first deportation. They put all the people in the marketplace and selected. Some went back to their houses in the evening, and some went on wagons—the boxcars.

They took my grandmother and grandfather to Sobibor, a death camp. They gassed them and burnt them. My grandmother was fifty-six. My Aunt Sara and her husband, Sam, their daughter Aika, Aunt Rahel with her son, Nachum, all went to Sobibor and died there.

We knew the first transport had died. We paid Poles who worked on the train to find out. They said nobody comes out from there. We didn't believe them. We said the Poles are anti-Semites, that's why they tell us these things.

The second Aussiedlung was October 1942. One day after Yom Kippur. This one went to Treblinka.

They called everybody out, again they made a selection. There were special SS troops in black uniforms. They took older people and children, and even young people if they didn't like them. It was a terrible thing, they shot a few hundred people that day.

My mother's youngest sister, Pola, had a girl, six or seven, and a one-year-old boy, who was blind. The boy had been sick with measles, and in the war they couldn't get the right medicine. He developed an inflammation of the brain. The only potion they could get cured him but made him blind. He used to listen for his sister. When he heard his sister come in the house, he used to dance in his playpen.

That day Pola put a sock in her daughter's mouth to stop her screaming when she heard the gunshots. Six months later, my aunt was taken to Treblinka with the two kids.

In 1942, somebody came back to our village from Treblinka. His name was Spivak, he escaped by hiding in a wagon full of clothing. He described what was going on there, and said he got crazy from what he had seen. We didn't believe him, we didn't believe in the crematoria. We thought he was a madman telling an unbelievable tale. How could such a thing be happening in our world, our modern world?

"Do you think in fifty years anyone will believe it? Will they say it is just propaganda?" Miriam asked me once.

I had an uncle, he was a jeweler in Warsaw. His wife was a beauty. They had a beautiful baby girl.

One day the Jews there were called out for a selection by the Nazis. The wife knew they were taking small children. So she put the baby in a large pocketbook, gave her opium so she would sleep quiet, and zipped up the pocketbook and took it with her. But they were standing out there for many hours—all day—and the baby woke up and started to cry.

A Ukrainian soldier came up to her and said, "What do you have in the bag? Open it!" She opened it. He looked in and saw how beautiful the baby was. He zipped up the bag and told her, "Quick, get to the back of the crowd." So they were saved that day.

But my uncle was scared. He had a friend, a Polish judge in Warsaw, not Jewish. This judge came to where we were living to ask if my uncle should come to us with his family.

My father agonized. "How can I advise him? Either way it may work out wrong. I cannot tell him what he should do."

So that judge went away, and within a few days, my uncle and aunt were deported and killed. After my uncle was taken, we got a message that he had something to tell. But no one could get to him. We believed, from what others told us, that the baby didn't go with them. We think that this judge has that baby. But my mother and I think and think, and we don't know his name. We couldn't find him after that.

We think my cousin is alive, but we don't know where she is.

Maybe she doesn't even know she is a Jew.

Each holiday brings its own special offering: apple cake for Rosh Hashanah, the Jewish new year; dark, moist honey cake to break the Yom Kippur fast. Hanukkah sugar cookies cut into holiday shapes—dreidls, menorahs, six-pointed stars. Three-cornered poppy seed *hamantaschen* for Purim, cheesecake with yellow raisins and cheese danishes for the spring harvest festival of Shavuot. Passover, when no yeast or leavening may be used, brings artful ovencraft: sponge cake, fruit-and-nut cake, flourless chocolate cake. Never less than three of Miriam's cakes, along with the special dried fruit *kompot,* for our Passover Seders.

In a cupboard under the telephone, Miriam may keep chocolates for the children, Israeli candied orange peels or lightly frosted wafers, hard candy, maybe M&Ms, just in case things are not sweet enough. As a new mother, I pursed my lips and looked stern. Thinking of teeth, calories, lifelong habits, I handed down a no-sugar, no-cake ukase. Those were the early days. I gave in years ago.

I blush now to think of Miriam, waking from nightmares, sleepless at dawn, with nothing to turn her hands to, and then no sweets to offer her only grandchildren. Her hungry heart must have wrung itself inside out.

"Someday," she warned me, "you will know what it is to be a grand-mother."

We were deported to Chestochowa in June or July 1944. The Russian troops were almost standing already in our village, they were about a mile away, and we were in the boxcars. We were lucky to be going, because whoever escaped got shot.

It took us more than a week or maybe two to get to Chestochowa. The Germans were fleeing the Russians, so they kept putting us on the side to let the German troop trains pass. While the wagons sat there, the local Poles would come in, and demand our money and any goods we had. We were scared. The door was unlocked but we didn't run away, because we were afraid to be shot in the woods. My Aunt Sesha did run away with two girlfriends, and they were captured with some Polish resistance fighters. They were sent to Auschwitz, but to the work camp, not the death camp, so Sesha survived.

I met my husband in Chestochowa.

I was beat up in Chestochowa. They wanted to take my father away. I held on to him—like this, and I wouldn't let them take him. They were beating me and beating me but I wouldn't let go, and they didn't take my father. I didn't even feel it that time, the pain, I was so excited. I could only think about keeping my father with me. But when I got back to the barracks my whole neck and back were black. Afterward, it hurt me. It got worse every year.

Now, it's something terrible, I can't do what I used to anymore. I can't take the vacuum cleaner even. Jacob is doing the vacuuming for me. After ten minutes my back is hurting so much I have to stop. It has a name, what's wrong with me. The German doctor wrote it. I forget what it is called.

Later they took my father away, to Buchenwald. He was very sick and hungry. He died a day before the American army came.

"Eat a piece of cake, *mamele.*"
"*Nem* a cookie, *oytser sheyner.*"
"What shall I bake for you next week?"

BUTTER CAKE

Batter

1/2 lb. butter (2 sticks)
2 coffee cups sugar
6 eggs
1/2 teacup buttermilk (3 oz. total)
3 tbsp. sour cream

3 1/2 to 4 coffee cups (7 oz. each)
   flour
4 tsp. baking powder
Pinch salt
2 packs vanilla sugar
Cocoa

Preheat oven to 350°F.

Combine butter, sugar, eggs, buttermilk, sour cream.

Sift flour with baking powder, add salt.

Add flour mixture and vanilla sugar to butter mixture, mix until homogenous.

Spread half into greased 12-×-18-inch pan.

Sprinkle bare layer of cocoa, spread rest of batter.

Top with crumbs. (See below.)

Bake at 350°F. for an hour. Test with clean toothpick for doneness. Cool and slice.

Crumbs

4 heaping tbsp. flour
2 tbsp. butter, cut in small pieces
2 tbsp. margarine, cut tiny

1/2 tsp. baking soda
6 tsp. sugar
1 tsp. vanilla sugar

Mix above ingredients together.

GRANNY'S DOG BISCUITS

5 cups flour
3 level tsp. baking powder
Dash of salt
2 sticks margarine, softened

2 cups sugar
1/2 cup vegetable oil
5 eggs
3 packs vanilla sugar

Preheat oven to 400°F.

Sift flour and baking powder. Add salt and make well. Put margarine, sugar, and oil in well; mix well so there are no margarine lumps. Add eggs and vanilla sugar and knead. Squeeze through food mill attachment or cut into shapes.

Bake for about 20 minutes or until lightly browned. Finished cookies are about 1½ inches wide by 4 inches long and flat.

HONEY CAKE

1 heaping cup honey
$^1/_2$ cup oil
1$^1/_4$ cups sugar
1 egg
3 cups flour

1 heaping tsp. baking soda
6 tsp. instant iced-tea mix
$^1/_2$ tsp. cinnamon
Dash ground cloves

Preheat oven to 350°F.

Mix honey, oil, sugar, egg. Sift flour with baking soda. Mix instant tea with enough water to make 1 cup (or use 1 cup strong tea or strong coffee). Add tea to honey mixture. Add flour mixture, cinnamon, and cloves. Mix.

Grease round bundt pan with margarine. Bake at 350°F. for about an hour and a half (top rack) until nicely browned.

PINEAPPLE CHOCOLATE-CHIP CAKE

*6 egg yolks (reserve whites for
   "snow," below)*
1 cup sugar
1/2 lb. sweet butter
Juice of 1/2 lemon

2 1/2 cups all-purpose flour
2 1/2 tsp. baking powder
*12-oz. package of semisweet
   chocolate chips*
*20-oz. can crushed pineapple,
   drained*

Preheat oven to 350°F.

Mix together egg yolks, sugar, butter, and lemon. Sift together the flour and baking powder. Add to egg mixture.

Grease ovenproof glass baking dish (9-×-13-inch), spread dough with wet hands. On top of dough in pan, spread the chocolate chips and the drained pineapple.

Topping

6 egg whites   *3/4 cup sugar*

Make a "snow": beat stiff the egg whites and the sugar. Wet hands with water and spread meringue over cake. Use rubber spatula to make a design in the meringue. Bake at 350°F. for a little less than an hour on a high rack. Watch it carefully. Meringue should be light brown.

March

MIRACLES

March

I resist assimilation, but that is a negative identity, not a positive one.

I recover the communal-cultural-folk tradition, but this is not a lasting recipe.

I embrace the values, but values can be taught without ritual.

I follow the ritual, but at a distance.

Shall I set myself toward something more? Commitment? Study? Belief? Where does the road lead?

The impossible existence of these questions, after thousands of wandering years, renders them insistent. I can't drop them. If I don't answer the questions, my children may.

Questions are not such a bad way of life. Maybe questions are the point of it all.

A *SIMCHA*

*F*rom New York and Florida, from France and Montreal, and from Akron, Ohio, Miriam's cousins and friends have come here: to a hotel in Georgia for a *simcha,* a celebration. Tomorrow there will be a wedding.

The bridegroom is Miriam's cousin. He was born in a displaced persons camp in Germany after the war. He has been a student of law in Ohio, a studio musician in Nashville, a medical student in Mexico, and a country club tennis pro. He has lived in Paris, in New York, in Tel Aviv. He speaks six languages fluently. He has competed in tournaments of chess and golf.

The groom, Daniel, is a handsome and charming man. The world is disposed to offer him second chances—an unlucky brand of good fortune, in the end. A year before, working in a last-chance hospital in rural Georgia, he passed his medical board exams, brilliance finally overcoming self-destructiveness. And now he has found his bride.

When the groom was a small boy in Germany, before the family moved to the States, he had one toy, a stuffed bear on wheels. You could ride it, push it, hug it, sleep beside it, and imagine its personality. The groom as a small boy did these things, in the meantime rubbing off most of the plush. His mother saved the bear all these years. It is packed in a box in Ohio waiting for a grandchild.

The mother, Miriam's aunt, is not here for the wedding. A few years ago, she stored the bear with a cousin, and moved from Ohio to Tel Aviv, perhaps tired of waiting. Now, she, a widow, has come to fear flying almost as much as she fears losing her only son to an unknown wife.

The cousins who have gathered in Atlanta for the *simcha* are happy to believe that the groom, in his forties, is settling down. They have shaken their heads over him for many years, meanwhile looking forward to his visits. Here was a young man, the same age as their assimilating children, who could tell a twenty-minute Warsaw joke in Yiddish and follow it up with a Bach suite on the violin. Had they known that the marriage would unravel in five years, they still would have journeyed to Georgia for this wedding.

The cousins have gathered in Miriam's hotel room, the night before the wedding. The women have luminous faces animated by this reunion, skin glistening with the moist kisses they have exchanged. They have shimmering manicures and gold jewelry and blond domes of hair. Their perfumed greetings fill the room like peonies. They are alive, joyous. *Oyf simkhes,* only *oyf simkhes,* they cry: We should always gather in joy, and not in sadness. Amidst all this female sparkle, their husbands lean into the wallpaper, in their jackets and ties.

The groom and my husband and I go off in Daniel's car, a leather-upholstered convertible, to buy pizza in a Georgia saloon. I, having known the groom for years, try not to think of girlfriends in his past.

"She's got the cutest mind," Daniel says of his bride, who has a distinguished career and several graduate degrees, and who looks like a china doll. "She's funnier than hell, and her Spanish is better than mine. She thinks she can cook, but she can't."

I, enormously eight months pregnant with Miriam's first grandchild, make my way through narrow aisles to the restroom, brushing the chairs of beer-drinking revelers. The groom and my husband order pizzas with cheese and mushrooms and peppers and olives, but never with pepperoni, never with meatballs or sausage. Thus they respect the strictures within which Miriam and her cousins were raised: to eschew pork, to avoid mixing meat with cheese—rules learned in a vanished Poland *shtetl,* a Jewish village, but flexibly applied to a Dixie pizza. Such were the ways of a people that Satan's army tried to eradicate, through death, mass death.

Returning, we open the door. The hotel room, light and gay, *freylekh,* buzzes with Polish and Yiddish. The women, happily relaxed, have taken off their shoes, relieving bunions, corns, and pinched toes. They pad about the room, in a festive manner, women's feet sheathed in powdered nylon stockings. They hover, *balebatish*—like busy, capable housewives—over the pizza boxes, serving one another greasy slices on paper plates with plastic knives. They serve their men, still in their ties, with pizza and deference and hotel glasses of ginger ale, bubbly as champagne.

My husband runs down the hall for more soda, more ice. We open bottles and cans. Some of the women take naughty sips of beer.

"I'm going to be a *shiker* already!" says Cousin Gussie, threatening alcoholism after her second sip.

Miriam sits on the bed with Cousin Gussie. Gussie leans against the pillow, holding an inch of beer in a plastic glass smeared with pink lipstick.

Miriam's shapely legs are tucked up beside her. They look like two girls at a slumber party. Gussie was young, only seven or eight years old, when her mother left her with a wealthy Christian family in Warsaw, a pretend orphan with a phony Christian name. She was the only one of the three children to have blue eyes, and Warsaw was a big city, so she survived, Miriam told me. The two brothers also were sent away, in one direction, in another.

Gussie has a round childlike face and big eyes. She lives in Montreal because that is where her elder brother landed after the war. The brother found her through the Red Cross and sent for her, by then a genuine orphan trying out her real name again. Gussie went to work for the Red Cross, and she never stopped searching for her youngest brother. Whenever an envelope went from the Montreal office to Poland, she included a personal note. She wrote to all the orphanages, Miriam told me, "asking if they had such a boy." He had been five years old when the war began.

Miriam is asking, and Gussie is telling. Then Gussie is asking. They have news of a network of family and friends, of acquaintances who became like family after real families were shattered. It has been years since Miriam saw Gussie, and in Gussie, Miriam sees her brief, lost youth.

Miriam remembers their village: she was older than Gussie yet young enough to openly study the world around. Her mind has held fast to every detail, each face. Pictures are slipped from pocketbooks in the hotel room, photographs that once were smuggled across borders or dug out of hiding, photographs that had been sent as postcards to the relatives in America before the war, dog-eared, faded, handcolored pictures. There are pictures of children who were shot in front of their mothers, and pictures of heroes and sages and bakers and carters in a long, bearded line, and Miriam knows them all.

The bridegroom is asking for a story, and Miriam tells the story. She remembers the bridegroom's grandparents, the cousins and uncles and aunts, the braggarts and schemers and leaders and followers who all became in the end one thing: Jews. She remembers Daniel's father as a young man in the village, a man of vast talent who could play any instrument and speak any language, who passed these gifts to his son along with the damage sustained in Hell.

Miriam remembers, above all, the mother of this bridegroom. Indeed, on the groom's unworthy head, she has long lavished the adoring love that she, a girl growing up, felt for her youngest aunt. By the 1930s,

enlightenment could be whiffed in her Polish village as well as the smell
of Sabbath stews and the distant scent of danger. Miriam's aunt, the bridegroom's mother, was the girl who would lead the way into a modern age.

She was the first girl in their village to go to *gymnasium,* Miriam tells
me, riding a bicycle to the secular high school three towns over. The
woman who could not fly to her own son's wedding was going to attend
university, to study medicine. She was strong and lithe, good in science
and math.

"And then came the war . . ." It is the way many of Miriam's stories
end. The Jews were dismissed from *gymnasium.* Yet we are here for a
simcha, so that was not really the end.

There are stories and jokes. It is hard for me, alone in my English, to
follow it all. My husband is listening intently, laughing hard. No one will
translate enough. The groom mentions that his bachelor party, a southern
conclave of motley genius and vague commitment, awaits at a speakeasy.
He knows that his friends will wait all night if they have to, and well they
might. No one can leave this spellbound room, as the women shout and
interject and clean up the pizza boxes, and their husbands at last lift
crooked forefingers to loosen their ties.

And what of Gussie's younger brother, the five-year-old boy pushed
into a wagon one night with a lump of sugar to suck and his mother's
fierce loving admonition that his name was no longer *Itzhak* but John?
The peasant drove off with his fee, a bag full of jewelry and coins, for
taking this risk, and the boy cried himself to sleep in the bumping wagon
on the way to a new home. Then the boy was found out and arrested, and
somehow he escaped. He ran with the dogs, stealing food, cadging shelter
until he was discovered, asleep in a farmer's barn.

"They let him stay," Miriam tells me, in whispers that night, as I beg
for morsels of history. "They were old, a farmer and his wife, and they
wanted a boy to do the work. They hid him in the barn, and they beat
him, and they fed him just like the pigs, and they told him they would kill
him if he ever showed himself to anyone else. But they kept him alive."

How could he keep track of time, or even remember his real name? I
look at the childlike Gussie, at the diamonds on her hands, and the pink
lipstick, and I think of those hands writing letters, writing letters, every
month, to Europe after the war, for news, any news. Year after year . . .

While in the back country of Poland, John who used to be *Itzhak*
heard the sound of a motor car and ran to the road. He saw: a long line

of soldiers marching behind shiny, black automobiles, a slow parade of authority, and he summoned his guts and ran to a uniform, its lapel splashed with red.

"Is the war over, then?" he asked breathlessly in Polish, straw in his matted hair. He was illiterate and filthy, and thin as a stick. He had never used a knife and fork. The startled Russian soldier stepped out of formation. The war had ended years before.

"*Du bist oykhet a Yid?*" asked the soldier, recognizing a fellow Jew, and he took the boy away.

"At the end of 1951, or maybe 1952, Gussie got a letter from England," Miriam tells me, before her attention is claimed by a cousin with a point of information to request I look around for my husband, who may have left for the bachelor party with the groom.

But Gussie is at the door, greeting a dark-haired young man in glasses, slight and tall. She guides him into the room and turns to me.

"I'd like you to meet my nephew from England, the son of my brother John."

It is nearing midnight. I yawn, forty pounds pregnant, with swollen legs. One of the husbands sits snoring in his chair. Ours are the only signs of fatigue. One of the women is singing, a few others join in. Yiddish songs for dancing, lighthearted songs. Laughter ripples across the room. Tomorrow we will have a *simcha,* but there is no point to waiting. You never know what tomorrow will bring.

KOSHER STYLE

$\mathcal{A}$s she went along, my mother made up the rules. These were not consistent, were not legal, were not the cumulation of centuries of rabbinical thought. Our practices, when I was a child, reflected that which my parents chose to remember, or with which my mother could not bear to part. They were vestiges of their own upbringing, aesthetic in the end. They had to do with comfort and familiarity and perhaps just a bit of superstition. Commandment and community pressure, which had kept our great-grandparents in line, had fizzled out in the long march of the twentieth century.

For a long time, we children thought we were kosher. Most of our friends and acquaintances, Jewish or not, ate spare ribs, pepperoni pizza. We, however, never drank milk with meat, or ate anything made with cheese or cream at the same meal as chicken or lamb or cow. The chickens, lambs, and cows were killed according to Jewish law. There never was pork in the house, never hindquarters, never a cut of meat called butt or rump or loin. It was unthinkable, too, to cook meat without garlic or onion; I figured this was a law of *kashrut* and felt nausea at the smell of nude frying steak in a strange kitchen.

Strictly speaking, though, our *kashrut* was a fiction. We had only one set of dishes, not two. Shrimp came home now and again, and I knew no sense of transgression. My mother, raised to eschew sea creepers and creatures, to eat only swimmers with fins and scales, had long since declared the dichotomy a gloss.

In restaurants, we ate what we wanted. I accepted unquestioningly, as have so many others, the schizophrenic distinction between "eating home" and "eating out." Shifting tables, one became a different person. Existential, this.

Thus we did not forgo Sunday dinners at our favorite restaurant, where one draw was the thick-sliced roast beef and another was the banana cream pie. The patrons themselves, blurry with blue cigar smoke and red lipstick, made this an *ekht* Jewish place. We had our cheese blintzes, large and savory, on Saturday mornings in Eastern Market, ignoring the sizzling bacon and country sausage as we slid trays along a cafeteria line beside the grocers, wholesalers, and farmers. We always greeted the owners, Jews like ourselves, and paid them in cash on *Shabbas*.

I now know a term for what we were: "kosher style." Back then I knew the phrase only to describe a delicatessen showcase filled with corned beef and *kishke,* stuffed derma—East European Jewish cuisine by way of New York, but graced by no certificate of rabbinical approval. Although my parents carried home only kosher corned beef, dining out we were liberals. The kosher-style places were nicer, newer: the big Jewish money was Reform in our town.

My parents followed their *landslayt,* north and west on Sunday nights, as the suburban frontier expanded to encompass mushroom barley soup and sandwiches of pickled tongue. It was more important that the thin slices of tongue be stacked on caraway-sprinkled Jewish rye and slathered with brown mustard than that its provenance be approved.

If you were strictly kosher, if you carried around your standards all the time, you would have had fewer choices. In midcentury America, that's what the good life was all about—choice. And the good life was what the immigrants wanted for their children and grandchildren. That's why they had come to America in the first place, those immigrants, schlepping their candlesticks and featherbeds. With freedom and opportunity came new undreamed-of choices—to believe in your grandparents' religion, or to believe in nothing, or to believe but eschew the trappings, or to embrace the trappings with all your heart, and make a corned beef sandwich on "Jewish" rye the only religion you need.

"What's kosher style?" jibed a young columnist, posing a witty rhetorical question in a Detroit campus newspaper somewhere around 1969. "It's got the taste, but not the blessing."

Leave it to a black man in Detroit to put it best. He would know; neighborhoods that had cycled from Hebrew to Negro were littered with Jewish remnants. As you moved northwest from the old East Side, many a Baptist church had been a synagogue once. You could tell because the cross looked tacked on, or there was no cross. You just knew that the movable letters on the outside signboard that spelled out ARE YOU SAVED? COME HOME TO GOD'S HOUSE, once said MAARIV SERVICE 7 P.M. RABBI MORTON GOLD. Delicatessens, stuck in the landscape like so many pushpins, still purveyed their spicy hot dogs and hot corned beef to a receptive community, kosher style.

The taste without the blessing. That was us. Our Magnavox played Yiddish singers, along with *Songs of Social Justice,* and sometimes it thundered the stirring speeches of Israeli figures of state. We had a mad scramble to clear laundry and papers, to run a dustcloth, in a Friday afternoon cacophony of piano practice, pot lids, and silver polish. At dusk, we stood before the mantelpiece as our mother lit candles, a white handkerchief on her head to show respect to the folkways.

My father kept track of the family *yahrzeits,* anniversaries of deaths, on the Hebrew/English calendars the kosher butcher distributed every year. He took his ritual glass of schnapps on *Shabbas,* and we cheered, *"L'chaim!"* At his workplace, where the Jew, a rare species, engendered suspicion, my father made an explicit point of staying away on Yom Kippur, although he never spent the day in prayer. We had our grandmothers, spinning their traditional webs in their far-off kitchens. Also, we went to Hebrew school, a small Yiddishist, Labor Zionist *cheder* to be sure, but it was serious, four days a week, not just Sunday school in English.

Yet in all of this, neither commandment nor community seemed to play a role. My mother, whom I always suspected of belief in *something* supernatural, claimed to have lost her faith when reports of the Holocaust moved somberly west. My father, damaged as a teenager by illness and once devoted to Marxism, was both too aggrieved and too rational for God. We had a *mezuzah,* a little inscribed parchment encased on the door frame, but we never gave it a bit of thought. A Jewish household has a *mezuzah,* that's all there is to it, *shoyn.* We did all these things, like Marrano families discovered in Mexico, generations after their forced conversion in the Spanish Inquisition, who still would fast one autumn day and light eight candles in December, although they had no idea why.

In our neighborhood, the Jewish population dwindled, then vanished. We stayed. We never joined a synagogue or attended Jewish summer camp, never traveled to Israel or marched for Soviet Jews. Jewish meant holidays, books, civil rights, and corned beef. God and *shul* had nothing to do with it.

This is what I mean by "kosher style."

My mother, a returning student, was in college when the columnist's wit came my way. I already was in high school then, avidly reading the publications she brought home. The radicalized college paper had become a hotbed of Black Panther sympathizers, of anti-Zionist rhetoric. One of its missions seemed to be to provoke with diatribes against bad Jews—slum landlords, exploitive business owners, and the press establishment, old canards dredged up afresh by the New Left.

My Old-Left parents shook their heads over the rift between natural comrades. They were alarmed by the attacks on "Zionism," hearing a euphemism for anti-Semitism. My father supported Israel, a stance that cost him, in those years, friendships on the Left.

"When fascism comes to this country, I want to have a place to go," he said.

I read the papers my mother brought home, winnowing the rantings. I tried to excuse overt hostility, reminding myself of evil stereotypes I had heard from Jewish lips. I tried on Jewish self-hatred, a specialized variety of the abounding white self-hatred of the time.

Back then I still thought that a hot corned beef sandwich grabbed to go, and enjoyed while waiting for the Dexter bus, was some sort of Esperanto—tasty, filling, holding out utopian possibilities for one big happy world. Later I widened my lens and thought that everyone should also eat pork ribs barbecued all day over half an oil drum filled with briquettes, and basted with homemade sauce until the tender meat was falling off the bone. The best was simply the best. Was it a mirage? Look at us, like relatives who bickered constantly, the subject of one another's worst jokes.

"Being oppressed doesn't make people hate oppression." This was my father's tart take on things. "It only makes them know they don't want to be the ones to be oppressed." The sad part was, that Jews and blacks were lumped together in everyone else's worst jokes.

There was a black-Jewish link through time in Detroit. Every generation of Jews had its signature high school. Within their echoing halls and funky locker rooms, every half generation had what passed for integration, but was in fact transition from white to black. Still it was contact, sometimes powerful.

All my life in Detroit I knew black aficionados of Jewish culture and vice versa—Pentecostal grandmothers who would only buy kosher meat, black teenagers who knew the right Yiddish word, countless Jews aspiring to soul music, and later, to nonwhite righteousness. Our neighborhood, a cauldron of instability, produced many a crossover confection. One lad shocked his family, a pillar of the black middle class, by renouncing

Christmas and trying out life in Israel. Another let his red, frizzy, Polish hair go natural. His friends called him "the albino."

By the end of grade school, as the Jews left our neighborhood, life for me had become increasingly layered, rich. In music class we sang Christmas carols and twelve-verse sea chanteys. On the playground, I tried to learn black syntax and new, complex rope-jumping rhymes. After school, I was faking Hebrew and Yiddish to somehow get through extended Jewish afternoons. At home, my mother, orthodox on the English language, corrected my grammar. "Hopefully" will never be more than an adverb to me.

Oh, I dawdled on the way to school, avoiding the moment of encounter, singing "Two steps forward, one step back," like some little mad Russian populist. Often, I was late. I brought home clichés of the red peril, anti-Communism being the prevailing ideology, and I returned to school with kitchen-table indignation, repeating my father's ripostes. I championed human rights in earnest paraphrase, but this won me no close friends, white or black. Popularity eluded me; I rambled home through the wild alleyways, a disguised fairy-tale princess in heavy oxford shoes and arch supports among the blooming four o'clocks and steel garbage cans.

We were outsiders to every constituency, even to those who were outsiders themselves. Our kosher meat, my father's idiosyncratic views, and possibly my mother's taste for fine leather goods set us apart from the Left. We were too Jewish. My parents' political background, their atheism, our rented flat in the city and tangential connection to institutional life, divided us from the Jewish community that had left us behind.

We were the last whites on the block, and our front lawn was the worst on the block. We weren't homeowners or joiners; the black middle class moved on, and our address was déclassé. We didn't even have a color TV, but had to watch *Walt Disney's Wonderful World of Color* in black and white. I can still visualize the NBC peacock, fanning out its stylized tail feathers in many a proud shade of gray.

I could be myself in a Detroit delicatessen, waiting for a seat alongside the cool glass showcases banked with pepper-crusted pastramis, roasted turkeys, chicken salad, chopped liver sprinkled with chopped hard-cooked egg, potato salad, cole slaw, pickled green tomatoes, sour pickles, new dill pickles, frankfurters linked together by casing and string. Customers buying cold cuts to take home pressed their fingertips against the glass. They craned up to look at the scales or bent to see what was going on behind the counter: "Extra lean, from the small end—no, not that one, this one!"

There was a list on the wall indicating the price of buying by the pound and the cost of a carryout sandwich. A counter near the door held a cash register, toothpicks, mints, gum, candy, cigars. There was a cigarette machine. There were vinyl banquettes and metal-rimmed Formica tables, and tall menus for those staying to a meal.

As neighborhoods changed and the Jews left, the delicatessens were the last or among the last remnants of Jewish communal life. They stayed if they could cater to a varied clientele. There might be a daytime scene, business owners who still had warehouses in the old neighborhoods, nearby office workers, the old folks who couldn't afford to move, treating themselves to a frankfurter and a cup of tea, maybe college students or hospital staffers or cops.

Some of the delis came to sell liquor or offered late hours if there was a movie house or nightclub nearby. One served the county courthouse, another boasted of custom past by Lenny Bruce. But the mainstay of these places became the new neighborhood dwellers, usually black, who inherited houses and street infrastructure as the Jews followed WASPs northwesterly and then forged ahead into brand-new neighborhoods across Eight Mile Road, the city limit. The black community, the Jewish community, doppelgangers, bound together from deli to deli, Mile Road to Mile Road, through time.

At some point I realized that we weren't really kosher. What a letdown. I wanted something recognizable to wear as an I.D. badge. I had to admit to the BLTs on the way to New York for Passover, although my parents always asked for the bacon "extra crisp" as if that took the pig out of it. At home, we children clamored for two sets of dishes, two sets of pots, two sets of spoons and knives and forks, a kitchen arsenal to objectify our leanings, to tether us to a solid post. No dice. My parents had known all of that, they were drawing their lines in the sand as they chose.

In my house, we were against "prejudice," a quaint euphemism now that once covered the gamut from economic exclusion to hatred of minority groups to ethnic jokes to calling the Negro maid a *shvartzer*. Once, this

Yiddish word meaning "black" described a swarthy, dark-haired Jew. Every Schwartz alive must have had such a one on the family tree. We children, taking a cue from our mother, cringed at the vulgarity of the term when Jews spoke it pejoratively, to mean The Negro People. There was one wonderful year in our lives when my mother had weekly household help, a tall dignified woman of color who was a regal sight ironing curtains in the living room. My mother addressed her as Mrs. Woods, referred to her thus. It never occurred to us but to do the same.

My mother must have spoken to us on the evils of prejudice. My father simply hated the concept of "race," which he thought unscientific. One time, our family visited Chicago for a weekend and stayed in a hotel, the sole pure vacation I can remember from my childhood amongst the many trips to Toronto or New York to visit the grandmothers. The high point (other than the Olde Towne restaurant where the steak was served with *Gott* help us a pat of butter melting atop the meat) was our tour of the Museum of Science and Industry.

In the Hall of Man, the Caucasian race was depicted by a tall, straight-backed mannequin or maybe skeleton, while a stooped, slack-jawed, simian figure represented the Negro race. My father let us know it was a bunch of stupid malevolent lies, the sort of thing Hitler had used against us, the Jews. There was no such thing as race. The gene pool was big. We all stormed out, indignant and pissed off, and we never went back to Chicago. When the 1968 Democratic convention blew up, we thought we knew why.

I knew that my parents were civil rights partisans. I was proud of the night my father had spent in jail in the 1950s, arrested and charged with "inciting to riot." He and a buddy had stood on a front porch in a white part of town, trying to protect the new black homeowners within from a rock-throwing mob on the lawn. It seemed the Jewish thing to do. I could never understand people of the Book lapsing on this front. Better you should eat bacon.

I think we children probably were rare and lucky: We, though white and Jewish, shared life with nonwhite friends, neighbors, teachers, associates, in as casual a way as was possible then. Our parents, like those of our black classmates, had grown up in an essentially one-color social spectrum. Our experience was different, and this was valuable, despite our sometime sense of isolation, of not belonging, despite our self-consciousness, despite the turmoil of the time and place. Yes, it was painful and lonely for me at times, but it was a painful time for many. I froze and burned for our first brown-skinned girl, ordered by the unfeeling teacher to "tie back your wild hair" in front of the whole class as we returned from a wind-blown recess. I always think of her, and wonder how angry she might have become.

As children, we experienced something of what this American experiment is supposed to be about. Had we lived in the Jewish neighborhood, gone to synagogue, had the "blessing," we would have had other things, but we wouldn't have had that, not in the same way. I hope, I just keep hoping, that the renewal of religion, of ethnic identification, of communal ritual, will not preclude the experiment continuing. I consider my own efforts to link past to future, to graft something timeless onto the rushing days, and I worry about the particularism my life is thereby coming to. If each little group identifies with itself first, what happens to the democracy of the village green?

In my parents' last city years, when they clearly became white targets of what my Marxist father called lumpen elements within the black community—a community undergoing its own class shifts and pressures— there was never a racist cast to my parents' complaints. Trash was dumped on their lawn, the house was broken into, my mother was mugged on her way home from the bus. My father would always say that the chief victims of crime in the city were black. As one of the victimized neighbors, though, he became a proponent of more "law and order" than suburban white liberals could abide.

I don't know if life, lived on those many planes, was complex or simple. It seems complex looking back, but I was a child then. Twice weekly I faced the matchless paradigm of Franz and Gladys. Franz, the men's locker room attendant at the Jewish Center, had a gold tooth, scant hair, and a concentration camp number tattooed on his arm. Year after year, he worked beside Gladys, the women's attendant, a coffee-skinned woman with a soft southern accent. They occupied the checkpoint you passed on the way to the swimming pool, handing out towels and locker keys.

I learned what the numbers stamped on an arm meant at the same time I learned about prejudice, and I linked them, Franz and Gladys, in a felt locus of injustice. To my eight- and ten- and twelve-year-old mind, they were like a long-married couple. Perfectly parallel. Just belonged together. That was simple.

Then the world split apart. The Jewish Center moved away. Finally, so did I. Are a few old delis still hanging on in my old hometown, purveying corned beef to a multicolored world?

If so, and if there is a God, they have the blessing.

CONFINEMENT

*I*t's not a foot, it's a head, I told the doctor.

There was a hard, round part of the baby pressing itself into a sore internal organ under my ribs.

Oh, no, it is not a head, that is a foot, said the doctor. She insisted that the fetus, at eight and a half months, had flipped itself over and was aiming for a headfirst exit.

What did I know? I kept on going to childbirth preparation classes, leaning against my husband and directing little puffs of breath at an imaginary lighted match. This being New York City, our instructor regaled us with tales of celebrity deliveries she, an obstetric nurse, had overseen.

We students were bent on perfect deliveries. No painkillers, no drugs, no intervention. When I learned that the baby, my first, was indeed in breech position, and would be delivered via cesarean section, I wept. It was the first inkling that life was out of my control.

The anesthesiologist gave a spinal, not an epidural. The recovery nurses refused to come when buzzed. But the baby was perfect, and after five days we went home.

I had heard so much about women back to work the next day, or in their bikinis the following summer. I shuffled into my apartment with a throbbing abdominal incision, forty pounds to lose. . . . The whole place had to be reorganized. I had things to buy, telephone calls to make . . . and all I wanted was to get into bed. I was a failure.

But the baby was perfect. Only, the baby seemed always hungry, and I worried. Is she getting enough milk? Am I replenishing supplies? The books say every two hours. . . . I began charting waking and eating times, searching for patterns. I cried with fatigue and confusion.

My mother came from Detroit. She had nursed three babies in the 1950s, while doctors and neighbors frowned. Her mother had nursed six, from 1920 to 1940. She knew what to do.

"Get into bed," said my mother. "Let me bring you something to drink."

Lign in kimpet was the Yiddish phrase she used. Lying-in, confinement.

Most cultures have this concept: rest the body, hold the baby, stay in, let the milk flow. Strange day, when women expect to get back into slim clothes at once, when nursing ties you down.

"Just stay right there," said my mother, bustling off to boil water for tea. In the next few days, she brought me tea with lemon, tea with milk and sugar, herbal tea, hot water with milk, barley soup, vegetable soup, chicken broth, seltzer and water and ginger ale and buttermilk and eggnog and chocolate milk shakes. Whenever she saw me pick up the baby to nurse, she pulled up a footstool for me. She brought a pillow. She positioned a makeshift table nearby and set a drinking vessel thereon.

"You have to get your strength back," my mother said.

"You have to keep up your fluids . . ." said my mother.

". . . replace your calcium . . ."

". . . keep your insides warm . . ."

". . . make plenty of rich milk for the baby . . ."

". . . she's on her schedule, not yours. Every twenty minutes if she wants it . . ."

"Let the laundry sit there," my mother said. "Have some nice warm tea."

"Just get into bed and rest," said my mother. "Take the baby with you."

These were the things her own mother, I believe, had said to her when I was born. I could liken the *bubbe,* my mother's mother, to a telegraph, transmitting information from a distant place: Poland, the *shtetl,* the old country. *Lign in kimpet*—that's what a woman did after childbirth, and the whole community mobilized to make sure she didn't have to do else but this. There were superstitions attached, but this was also science. Empirical evidence said a woman should rest and drink.

My mother-in-law Miriam arrived with covered dishes: split pea soup, cream of cauliflower soup, prunes dipped in chocolate imported from Poland. This was for me, but also for the baby, her first grandchild.

This was no time to start a diet.

"My mother always called this *lign in kimpet,*" said my mother to Miriam.

"Sure," said Miriam. "That's what it is."

"Would you like a drink?" asked my mother to me.

"Maybe a piece of cake with tea?" added Miriam.

"I think I would like half a beer," I said. It was late afternoon. Someone had told me beer was good for nursing at the end of a tiring day.

"It's very good, beer, for nursing," commented Miriam. "The dark beer makes good milk."

"Beer is good for nursing?" asked my mother.

"When my son was born, mine husband brought me a whole box of beer," said Miriam, "a big box like that." She moved her hands along the sides of a cube of substantial remembered space. "We were in Israel that time, he went to Holon with the bicycle. Twenty-four bottles of dark beer, liters, like that he brought me." She marked the height of these bottles with her hands. "I drank one or two bottles every day."

Miriam paused, thinking about being a new mother in a new country. I thought of Jacob, a first-time father, maneuvering a heavy case full of beer bottles on the handlebars of his bicycle. My mother thought about a tall bottle of dark beer, rich and spicy.

"My, my," said my mother, with a touch of envy. "You had a good *kimpet.*"

"I think there is dark beer in the fridge," I said.

It took me a year to lose that weight, but so? My daughter's teeth are white and straight. She is growing out of her shoes. "Have another one, Mom," she urges from time to time. "Another little girl. You can do it."

April

FEMALE RELIGION

April

I've been ignoring it, with a mixture of advance regret and resistance. What's hard is that it rolls around every year. Every year to excavate, clean, change over, cook, return to normalcy. Renewing, uplifting, etc., etc. But definitely exhausting. I can either write about it or do it, but not both. I'm not doing Passover this year.

I'll wipe down the counter and use paper plates. I'll buy a box of matzo. It doesn't have to be a big production. I'll simplify.

We'll have a simple Seder. I'll buy a few bags of groceries, the basics— that's it. Five boxes of matzos, a box of matzo meal, a couple of cans of macaroons, soup nuts, a dozen eggs, odds and ends. Parsley. Everyday plates.

We must have a Seder. Miriam will do some cooking at home, and we'll hold the dinner at my house. I told her to keep it simple and she sort of shrugged. "We have to eat something," she remarked.

I can't put Miriam's Passover cooking on an everyday plate. What was I thinking? I have scruples.

I suppose I will unearth the Passover dishes, gingerly balancing as I creak down the attic steps. The boxes won't be properly labeled: I won't be sure which are dishes, which pots and gadgets, so I will take down all of them.

I will need a place to put the Passover dishes, so I will empty a cabinet, just one, pack up the everyday dishes and move them downstairs. I'll wipe out the shelves and line them with paper. I have to wash the Passover dishes, so I will kasher *the dishwasher, by running an empty machine through a boiling hot cycle. Then I will load the Passover dishes.*

I can't let Miriam stand on her feet and cook everything. I'll have to cook something. I guess I should unpack the Passover pots. I will take just the minimum—a couple of mixing bowls, and a big soup pot, and another pot for matzo balls. I'll need a few pans, for roasting chickens and potatoes. ''hickens are already in the freezer.

I'll need a few more things at the store. Seder plate, symbolic foods. Horse-radish root, greens, roasted shankbone.

Oh, no, I forgot to order a shankbone when I bought the chicken, every lamb shank in New York State must be spoken for by now.

Roasted egg on the Seder plate. You boil it then hold it over the burner with tongs to brown it. Eggs in salt water for the Seder meal: Better get an extra dozen eggs.

I enjoy making haroses, *the heap of chopped fruits, nuts, and wine that stands for the mortar used by Hebrew slaves in Egypt—that to me is Passover. Put walnuts, sugar, apples, sweet wine on the list.*

Passover wine to drink. Grape juice for the kids. Add beverages to the list.

Soup. I've been to the butcher for broilers but forgot the pullets for the soup. Have to go back anyway for the shankbone. Call for that shankbone RIGHT NOW.

Must watch Miriam make egg noodles this year.

I'll have to do the utensils. If we're using the Passover pots, we'll need turners and slotted spoons and soup ladles and silverware and chicken shears and a grapefruit knife and a strainer and a chopper and a good knife. I'll need to Passoverize a few everyday utensils.

Pickles.

Dried fruit for compote.

Fresh fruit. It wouldn't be Passover without grapefruits, oranges, strawberries, and bananas.

Why would I want any life to live other than a Passover week with my family?

I'll buy a few fresh packages of salt and pepper, coffee, tea, ginger, paprika. I guess I'll sell the spices, the whiskeys and liqueurs, that a Jew is not supposed to own on Passover. I know it's a legal charade; authorizing the rabbi to sell these items, too expensive to give or throw away, to a non-Jew, and then arranging to buy it all back.

Where is that legal form from the rabbi?

I will need a new bag of sugar and new cinnamon for the bubelekh— *matzo meal pancakes—and for the matzo* brei. *Take out a Passover frying pan. Can't use everyday oil in a Passover pan. Add oil to the list. And—yes, another dozen eggs. For my children, I'll make* bubelekh *for breakfast.*

I should make the stove kosher for Passover, burn out the oven to clean it, take off the stove knobs and soak them, sear burners in their own flame. I should move out the stove and see what's underneath. Under the refrigerator, and under the sink.

I'm not going to put Passover things down on this counter, where I've been slicing bagels for fifty-one weeks. I'll just scrub and cover it. I'll pack away the toaster oven, as long as I've done all of this.

I might as well invite a few more people to the Seder. I'll have to clean up a bit around the house. I'm in my living room, and there are hard, stale cookies under the cushions. The floors, the corners, crumbs everywhere! Hand me that mop, that bucket, that rag!

We're finishing up the hametz, leavened foods banned during Pesach. *Eating the last crusts of bread, the last frozen bagels, the Greek spinach triangles and crescent rolls. We're having rice crackers for breakfast and soba noodles for lunch. We're baking chocolate chip cookies to use up the flour. We're making corn bread, five days before* Pesach.

Enough, already. I will bag up these packages of pasta and rice, and give them away to the soup kitchen, the one at the Methodist church.

Add it to the list: Church.

I will make Pesach.

BABY NAMING

*W*hen my daughter was born, I learned from my mother-in-law, Miriam, that we must have a *Mazel-tov,* a celebration for the baby. In Yiddish, *mazel* is luck and *tov* is good. The phrase embodies the English "congratulations," and also a forward-looking, slightly superstitious "good luck."

The *Mazel-tov* in Miriam's mind was an official baby naming in the synagogue and a party to go with it. Boys are circumcised on the eighth day of life, and this male occasion, the *bris* or *brit milah,* calls for rejoicing, wine, and food. The guests must be fed, it is even written down somewhere, and the arrangements are the father's responsibility.

The baby naming for a girl is pure tradition, not obligation, one of those distinctions that makes a girl seem less valued than a boy. This is the sort of thing that made me write off religious involvement for a long time. When pregnant, though, I did not trouble myself about any of this. I knew not from baby namings, raised as I was on the fringes of Jewish communal life.

I suspected Miriam's namings were modern inventions, and asked my mother if this was so.

"Oh, no," objected my mother, taken aback. "My mother named you in *shul.* She named all her granddaughters."

I never knew that. My parents were not involved in my synagogue naming. They did not join with friends and family to formally welcome me in. No community gathered to celebrate with a schnapps, herring, a piece of sponge cake. Yet my mother's mother, the *bubbe,* assured that a delicate thread of female connection was worked into the generations' embroidery, on my behalf.

While the Torah was open, when my mother's mother believed she had the attention of God, she recited a blessing. She stood at the hand-lettered parchment scroll and stitched her mother's name, Libe Beyle, into her prayers for me, the namesake—in the way of the Ashkenazim, the Jews of Eastern Europe, who keep names alive after loved ones have died. A name without a life to live it is a restless, wandering thing.

The *bubbe,* it seems, went to the synagogue to have seven grand-daughters properly named in the 1950s. On seven Sabbath mornings, alone, or perhaps with her youngest, then-unmarried son, she went. She walked with her determined, rocking gait, to the neighborhood *shul,* in Toronto—hours away from our home in Detroit, and across a border. She whispered to the rabbi, planned to offer a few dollars for charity.

She would have spoken the Jewish names, and recalled the dear dead that we girls were named for, and said a Hebrew prayer. My mother's mother could read Hebrew, although she was not educated in the Texts. Girls weren't, by and large, in the Warsaw of her childhood. That, too, we can abhor. We can fan our complaints into great flames, but one truth is fireproof: those girls knew what they knew.

When it came to my cousin Carlotta, who would be raised Catholic by her Mexican mother after the divorce—my grandmother must have wept, yet named her a Jewish name. What that name was, I don't know. My uncle, Carlotta's father, died long ago. Yet a Jewish name for this cousin was given, it must exist, afloat someplace in the galaxy.

The eighth granddaughter, born after the *bubbe*'s death, was bestowed with her grandmother's very name, Malke. And now there is another Malke, a sturdy, beautiful toddler with dark ringlets of hair and a heredi-tary crossed toe on her foot, my sister's child.

While pregnant, I had two lists of baby names, boy and girl. These were variations, translations, and evocations of the Hebrew and Yiddish monikers of family members fallen and affectionately recalled. I took the male list less seriously. Among all the women offering opinions on the baby's gender throughout my pregnancy, only my Ivy League–trained obstetrician predicted a boy, a large one at that.

Any other woman in any way connected to a folk tradition, anywhere in the world—the West Indian checkout clerk at the supermarket, the Harlem-reared secretary at work, the Chinatown peddler, the Hispanic woman on the bus, and of course, Miriam—these women unanimously appraised my complexion and the configuration of the weight I was gaining, and stated definitively, "It's a girl." Middle-class friends, too far removed from female folkways, had no way to guess. Nor had I. For what it is worth, though, at night I dreamed Girl.

I wanted a daughter, first time around. Her name was a delicate matter. My husband's sister, loved and cherished, had died young, and her name hovered over our heads. But my husband feared the daily pronouncing of her name again. He worried that the name might never become fully our daughter's, that its sound to him might always be conscious and heightened. He worried, too, about assigning the sadness and regret and unfulfilled expectations of a tragically shortened life to a new, pristine baby.

I love the old tradition in which given names in a family reach endlessly back through time. We live with our legacies, imperfect or tragic, and life is made dimensional thereby. Pain and joy coexist; children grow up with history, good and bad. Those who name move on, and the naming, I thought, might help with this. I saw a purpose to this naming, for parent and child.

But it was his little sister, his black-eyed sister, the person with whom his childhood was shared. He had pulled her about in a homemade wagon, and later, visited her in the hospital. I had never known her. My husband had the memories. I was for it, but the decision had to be his.

I went through my ungainly ninth month with the baby's name still unresolved. I was becoming an expert on names and their origins, buying books and cross-referencing with yellow stick-on notes. Whether to name after, and in what shape naming after might take, these matters took time. We had to consider whether to bestow two names, a ritual Hebrew name and a secular name as well. We could anglicize a Yiddish name. Should we choose an English name with a meaning or sound similar to the Yiddish? Should we carry over only the initial? Use Hebrew for the middle name?

In the process of becoming an expert, I developed some prickly opinions—among them, indignation at the general popularity of names indigenous to my family. Others had no right to my family's interesting, beautiful names.

When not obsessed with the names, my concerns were equally obsessive: breathing, contractions, maternity leave, the constant soreness under my right ribs, where the baby was resting what my obstetrician called a foot but turned out to be a head, on my liver. Since she never saw fit to rotate herself into a head-down pose, my daughter's first day of life and my first day of motherhood found me flat on my back in a hospital bed after excessive anesthesia and a cesarean section, in a state of exhausted disbelief.

This was when I learned about the *Mazel-tov*. In the next few days, I was pressed into arranging this affair. My father would be in town only a short time; it must be soon. Miriam was insistent.

I was resentful, uncomfortable, drained. Where the warm bundle sucking away in a football hold at my side was concerned, my mind was focused clarity. All else was blurred and surreal. I learned to diaper and bathe the baby, to move about on my feet again, to catnap. I wanted to stare at the baby for hours, and then, to sleep, to sleep.

To such all-consuming purpose was added the detail of arranging an affair for forty or sixty people, the necessity of which I had to take on faith. A yellow legal pad and a felt-tip pen materialized in the hospital, and I began to make lists. I used some autonomous circuits of the brain, I think. I set down names and phone numbers, second cousins and friends, bakeries, purveyors of smoked fish, the endless details that women expect themselves to know: plastic shot glasses, cutlery, tablecloths, ice. I noted prices, made bright telephone calls to people I had met at my wedding, gave directions.

None of Miriam's crowd had answering machines or call-waiting services. I had to listen to busy signals, to phones ringing out into empty kitchens and bedrooms, to keep track, to call again. Through it all, nurses came by with forms to fill out, birth registration forms. They reminded us daily. The paperwork sat on the nightstand. I was planning a naming, but we still had not decided on the name.

This was maternity leave; my time to rest and reorganize myself, to set up the apartment for its new little resident. Nothing, by the way, had been done for the new one in advance. In my husband's family, you don't get ready for a baby, you only wish for luck, and others so wish on your behalf. There are no baby showers, no placing orders for towels and cradles, no wallpapering the nursery walls with darling duckies and beribboned cats. To set up for a baby is to tempt the evil eye.

"Don't do anything, please," Miriam had pleaded with me.

Irresistible nesting urges had forced me to prowl baby equipment stores, those bewildering, perfect retail worlds where dressers, cribs, linens, towels, mobiles, wall hangings, changing tables, carriages, and jumpsuits coordinate perfectly and play a tinkling rendition of "Small World." I could do nothing with it. Also, Miriam screamed every time I reached for a glass on a high shelf, and she sighed bitterly as I continued to take the subway to work. I was frustrated, angry. Trying to figure out childbearing anew, I was roped in by the *ancienne*.

"Do you really believe in all this?" I accused my husband, seeing him with new eyes.

"Do you really want to take a chance?" he countered, unsympathetic.

Miriam, as a young bride in Israel, had suffered a miscarriage: "Once I prepared everything, and I came home with empty hands," she told me.

What can one say to the unanswerable?

"But what will the baby wear?" I wailed. I expected, before the fact, to be home from the hospital in forty-eight hours, with a naked infant.

"Don't worry," my husband told me, again and again. Sure enough, I had a C-section, and the baby had jaundice, and my hospital stay was extended to five days. This gave my husband time to drive the two new grandmothers to Brooklyn for the purchase of an extravagant layette. Gaily, they reviewed for me their triumphs, unwrapping the little pieces, holding them up by their wee shoulders and dainty hems, refolding them on the hospital bed—wonderful little things, washclothes, crib bumpers, stretchies, although perhaps not entirely my taste . . . I set back my head on the pillow and wondered if anything would ever again be within my control.

Ten minutes before checkout, as our baby regarded us with wise baby eyes, we registered her birth, with a Hebrew name, that of her father's sister. We dressed the baby's perfect six-pound body in the going-home clothes provided by the grandmothers: a *hemdele,* the little undershirt, fastened lightly with ribbon ties, a red velour stretchy, with an overedged collar and teddy bear appliqué, a cotton cap, a hooded white cardigan sweater embroidered with small red strawberries, and matching *kleyne hoyzn mit fiselekh*—leggings—and a patchwork bunting sort of thing that zipped and snugged. Around all of this was wrapped a soft blue blanket, the one item my father, along for the ride to Brooklyn, had picked out.

"The saleslady raised her eyebrows at blue for a girl," my mother remarked, "but Dad didn't care. It's his favorite color."

It took us twenty minutes to dress the baby. Then we sat in the overheated hospital lobby for another half hour, waiting for a taxi, debating whether to unwrap the baby, who was now wailing, and quarreling gently as to whether we should have purchased a car seat in advance. We grasped her tightly in the back seat of the cab, bracing ourselves against potholes, and we urged caution on the driver as we crossed Central Park and turned north.

When I got home from the hospital, there was a place for the baby to sleep. Miriam had gotten her hands on someone's rocking cradle. There it was, softly cushioned, and ruffled in snowy eyelet embroidery, at the foot of my bed next to the TV, surrounded by shopping bags. I wasn't sure it was safe, or quite the thing for my infant, but there was nothing to be done. I wanted to wrap up into a cocoon with the baby, not see nor hear anyone else. I itched to do for the baby. It seemed to me all the furniture needed to be rearranged, the closets cleaned out. It was too late to be prepared.

Instead I tackled the *Mazel-tov,* weeping daily in a blue postpartum state.

I had no idea about the ritual, where or what. But my husband had a synagogue. Some months before, he had begun dropping into Saturday morning services now and again for refreshment, contemplation, as a way to cope with the dark forces of materialism that are so much of life's warp and weft. He had found an interesting rabbi who would oversee the naming of our daughter.

I remember calling this rabbi to arrange things. I had been home a day or two, and was barely getting into clothes by lunchtime, and shuffling no farther than the bathroom. The baby lived in bed with me, trying to nurse nonstop in a damp nest of pillows. My parents were staying in town. Every day my mother would come, bring me soup and tea, and look askance at the log I was keeping on the baby's sleepings and feedings.

It was February, stone cold in New York. I had no wish to go out until May. I certainly had no intention of sitting in a synagogue pew with a fragile two-week-old baby. She and I would stay home, while my husband took care of the synagogue part, I thought. He would go and do whatever men do in *shul.* But I hadn't reckoned on this particular rabbi, who had been the spiritual leader of the Jews of Argentina during the years of disappearances there, and who was revitalizing a long-languished neighborhood *shul* with a mystical brew of intellect, egalitarianism, social consciousness, and charisma.

The rabbi took umbrage at my lack of interest, and at my sexist expectations.

"The parents read the blessings together. They get called up to the Torah together holding the baby. It's a beautiful service, the way we do it, and the mother should be there," he said heatedly.

"But I just had a C-section . . ." The conversation was embarrassing. A man was arguing feminism, while I claimed for biology, feeling a lump in my throat. I wanted to stay home, my logic had told me to delegate the formalities. Having made the actual ceremony into a line item on my

To Do list, I was thrown off by this rebuke, this inclusion. I felt moved, and confused, one of those cosmic states of confusion that set chains of events in motion. I've felt the reverberations now for a long time, and I've often thought about that rabbi, who died a few years ago.

I *had* to stay home. The reality was that forty or sixty people were coming to my apartment after *shul,* and I wanted everything to be right. Crates of smoked fish, cheeses, bagels, and pastries had to be unpacked and set forth. Ice cubes had to be cracked out of freezer trays, fresh towels had to be hung at the last minute—female religion. This was Miriam's occasion, and Miriam had asked only that I arrange the background, prepare the canvas. Indeed, there was plenty to do. Yet suddenly, from nowhere, I was drawn to the canvas, to participation in the ritual itself.

I had a daughter. Her name was about to be threaded into the tradition. What was her place in that fabric to be? What was mine? Was it only about duty, obedience? Was it only about being a woman in the kitchen?

I did go to the synagogue, carrying my wee bairn in her strawberry sweater, calico bunting, and blue blanket, on a frosty Saturday morning. I wore my favorite maternity outfit. I sat on a wooden bench under an ornate ceiling, stood, sat, as protocol demanded, sat, stood, on my still-swollen legs. I thought of my *bubbe,* her six children, her busy kitchen, her swollen legs, naming the granddaughters. Each naming: once in a lifetime.

The morning was a revelation.

There were women in prayer shawls and skullcaps, men in casual clothes; there was practiced prayer, fervent discussion, intelligent argument. There was a bat mitzvah: a simply-dressed, thirteen-year-old girl chanted the *Haftarah,* the week's section from the Prophets, and then engaged the rabbi who had taught her in a thoughtful exchange about the reading. It may have been hormones run amok, but I dabbed at my eyes with a burp cloth. One day, an unimaginable span of years hence, that could be my daughter, I thought, amazed. Not in the kitchen, but here.

My husband and I bore our bundled baby to the pulpit, or *bima.* It was my first *aliyah,* the very first time I had ever been called to the Torah, and it was my turn to be indignant, just for a moment, when the rabbi handed me an English transliteration of a blessing I found I still had by memory, in Hebrew, from my Hebrew school days.

But petty notions slipped away. We prayed that she walk in joy, righteousness, and virtue, along the road of our matriarchs, and that we would see her under the marriage canopy one day. And my daughter had her name, she was altered and completed. The name of my husband's beloved sister lived on.

Back at the apartment, there were toasts of *l'chaim!* with glasses of whiskey and wine. There were unbelievable heaps of baby gifts—not a shower but a deluge. There were relatives and friends, fussing over a baby with a name. The festive food was plentiful, perfect. Platters of smoked salmon, sable, whitefish, tomatoes. Egg salad, made by Miriam with three dozen eggs. Tender herrings, displays of cheese. The colors fanned out on the blue tablecloth like a shimmering coral reef.

Bagels, carefully halved, spun in their baskets; ice glistened in a bucket. The kitchen smelled of coffee, cinnamon, and cake, sliced and ready on a silver serving tray, as I opened the apartment door and walked in with the crowd.

Some might say miracle, and others wag, "You see? Nothing to worry." But there is always more to truth than this, and it's often a woman in the kitchen. While I took my baby to the *bima* on that thrilling journey, infused with the power of what we might become, my sister and my brother's wife stayed home. The rabbi was right, the service was beautiful. The baby girl's aunts, however, missed the entire thing.

PUBERTY

In my grandmother's house in Brooklyn, in the bedroom in which I slept, there was a painted dresser. One drawer of the dresser held pale blue sanitary napkins, year after year.

These came in handy one year. Visiting, I got my first period—far from my mother, who had remained in Detroit to study for college exams.

I confided in my grandmother. She smacked my face.

I looked to her for a reason. I saw an ironic, apologetic little smile, heard a caught breath that might have been a decimal place's worth of secret amusement or inner regret.

She said: "Now you'll always have rosy cheeks," then went looking for a contraption, elastic and clips.

I knew this slap came out of the past, and she was just doing her duty. I sensed that her investment was less than complete. The smack was not painful, yet burned on my cheek like guilt, like innocence—something she felt was fitting, and I knew was unjust.

Later I stumbled on written words parsing that *shtetl* gesture. Thus mother warned daughter, time out of mind, not to compete for the father's attentions; thus mother taught daughter the shame of Eve. I may have been the last in my line to be punished in advance for sexual sins, mine and those of every mortal woman.

PASSOVER

$\mathcal{I}$n the beginning there was Brooklyn, and it was Passover. We had journeyed east in our Plymouth from Detroit. We brought school books, and our spring coats. The call of our rich tradition had been heard—*Next year in New York!*—and heeded. We, the destined ones, would miss an extra week of school, right after Easter vacation.

We sat at my grandmother's dining room table, on stiff mahogany chairs upholstered in blood-red velvet. Candle flame flickered, chandelier glowed, crystal refracted, the dark of evening gently fell. Above the Belgian rug, my feet dangled in navy blue maryjanes. They weren't as fancy as patent leather, but you could wear them to school. A wineglass stood at every place, with an extra goblet for Elijah the prophet, who visits every Seder table. At the head of the table, my father, impressive in his high, boxy, black skullcap, resembling an Eastern Orthodox bishop, performed the Passover recounting, the Haggadah, in rapid, rusty, musical Hebrew.

We followed the English in our Haggadah pamphlets, the ones distributed gratis by Maxwell House. I, enrolled in Hebrew school, could sing the four questions in Hebrew. My cousins, Selina's children, in their miniature prep school blazers and gray slacks, read them in English, since they were being raised with no religion.

The four questions, posed by children at the Seder's start, never seemed entirely apt. *Why do we dip twice?* Why would you ask that before any dipping took place? *Why do we recline?* We never reclined. On my grandmother's slippery velvet chairs, the hard springs forming a dome in the seat center, reclining was problematic.

"Teach your children to remember," commanded God. And so my father would begin: "Once we were slaves in the land of Egypt," as parents had done for thousands of years. On to the pages of commentary, Talmudic scholars arguing interpretive points. "Rabban Gamliel used to say . . ."

"Let's go, Edward," spurred my grandmother. She had been cooking, cleaning, and changing dishes for days with my mother's help, and didn't want the roast chicken to dry up.

My father would charge through the Haggadah, reading ahead from right to left, letting his mind become a vessel of subconscious memory to recover the Hebrew studied until his thirteenth birthday, to embrace the tune, the cadence. He did recover it through force of mind. His voice enfolded us like smoke.

At points, he paused, performing the rituals as his father had, or as close as could be remembered. He was transformed in the Seder to teacher or priest, to Someone Who Knew, to the keeper of mysteries, serious things. I was transformed by the Seder, by candles and silver and ancient language and melody and the incantatory realization that this was my birthright, this belonged to me.

My father said when to raise glasses, and when to drink the four draughts of wine—or grape juice—draughts that a free person, celebrating redemption, can drink. He washed his hands ceremoniously, reciting the proper blessing. He pointed to a roasted lamb bone, which had been set on fire over the gas burner earlier that day, displayed as a symbol of the animal sacrifices practiced by early Hebrews.

Holding out his strong, freckled hands, my father broke matzo, the unleavened bread baked in speed by the escaping slaves, and we handed around the crisp pieces. During the eight days of Passover, or Pesach, one may not eat regular bread, or anything prepared with or touched by a leavening agent such as yeast or baking powder. We didn't miss it; the Seder's first matzo wipes bread-hunger from the mind.

Next came the dipping, once and twice. My father dipped parsley, a token of green spring and new beginnings, into the salt water that stands for Israelites' tears. Down the table the dripping sprigs were passed. Raw bits of horseradish root, to recall the bitterness of bondage, were dipped in *haroses*, a sweet, wet gravel of finely chopped apples, raisins, cinnamon, and wine. This *haroses* symbolized the mortar with which the slaves toiled under the cruel sun-god. "We built the pyramids!" I breathlessly discovered. From then on, history was personal.

Green-sprouted horseradish pieces were passed. Brave children, dying of hunger by then, tried the bitter herb, yelped, gulped water. Red-eyed, we fanned our open mouths. The physic worked. They taught their children to remember.

Finally, finally, the festive meal. Fruit salad in dishes of gold-rimmed glass. Invariably fruit, though I don't know why—for spring? There were grapefruits and oranges, chunks of pineapple and peeled apples marinated in lemon and orange juice, strawberries, bananas. I had watched this salad prepared. My father, sitting at the kitchen table with a paring knife, peeled and sectioned the citrus fruit. My mother hulled boxes of strawberries, berries selected each by each. The kitchen table grew juicy with brilliant color.

After the fruit, the hard-boiled egg, the pagan sign of life's renewal, served whole to each person in a bowl of saltwater broth. Under the big spoon grasped in a small fist, the egg skittered dangerously. I supposed it was forbidden to cut the egg with a knife. I never asked. I crumbled matzo over the bowl and rose to the challenge of nailing the slippery egg.

Chicken soup with matzo balls, or *kneydlekh,* as we called them, and toasty soup nuts, bought in a blue-and-gray box in the store, kosher for Passover, to float in the shallow dishes.

Ahhh. Here we breathed deeply, wriggled expectantly in our seats. I wonder at our appetites, the quantities we ate as children. I think we ate it all.

Next issued gefilte fish. It came from the kitchen, on a thin china plate, a thick slab of it, homemade, with a slice of carrot and the detested jellied broth. It was served with *khreyn,* grated horseradish root, flavored with vinegar, sugar, and salt. Outside on the stoop that afternoon, my father had rubbed the pungent root on a hand grater balanced atop an enamel basin. His eyes streamed with the hot smell of it. My sister and brother and I ran up for a sniff, a hilarious scream, pretending to faint and die.

Roast chicken, huge quarters of spring pullets my mother had cleaned and plucked, had *kashered*—made kosher, had massaged, according to my grandmother's direction, with a paste of crushed garlic, paprika, pepper, salt, and sage, had roasted in glass baking pans. Skin side down, covered, skin side up, covered, then the foil off to crisp, roasted certainly for hours until the meat nearly fell off the bone, and velvety chunks of potatoes browned in the drippings.

I cannot picture a vegetable. Perhaps I did give up at some point, or was there none? No, this is all I remember, save for a slice of cucumber pickle and possibly a little more matzo, until the stewed prunes, the sponge cake, the coconut macaroons, the chocolate-covered orange peels, the tea with lemon and sugar, the last bit of matzo eaten as dessert, and the final songs.

After the meal, we opened the door for Elijah, and ran back to the table: a quiver ran through his cup of wine. My father looked innocent.

Once in a time gone by, Passover Seders lasted until midnight or even beyond. In the Old Country, we heard, children collapsed on heaps of coats in the corners, while parents and grandparents drank and made merry. My parents could even remember such times in their childhoods. They had grownups who lived through the winter looking forward to Pesach festivity and pomp.

Now Seders, mostly done for the children, are arranged to end at their bedtimes.

The Brooklyn Seders I remember, a bit past midcentury, bridged the eras of way back and now. We children were still awake but very tired, flushed with food and happiness, as we sang the many verses of *"Khad Gadya,"* a song that traditionally ends the night. This song has been culled for meaning: Some say it stands for all of Jewish history. We sang it as a children's song, a medieval romp through weird and violent events unleashed by a father's purchase of a baby goat. In the end, God himself strikes down the Angel of Death.

It was the robust baritone of Uncle Charles, who was not Jewish, enthusiastically singing *"Khad Gadya!"* according to the Maxwell House phonetic transcription, and the counterpoint of my grandmother's droll laughter, that sealed and certified another Seder night for me.

In the kitchen next morning there was a lightness and cleanliness, a freshness, and Passover smells. New linen dishtowels hung on the rack. The kitchen table was spread with an ironed cloth. There would be eight days of matzo: matzo with whipped butter and salt, matzo sandwiches, matzo puddings, dumplings, *farfel,* sponge cakes, also egg dishes, and fruit salad, and stewed prunes. How many eggs would be purchased for Passover week? Eggs to boil whole, to mix into chopped liver, to make pancakes fluffy, to fry with onions. Five or six per person, per day? No one can do this anymore, but are we really more healthy for it?

My grandmother rendered chicken skin for the yellow fat, schmaltz. As we gathered round the fragrant stove like so many chubby fledglings, she gave us the cracklings, the *grivnes,* to eat.

She made a giant ginger-scented matzo-meal pancake, round in its iron skillet, half-fried, half-baked, dense, crisp-edged, and two inches high. This *fankukhn,* cut into wedges, lavished with sugar and cinnamon, was one kind of breakfast. She steamed matzos over hot boiling water, spread each limp matzo square with hot chicken fat, sprinkled it with coarse salt, and rolled it up, to be eaten with soft-boiled eggs. She poured boiling water over crumbled matzos and strained the pieces, scrambled them with egg, fried them in oil, and this was matzo *brei.* She poured sweet red wine into hot morning tea. There was a week of such breakfasts, a blissful week of spring.

During the days, we walked with my father and played in the neighborhood park, among spring puddles and sunbursts and chalk hopscotch boards. The only cloud in our sky was that vernal harbinger, the first sighting of the Ice Cream Man. Oh, we would badger my father for tempting wares we knew were not kosher for *Pesach,* or face an early crisis of consciousness. Sometimes we had to leave New York in an incomplete state, having partaken of no Good Humor bar.

The years rolled on, it seems so quickly now. One spring I remember teasing for an ice cream and being stunned when my father said, "O.K." The condition was it must be finished at the playground, before we strolled back within view of grandmother's house.

Was this, just maybe, what set our rites of spring so softly crumbling?

After this, my recollections blur. My father began to skip parts of the Haggadah, and to stumble on the Hebrew from time to time. My grandmother died. The family met in New York for Christmas then, not *Pesach.* Our small Detroit Seders drifted toward English, grew shorter. Teenagers tried for political relevance, dogmatic and sincere.

Gefilte fish came from a jar. We barely noticed when the green apple blossom dishes, our own Passover set, stayed packed up in the basement one time, then forever. When was the last bit of chicken skin crisped in the pan, the last *grivn* eaten?

My father still scoured the oven each spring. My mother made matzo balls. I don't blame my parents. One spring in college, I didn't go home for Passover, though spring break coincided with the new April moon. I wandered the empty campus, an exile from history, and I ate a burger in a bun. The tides were bearing my craft away from the high-church Seders I once loved, and I held the rudder.

At last the man I would marry brought me home to meet his parents, and they chopped gefilte fish by hand.

For years I was content to eat it, oblivious of the work involved, though I uttered empathic things. Now I am going to watch: Miriam, my mother-in-law, feeding chunks of whitefish and pike through an electric grinder. Long pinkish pulverized strings of mash falling hypnotically into a bowl as the face of the grinder goes round and round.

Father-in-law Jacob places two folding chairs seat to seat, covers this makeshift table with an old towel. On it, he balances a wooden board heaped with ground fish. Pulling up a third chair, he sits. He grasps a sharp-bladed cleaver with both hands, and begins to chop. Ten cuts this way, ten cross-hatched cuts, cleaving the translucent sea-flesh, twelve more this way, the ax-blade again mounding the fish, lifting high, weighing down, a lifetime of fine etched lines in the board, like lines on the palm of a hand.

I offer to help.

"Chop the fish?" Jacob, incredulous.

Miriam makes a face: "For what?"

When I insist, Jacob shrugs, a squint of humor in it. He still opens doors for me, hoists the shopping bags of Miriam's cooked food down their front stairs to my car. The implication of female frailty infuriated me once. Now I treasure Jacob, a good man who embodies his responsibilities, whose sense of duty is a kind of knowledge, one that indeed gives him eerie strength.

Where the fish is concerned, at least, I am about to be humbled. Leaning over the board to chop, my back begins to ache. My shoulder throbs with the up-down pulse of the heavy cleaver. Flying bits of fish stick to my hair, mashed pink fish works crazily to the ends of the board. The board wobbles unsteadily on the chairs. The handle grows sticky and hot.

Surreptitious, I glance at the clock.

"It's too hard for you," comments Miriam, her back to me, at the sink. She is cleaning the grinder with a toothbrush and toothpick, piece by shining piece.

"No problem!" I gasp. I scrape fish away from the edges of the board, pull fish into a mound, scrape, pull. I chop. My two red hands grip the cleaver. My shoulders burn, but pride keeps me chopping a good ten minutes, and it seems like forty-five.

"There!" I proclaim, unable to go on. I work the handle out of my claw.

"Thank you!" exclaims Miriam, wiping her hands. "Hmmm," she adds, examining the fish.

I wash my hands tenderly. Miriam sprinkles sugar on the fish. Jacob, wordlessly, resumes chopping. He had not bothered to sit down meanwhile at all.

"Couldn't you use a food processor?" I say, a bit plaintively, once my pulse slows.

"For the fish?" Jacob allows himself a rare, private smile. "Sure not."

"I tried it once," remarks Miriam, cutting onions into a pot with fish bones, a bay leaf, water, and pepper. She will mix the chopped fish with egg, matzo meal, seasonings, then shape oval patties in her palm with a knife to simmer in the broth. "The one you brought."

Oh, yes, I had forgotten. A gift, back when food processors were new, back when Miriam was still asking, "How should I call you to the family?" for I was neither wife nor fiancée, and her cousins and their children were busy with weddings, *mazel-tovs,* bar mitzvahs, and all the other communal demarcations and progressions. I had other things on my mind. "Friend," I used to answer, resolutely obtuse in the face of Miriam's sharp discomfort and longing. One son, and not a *boychik* either . . . living with a girl (though this was not quite acknowledged), and nothing happening. No grandchildren.

"You can have it, it's downstairs in the box still," she said. The food processor. "The fish didn't come out good." She thinks back. "It didn't— feel."

I watch Jacob and the shimmering fish mass, as it is heaped, divided, broken down, pulled together. The texture has gone way beyond chopped flesh. It grows—gelatinous, sponge-like, it glows and expands, gains mass and presence, substance. In a word, it feels. Jacob is one with his task, his wiry arms rising, falling, his face intent but composed.

"What about a chopping bowl? A hand chopper?" I ask faintly, entranced.

"This would be all right," she admits. "But I don't have the bowl."

Sugar in fish? My parents had their view: Never. Their families didn't, the Poles did. True, my grandparents were all, essentially, Polish Jews. In the nineteenth century, however, the map of central and eastern Europe was continually redrawn, towns and districts reassigned. I did not think us Polish.

One grandfather hailed from Lodz, but had a German last name, which might lend a bit of caste snobbishness. My grandmother, born in Stanislowa, perfect Poland, considered herself ethnically Galician, an earring-wearing Carpathian Jew, whose family drifted west to Bremen, Germany. Malke, the *bubbe,* my mother's mother, was born in Warsaw. But when she married her husband, a *Litvak,* Lithuanian, she crossed over the culture's wall. Like women through the ages, she changed the way she pronounced her *mame-loshn,* Yiddish, changed the names for the food she cooked and the way she seasoned that food. The *Litvaks* were, as they say, not from sugar.

Such distinctions once were so important: in a Lithuanian village, some of my people traced their line to an eighteenth-century wise man; Austrian Jews heaped *schlag* on their honey cake; Germans styled themselves heirs of Heine and some looked down on the Poles; Polish Jews enjoyed fish spiced with sugar. What does it matter now?

For many Passovers I sat down to Miriam's dense, miraculous gefilte fish wishing it were not sweet. I dressed it in sharp horseradish, while my husband's family corrected my spotty *Litvakish* Yiddish. Then one year it struck me that I had changed. I liked the fish sweet, and the horseradish sweet, and the red cabbage salad and the carrots sweet.

I guess it is only poetic justice and the debt the universe owed my *bubbe,* who must have been raised on sugar in fish. At an age when I moped around college libraries and worse, she was busy transliterating her husband's food preferences. She longed for more sweetness from time to time.

And so, I began keeping Passover, and hosting an annual Seder. I get ready for Pesach, little by little, and do a little more each year. Some of it is spring cleaning: I dust and wipe and shake out the rugs, and in a good year, I get to the windows. Then I get rid of improper food, the crumbs and crusts and anything not kosher for Passover: the *hametz.* I line drawers and shelves with new paper, and fit them out with Passover dishes. I scour the sink and clean the oven. I cover the countertops and kitchen table. All for a span of eight days, and then I box up Pesach again for another year.

The preparations are insane. They get under your skin. One night in September, near on to the children's back-to-school, I dream Passover will begin in one hour, and I have done nothing. I have not cooked, cleaned, covered surfaces, shopped. Many guests are expected. As with a math exam for which one hasn't studied, I have failed at the geometry of switching dishes, lining shelves, at counting out place settings, estimating servings, timing errands. To a dazzling repertoire of anxiety dreams, add this.

At last, though, the new boxes and jars, kosher for Passover, are lined up in the cupboard. The last night, we search the house with our children, hunting crumbs hidden in corners by candlelight, sweeping the crumbs with a feather into a wooden spoon. I always forget at least one location and have to search too, for the misplaced *hametz*. We burn these crumbs the next day, saying a prayer that admits that no one is perfect, but that we did our best. I say it with feeling, and the holiday begins. The doing is part of it. It brings back all I saw and felt and knew. It is not the same without the doing.

I thought long about changing dishes. A year came when I took the leap. My parents were visiting; we leapt together. My dad commandeered the wheel and we drove to a distant housewares outlet. I chose dishes, enough for the big multiple-course Seder dinner. I bought pots and pans, cutting boards, paring knife, spatula, outfitting a phantom kitchen.

My mother showed me how to boil my silverware, *kasher* my glasses, make Pesach in fridge and sink, remembering this and that as we went along. We packed up the everyday things. And then, only then, we began to make the Seder.

Everyone cooked. We followed the Brooklyn menu, and we followed Miriam's menu. My mother made chicken soup and matzo balls, and Miriam brought her Passover egg noodles for the soup as well, delicate crepe threads of egg and potato starch. I attempted Miriam's *rabinik,* which means "grated thing," a mystery to my mother until she recognized her mother's potato pudding. We boiled eggs, for serving in salt water, for chasing around the bowl with your spoon. Miriam brought the gefilte fish.

We invited the family. My father's sister, Selina, arrived with a *fankukhn,* in a gift box, tied with gold ribbons. Forty years after perfecting soufflés, she had spent the day destroying *fankukhn* failures and had at last got it, "Sort of," she said.

We went through the rites, Jacob in his thick glasses leading, trying hard to read slow and allow for English. We drank wine and retold the story, as children giggled and showed off. It came time for the entrance of Elijah, whose full glass awaited at the table's heart. Children ran to the door, throwing it open under a starry sky.

"If you want wine, come in now!" a child yelled into the night.

It was our firmest apostate, Aunt Selina, who found herself shocked at the joke. "I was the oldest, I used to have to walk down a long dark hallway alone, to let in Elijah. I was scared," she mused. "Imagine them joking about it."

I remembered my grandmother's hallway, long and dark, remembered Elijah's wine in its tall goblet, shimmering and moving as if invisibly sipped, as my father, straight-faced, jostled the table leg with his knee. There was a glowing solemnity about Passover then. I don't know if it will return. Yet for my children, Passover is not a mausoleum, and I like this, too.

GEFILTE FISH

12 lb. fish (usually 2:1 whitefish to pike; can use 1 lb. of carp
   if white)
4 tbsp. sugar
2 tbsp. salt
3 medium onions
5 tbsp. (heaped) sugar
2 tsp. salt
3/4 tbsp. pepper

4 eggs
5 tbsp. sugar
2 tsp. salt
1 cup (or more) water, to moisten
2 small onions, sliced
Fish bones
3 carrots, sliced
Cold water

Have fishmonger fillet fish but take heads and bones. Clean and wash fish. Marinate (with heads and bones) in the sugar and salt overnight. Grind fillets with the onions. Add sugar and salt. Mix well. Chop for 1/2 hour or more, adding the pepper, eggs, sugar, salt, and water. Place the two sliced onions, fish bones, carrots, and cold water in a large pot. Shape chopped fish mixture into patties, using cold water and patting with a knife. Stuff the fish heads with fish mixture. Place 2 pike heads on the bottom of the pot. Arrange patties. Place 2 whitefish heads on top. Bring to a boil. Lower to a simmer; partially cover. Cook 2 hours. Taste broth, add sugar and pepper, if needed. Cook 2 more hours. Remove fish with slotted spoon.

Yield: 25 patties (3-inch to 4-inch long, 1 1/2-inch-thick ovals)

RABINIK

7 lb. potatoes
4 onions, grated
2 onions, diced
Pepper
A strip of flanken (short ribs)
4 to 5 marrow bones

1¹/₂ tbsp. salt
4 tbsp. matzo meal
2 eggs
Potato starch
Vegetable oil

Grate the potatoes and 4 onions. Put in a sieve to drain. Dice and sauté the remaining onions with pepper. Bring to a boil the short ribs and 4 to 5 marrow bones. Pour off the water.

Mix the drained potatoes and onions with the sautéed onions, salt, pepper, matzo meal, eggs, and potato starch. Lightly oil a pot. Put in the boiled flanken and bones. Then put in the potato mixture. Pour ¹/₂ cup oil on top. Cover. Put in a 350°F. oven. Lower oven temperature to 325°F. when it boils. After a few hours check the *rabinik*. If it looks dry, add more oil. If too brown, place a layer of foil over the pot; then fit lid on top. Bake for 6 to 7 hours in all.

(You can make the same thing without the meat and call it "potato pudding.")

Yield: Serves ten to twelve, as a side dish

THE SOUL IN THE DUMPLING

"Call your *Bubbi* for the recipe and write everything down," I said to my daughter. It was just before Passover, and we were going to make *kneydlekh,* matzo balls.

In the old days my family made them together, batches and batches, some large, soft and fluffy, some small, round and chewy. The family was split in its tastes.

Before my time, my mother's mother had inserted a crisp bit of chicken skin, a *grivn,* in the center of every *kneydl.* This flavorsome crackling within the dumpling she called *neshome,* the soul.

My daughter calling my mother for the recipe? My mother who approximated her mother's recipe? Her motherless mother who re-invented her mother's recipe? The ancient and timeless matzo ball? Yes, that's my religion.

KNEYDLEKH

8 eggs, separated
1 cup matzo meal
Salt and pepper to taste

Dash of ginger
About 1 tsp. veggie or peanut oil

Crack open eggs (my daughter wrote). Separate whites from yolks. Beat whites till fluffy. Beat up yolks, add oil and matzo meal. Add salt and pepper. Put in ginger. Fold in egg whites. Add a little cold water—quarter of a cup. Mix it all around. Has to be a batter you can work with. Can't be cement. Can't be mud.

Taste it. *Must be good raw!* Add more seasonings if necessary.

If good batter, cover the bowl with plastic wrap. Put in freezer 10 to 20 minutes.

Boil either soup or salted water. Have a small bowl ready with cold water and ice cubes. Dip hands in cold water before each *kneydl*. Form *kneydlekh* and throw in boiling water. If you want small, hard *kneydlekh*, add more matzo meal and seasonings. For small ones, form marble-sized; for big ones—size of golf ball. (They grow.)

Cook for 15 minutes. Cut one big one in half and see if ready. (Look and taste.) Throw in colander. Let Mom and Dad do this. If want to keep warm, cover.

PASSOVER EGG NOODLES

$\mathcal{M}$iriam makes matzo balls from a mix. She makes them year round. They are an unexpected warming addition to split pea soup on our winter table.

On Passover, egg noodles go into Miriam's soup, into her rich amber *yokh,* the broth of chicken and one deeply flavoring beef bone. Flourless egg noodles made with potato starch, delicate pancakes crisped in a small frying pan and cut with a sharp knife into narrow shreds. However, I cannot give up *Pesach kneydlekh*—matzo balls. So, on Passover, we have both.

"First you take out the mixer," says Miriam, starting the egg noodles. "I used to have one with extra beaters for *Pesach.*"

"I can get you a set of extra beaters," I offer.

"No, I have no room. Where will I put it? I can *kasher* the beaters, they're metal. That's why I didn't buy."

Passover preparations are on our minds.

"And with the glasses I am putting them in water in the basement for twenty-four hours. Then any glass is kosher for *Pesach,*" Miriam states.

Miriam breaks twelve eggs, slides them into the mixing bowl one by one.

"How would I manage in an apartment with all these things I have?" she wonders. She is thinking about selling the house.

In a cup, Miriam mixes potato starch with water.

"Less than a quarter of a cup," she says, adding this to the unbeaten egg. "In Poland we got potato starch not in a box, but in a big barrel. You brought a sack to put it in. Now everything is easy." She considered for a moment. "But we used to get it all year long. Here I must stock up at Passover."

Miriam turns on the mixer, at a high loud speed. She stops it to check. "Mix very well so that no white is showing. Mix so it foams, so there is a *shom* on top." She turns on the mixer, then stops it again. "You have to put in the water, starch, and eggs first, then mix. Once I beat the eggs first—don't ask.

"Everything is experience," Miriam says.

Vegetable oil is poured in a saucer. Miriam gathers a sheet of paper towel into a little sock doll shape, and secures it with an elastic band. She dips the doll's head in the oil and greases a small frying pan.

"It has to be very hot." The concept is something like crepes. She fills a small ladle with egg mixture, and pours it into the hot pan. "Take less than you need to cover the pan, so it wouldn't be thick. Swirl it thin, very thin, and brown on one side, then turn it over quick."

Each little pancake should be golden brown and crisp. "Then take it out, let it cool on the side." Move on to the next pancake. "In between you *shmear* more oil."

I am trying it. "Thin enough, *Ema?*" I ask, confident of my frying skills.

"It is a little—" begins Miriam. Diplomatically, she continues, "But for the first time, it's very good. The color is just beautiful."

"Now you can stack several pancakes," instructs Miriam when the frying is done. "You roll them up tight, tight." I roll them. "Sit down, it's easier."

"Now you cut, very thin." I am holding a knife, slicing the pancakes into golden threads. "No, thinner," says Miriam. "Thinner."

I cut slowly, precisely. "Like this, *Ema?*"

"My mother used to do it so quick," says Miriam. "*Gotenyu.* You can't imagine the things she could do."

PASSOVER EGG NOODLES

2 tbsp. potato starch   12 eggs
2 oz. water   Oil for frying

Mix potato starch and water. Crack the eggs into a bowl; add potato starch mixture. Beat until foamy.

Heat a small greased skillet, swirl 2 to 3 tbsps. egg mixture, forming the thinnest possible pancake. Fry over a hot flame quickly. Brown on both sides. Set aside to cool. Repeat until all egg mixture is used up, greasing the pan between pancakes. Stack 2 to 3 pancakes, roll tightly. With a sharp knife, cut rolls into the narrowest possible shreds. Place cooled noodles in a soup dish. Spoon hot broth over the noodles.

Yield: 24 servings

SALT-FREE

$\mathcal{M}$y grandmother's last year of life was a suffering sickness. Her arms grew thin and frail, but her belly swelled with fluid. She was still her own stubborn woman and insisted that she did not need to move into her daughter's house.

"She has a right to die on her own kitchen floor if she wants to," said my aunt, ever her mother's daughter. Later, many years later, she told me how much her mother had loved that house, that kitchen, the blue-and-white tiled floor. "She used to scrub that kitchen floor at night, the last thing," my aunt recalled. "Sometimes she was so tired, she would fall asleep on the floor."

There were many compromises with failing health. Near the top of the list was the special diet. My grandmother was barred from eating salt. Thus the medical men believed fluid retention might be reduced. What hardship this was. There were special foods predicated on salt that my grandmother's Ashkenazic palate relished: dill pickles, corned beef, schmaltz herring, lox. Then there was the kosher meat, itself saturated with salt that could never quite be totally rinsed out, and she had to sharply limit that, to eat meat boiled not roasted, stewed, or broiled.

Here was a woman who, cooking, would sip and taste and add a pinch, deliberate and focused, to draw out the essence exactly right. Now my grandmother could no longer salt a chopped egg, a boiled potato, a cup of soup. *Feh.*

Worst of all was the wreck of that most basic of foods: flour of wheat mixed with leavening and salt. No longer could my grandmother enjoy her *kiml* breads, corn ryes laced with caraway seeds, or a salt stick, or a decent piece of cake. Salt-free baking is as bleak and drear as the old fairy tale at the heart of *Lear* had it.

There was only one kind of salt-free bread she could eat, and it was baked in Detroit. My father had found it. The loaves were pale and cylindrical, sliced into rounds, packed in plastic bags and twisted shut with a *bendl,* a wire tie. My father would buy them and send them in the mail, a gift of his helpless heart traversing the miles.

And there was but one kind of pastry for my dying grandmother, and it was baked by her sister, my Great-aunt Dora.

My grandmother's eldest sister, Dora, doted on my grandmother. They were sisters all their lives: once there were telephones, they talked together on their telephones every day. They shared the tribulations of their lives in complete, enjoyable trust.

Dora was a splendid baker. One of her specialities was the butter horn, a yeast dough rolled out and twirled up with cinnamon and butter into the shape of a crescent, then dusted with sugar crumbs. For my grandmother, Dora concocted a salt-free version. She made salt-free butter horns, and they were delicious.

"It is the only salt-free pastry that tastes good," my grandmother told my father, time and time again. "The only salt-free baking I can eat."

"That's wonderful," said my father to his mother.

"I know why they're so good," my father said to me.

"Aunt Dora," asked my respectful father, not one to interfere, "tell the truth. Do you put salt in Mother's butter horns?"

Great Aunt Dora looked her nephew in the face. She stood for a moment, silent—short and plump and dignified, her eyebrows arched; defiant, proud, and stubborn, a woman of her tribe. Her contralto voice spoke.

Aunt Dora said: "What do the doctors know?"

May

DECISIONS

May ～

Here are the things I have to give up.

Lobsters in New England, oysters sensually slithering down my throat, the French butcher. I give up calamari on Christmas Eve with a favorite friend, a traditional meal that links her to her Italian grandparents, and thus connects me to my friend's childhood. I sacrifice bacon at my aunt's house, crisped and greaseless beside a home-baked corn muffin, forgo Western omelets at diners I once loved to frequent.

I give up being able to eat comfortably anywhere, able to make casual assumptions. It is like being an immigrant, maybe; never quite feeling at home.

Once I knew I was a certain kind of Jew and I was comfortable in that identity. My heritage was Jewish, I was culturally a Jew. My cultural memories were Jewish. But I was Jewish and American, and the identification with my hybrid roots was also strong. I strove to be pure hybrid.

Ten years ago in my life, I would have found it unthinkable to divide my activities and concerns into the secular and the Jewish. Now I do, almost reflexively. I think about shaping everyday life according to principles not of my devising. Now I don't know what kind of Jew I am and what I am becoming. I only know that my two grandmothers had sixteen grandchildren between them, none of whom so far are raising children in a kosher home. I need to do something about this.

In striving to give my children their history, I take risks. Establishing their differentness may strain their sense of belonging to this American society. Connection to their tradition may lead to dissociation: a paradox. Plug in here, disconnect there.

What if one of my children says to me, someday, "There is nothing here for me"?

Those words imagined chill me. It is Israel that lures them, and I shiver at the distance. My grandchildren will not speak my language. They will not grow up in my backyard, or share the reference points I take for granted.

My mother loved this American ground, twisted her Polish/Lithuanian/ Canadian self into knots to become a citizen. I call to my children in advance, shaking out a sack of Americana: Bill of Rights, blues, Walt Whitman, heartland, rustbelt, New York. Will all of this be like a melting ice cube to the vibrating heat of the identity we are forging?

I remember how strong the drive can be to connect somewhere but get away from here, when you are twenty years old. I feel as powerless to hold things together as we all finally are. The generations scatter, those who have gone turn to dust.

The traditions of our foreparents will lead my children away from me. But is this not as it should be? I should be giving my children the wherewithal to surpass me, to live life in a different way, to understand more, to go farther, to be responsible but also free.

I am building a floor under my children. I must live on it, too.

IRONING THE KITCHEN

I am told that my father's mother ironed her kitchen to make it kosher.

"That's how particular *she* was," says my Aunt Selina, who served me the first bacon I ever ate.

Though I never saw this, who am I to doubt? I can even picture my grandmother, stately in a ruffled apron, gold earrings, and thin, wavy brown hair, gracefully working a hot iron across a kitchen counter. But it is an odd image, and what does it mean? What did she iron, and why?

This is what Aunt Selina remembers: Her mother preparing the kitchen for Passover. Along one wall stood a deep porcelain sink, with a ridged drainboard on each side. She describes this, then stops to think.

"I really don't remember which side was meat, which was dairy," Selina remarks.

"Oh, sure you don't," says my father. He is skeptical that his sister has forgotten as much of her Brooklyn childhood as she claims.

"Where was the meat *kashered*?" he tests.

"I don't know," repeats Selina, after a startled pause. Well, it was sixty-five years ago.

"On the left," states my father.

The animals must be slaughtered according to law, then the meat soaked and salted to draw out the blood. Now the butchers do this as a convenience to the public. My grandmothers did this themselves, the soaking and salting, on drainboards sloped into deep kitchen sinks. Dressed in their cotton stockings, their large protective smocks, they leaned over the meat with damp foreheads, spreading salt, rinsing, submerging.

I can see it in my mind's eye: a white enamel *shisl,* or basin, filled with red, raw meat and water; or meat on the sloping drainboard, crystals of coarse kosher salt drawing blood and moisture out of the sinew, dripping pale red droplets into the scoured white sink. The drainboard sloped at the left side of the large double sink, at your mother's left side, as she stood in her apron and slippers with her back turned toward you. This at a child's eye level, week in and out—no, you wouldn't forget, you couldn't entirely forget.

"She used an iron, not the irons we have today, a solid piece of—iron—a flatiron, heated in the oven," recalls Selina.

The kitchen was hot, the oven was heating to burn away the last imagined traces of everyday baking, to purify it for Passover. In the hot oven, the flatiron heated. A huge cauldron of water was boiling, to Passover-clean small metal implements, to purge them of bread. In the early spring weather, kitchen steam billowed from the open window.

Outside, shrubbery bloomed green and unruly. Inside the kitchen, Edward, my father, was packing dishes, the everyday dishes, in newspaper first, then boxing them for eight days of basement storage. His sisters were lining the cupboards afresh.

My grandmother seized the iron's handle under a large padded potholder. She hoisted the heavy iron, and then set it down on the drainboard.

My grandmother ironed the white drainboards beside the sink. She pressed the burning iron against the ridged surfaces for a precise number of seconds. The heat soaked into the counter. She worked the iron over the counter, and then she ironed the sink.

This she understood as her duty. This is how she prepared for Passover each year, marking the spring, drawing an ancient history into her own time, experiencing the sources of connectedness.

An observant Jewish woman lives on many planes at once. We celebrate Passover to recall the bitterness of slavery, the dreariness of work that benefits a master, rather than ourselves. We recall our flight, and celebrate deliverance. We savor freedom, sing songs, stay up late.

How, in all this, does the preparation fit? Another set of complicated meals, fatiguing rituals, required forms of work that has little to do with freedom or choice. I suppose we are laboring for our families, for the perpetuation of our people, and that is the difference. But the skin of my hands still cracks painfully from plunging in cold water, hot water, dishwater. The veins on my legs still bulge from standing on my feet. The day after the Seder, I cannot move.

What does spring cleaning and clearing the house of crumbs have to do with freedom and history, anyway? Is it an artificial and self-serving way to attach importance to a housewife's ritual? Is it investing the everyday with spirituality? Do ceremony, excitement, and special food simply serve to lock ritual into a child's mind, securing it for the future? Without the meal and the commotion, the tradition of remembering the Exodus would certainly have died.

When Selina married Uncle Charles, she did not pack up the extra hand chopper, wooden bowl, and chicken soup pot. She bought copper molds, soufflé pans, and chafing dishes. She perfected crisp bacon, cream puffs, scalloped potatoes, crabmeat salad, chicken and morels in cream sauce, Yorkshire pudding, mince pie with hard sauce.

My mouth waters at the childhood memory of those then-exotic dinners, elegant and upper-class—not ethnic, and how I as a young person aspired to that state—served around her well-dressed table when my family visited New York. The menus were, or may as well have been, drawn to maximize her distance from the Brooklyn kitchen.

Each setting had its bread-and-butter plate, matched to a little monogrammed silver knife. Cold butter glistened on creamy butter-dishes, silver salt cellars stood always within reach. Selina did not chop eggs with onions, light a memorial candle, search for hidden bread crumbs with a candle and a feather the night before Passover.

But one March, she was in a frenzy to dust the books, as they did long ago before Passover. In Brooklyn, they had opened each book to the light. . . .

"I'm always aware of it, very aware of it," Selina told me.

How could it be otherwise?

"My mother used to iron the kitchen."

THE BOOK OF RUTH

*T*here are two harvest festivals in the Jewish calendar, spring and fall, for there were two growing seasons in biblical Palestine, as there are in Israel today. The spring harvest, Shavuot, or as our grandmothers might have said, *Sh'vues* or *Sh'vies,* depending on their birthplace, exists in only a vague way in my childhood remembrance—predominantly in the form of frozen cheese blintzes, thawed, fried, and heaped with sour cream. Dairy foods are traditional Shavuot fare.

The fall harvest is Sukkot, the spring harvest Shavuot. These are festivals, rather than holy days. I forgive myself, as a child, for confusing the two. I do recall a dairy moment each year, somewhere around May, when my mother would feel childhood memories stir. She would chop radishes, scallions, tomatoes, cucumbers, and parsley into cottage cheese and sour cream, season this dish with salt and pepper, and pronounce it "spring salad." She would fry the blintzes in butter, as if to evoke the ambrosial homemade blintzes her mother prepared from dozens of eggy pancakes rolled around sweetened homemade pot cheese.

In this annual dairy moment, we ate cheesecake. My father would be dispatched to a certain bakery, not his regular bread-and-pastry stop, to pick up a piece of special cheesecake. This cake had a short bottom crust, and a shiny top lattice. The thick filling was sweet, a bit dry, scented with vanilla, dotted with yellow raisins. It was baked in a huge rectangle, and my father gestured and directed, standing at the counter, negotiating for just the right piece, not too large, not too small, and from the middle, not a corner.

The ageless bakery ladies skillfully obliged, wielding sharp knives and flat servers. In a fluid ballet, they assembled pastry boxes, crisply lined them with paper, tied the boxes with brown string off a never-ending spool, and, as the finale, gracefully handed out cookies to all comers under the age of eighteen.

Who would be stuck with the corners and ends, I wondered? Now I know there must have been those for whom the cakey crusts were the calendar's best-kept secret.

My mother loved this cheesecake. I must admit I did wish it might have been, just once, the graham-cracker-crusted blueberry-syrup-loaded cream cheese glop that was a deli-style cheesecake—or even Sarah Lee.

I vaguely connected the spring harvest to the story of Ruth and Boaz, with Ruth gleaning among the sheaves in Boaz's fields after the reapers are through. Sheaves even sounds like *Sh'vies,* so I thought I might have filed it thus as a cross-lingual mnemonic device. There is a real connection, and it dawned into my ignorance one year: the Book of Ruth is read in the synagogue on Shavuot.

I still don't know what cheese has to do with the grain harvest, or by what miraculous transposition the spring harvest of a warm land in biblical times was preserved in the slushy thaw of a Polish equinox. But the Book of Ruth has become something of a feminist touchstone. Women are reading it in new ways, placing the emphasis not so much on the obedience of Ruth, or on her correct marriage to the much older Boaz, or on Ruth's genealogical place as the great-grandmother of David, the shepherd king.

Instead, these scholars focus on the love between Ruth and her mother-in-law, Naomi; Ruth's forsaking of Moab, her home, to follow the ways of Israel, her commitment to the Torah and to her adoptive family and religion. They ponder the story of a woman, a convert, whose love and faith were so decisive. Ruth, a widow, and childless, followed her downcast mother-in-law home, despite Naomi's repeated efforts to discourage her, after the deaths of Naomi's two sons.

Ruth *was* dutiful, obedient: on her mother-in-law's counsel, she gleaned in the fields of Boaz, a kinsman of Naomi, and then seduced him on the threshing floor. They married, thus securing, some feminists posit, economic security for the impoverished Naomi, and also giving her grandchildren. Ruth, a convert, became matriarch of a dynasty of kings, including the prophesied Messiah, an interesting note for those who view intermarriage as preeminent threat. Jesus, whatever you think of his claims, was of that line.

Perhaps the Book of Ruth in this cheese-filled season is an opening, an opportunity for me to find connection to the written tradition, the synagogue tradition. I am not an outsider. I knew the spring cheesecake, though I didn't know why. Still, a moat yawns between me and formal synagogue ritual. In what manner I may cross it, I am not sure. I cast about for a group of women that could meet to read Ruth and discuss it, but no one has time. No one I know seems to harbor a matching interest at this moment.

Perhaps I will go to synagogue, to hear Ruth read. I envision myself on the sidelines, among a smattering of weekday attendees, mostly retired men, listening to men read Ruth. I don't think I can bear it, just now.

I don't know what to do about Shavuot. At least, the tomorrow part of it, the day. Tonight, the eve of the holiday is a different matter: this belongs to Miriam, my mother-in-law. A holiday meal has been prepared, and so, on a Tuesday afternoon in May, I pack my children, their toys, pajamas, books, and supplies into my station wagon. We follow a herd of migrating semi trucks on the Cross Bronx Expressway toward my in-laws' steady, reliable light.

They are watching for us as we pull up. Jacob opens the door and is down the steep front stoop to help with our bags, to carry the baby. We are clattering up, we are in the front door. It closes, leaving the humming world outside. Now we are in a bright, small world that is ours alone.

The house is luminously clean. The white tablecloth glows as if aloft in its own light. Jackets and bags are whisked away. The high chair comes up from the basement. The children review the landscape—these pictures, knickknacks, cupboards, and corners. The children's likenesses are framed in gilt and glass. My husband races in from the express bus, caught on Madison Avenue an hour ago. And we begin. *"B'teyavon!"* Miriam wishes us in the unembarrassed Hebrew of the hungry Israeli 1950s. "Good appetite!"

Year in, year out, and always on Shavuot, Miriam brings forth her wonderful, completely fulfilled dairy meal, the *milikhdike* standard in a repertoire dependent on meat.

Fruit salad starts us, *kompot chai*. It is made of the ripe, the large, the sweet—strawberries, cantaloupe, kiwi, papaya, blueberries, pineapple, grapes, enriched with a tumbler of wine. We fill our pink-rimmed plates.

"The fruit is delicious," she reminds us.

"Wonderful," we agree.

The fruit is a meal. Our plates shimmer with juice, our forks are still in midair and on their way to rest, when Miriam, with perfect timing, speaks.

"Have some fruit," says Miriam, as if we yet had taken none. So we take, again.

Miriam is at the stove, serving soup, the *milikhdike* soup: a rich sour cream soup, lavishly full of potatoes, cauliflower, and tiny gratings of carrots. Heaped in pink-rimmed white bowls, with tiny red flowers, the dairy dishes.

Note to the French: You can do cream soup without chicken broth.

"It is good?" asks Miriam, her voice a tad anxious.

Mmm, we nod. So good.

"More soup?"

Can't.

"All right," sighs Miriam, the sound of resignation. She is a professional. We enter afresh into the script with every meal. "You will take it home."

We clear the soup bowls, begin to rinse.

"Don't do anything!" warns Miriam. "Please."

We sit.

"I have fish," she remarks.

A platter of thick flounder fillets appears, dredged in bread crumbs and gently fried. Giant fillets, what my grandmother called fluke, white, mild and meaty, just enough seasoning in the breading. This food is elemental. Food children love and adults cannot resist.

A few side things: deep-fried cauliflower, to melt in your mouth. Sweet-and-sour red salad: diced tomatoes, finely shredded red and green cabbage, vinegar, sugar. Never glasses on the table—they weren't used to drinking with food and still don't think of it. So we come, and set out glasses, and swizzle gallons of seltzer at every meal. But halfway through dinner, Miriam will say:

"Would you like some borsht? Or buttermilk?" I choose both, creamy pink borsht, warmed, a raw egg stirred in smoothly and quickly to blend with the beet soup—or tart cold buttermilk, always served in a delicate china cup.

We are slowing down.

"Have some fish. Please. Eat, people," implores the watchful Miriam.

Dessert: fruit again, this time cooked plums and peaches, in a round glass dish, a very small serving, please. Half that, please. *Oy, Ema.*

"Diet at your house, not mine." Miriam pulls a face. True, I have a problem. It's almost bathing suit weather, and I still have to overcome the latkes of Hanukkah, Passover matzo *brei,* a whole long winter of Miriam's meats, cakes, dumplings, soups.

Miriam aims heavy artillery at any thought of eleventh-hour resistance.

"You got very thin, so thin," says my mother-in-law, shaking her head in a convincing show of concern, bewilderment, admiration. "I don't know how you do it."

"She is just right," adds Jacob, unwitting co-conspirator, finishing his own modest portion and laying down his fork.

It is amazing how effective is this well-rehearsed script, or maybe it is just my mind that is weak. Whatever. Here is Miriam's cheesecake, a complex work of hands, cut from a giant tin pan: heavy, sweet, cake dough; heavy, sweet, vanilla-flavored cheese filling, dots of yellow raisins; brown cake lattice, shiny with egg yolk. It is the template for the bakery cheesecake I remember from the dawn of time. And here am I, middle-aged and thickened, and Miriam will press the whole cake on us to take home.

I pack up the cake, the fish, the cauliflower, the soup in plastic containers we pass back and forth all year long. I pack up the baby, and leave the older children for sleep and then *shul* with their grandfather in the morning. We are all full of cheese and cream, fruit and wheat, in a state of biblical turpitude. I am ready to sleep on the threshing floor, et cetera.

"You will be back tomorrow morning?" asks Miriam. "We have to bake the *danishkes*."

I had forgotten . . . the cheese danishes . . .

"What time will you be here tomorrow?"

Maybe if I run the whole fifteen miles back I can face danishes.

"Please, make it early," says Miriam.

I don't know, I don't know. I don't know what to do about Shavuot. I think about synagogue. I think about staying home. When the baby naps, I could read some of those books I've collected, learned expositions of the Book of Ruth. I'm full of food and my spirit is lagging. Maybe I will go to the gym, or clean out a closet, or take a hot bath.

Then I think of Miriam, faithfully baking cheese danishes every Shavuot, true to her mother's recipe, true to the calendar, true to her sense of right and duty. Every Shavuot, Jacob goes off to the synagogue, fulfilling a commandment on behalf of them both, and comes home to a lunch of freshly baked danishes.

I think of Miriam during the years when we lived in a different city, or were too busy to pay attention. That's the thing; for a long time, I didn't pay attention. I didn't have children. My interests were elsewhere. I didn't fully appreciate what Miriam had to offer—her history, her willingness, herself.

When my husband was born, Miriam was twenty—a young mother, a refugee, determined to live, and living a pioneer's life in Israel. Now my husband's hair grows gray and Miriam has looked at her hands and said to him, with just a trace of bitterness, "What I could have done as a fifty-year-old grandmother." How frustrated she must have been, how she bit her tongue and invited and smiled and cooked and lit candles and ironed her pillowcases and baked cookies for her husband and waited, waited, while we dawdled, figuring out what was important.

When Naomi comes home, with Ruth, she tells the gathered women her name is no longer Naomi, which means "pleasantness," but to call her Mara, which means "bitter." No husband, no sons, no grandchildren.

It is time to pay attention.

So early next morning, after a quick cup of coffee, I recklessly leave these behind: unmade bed, unfolded laundry, unanswered mail, unwashed coffee cup. I leave my unfulfilled notions of scholarship. I leave the matter of *shul* for another year. I pack up the baby and leave my home and set off for the Bronx, to make cheese danishes.

Whither thou goest, I will go.

DAIRY MEAL

The Soup

4 large Idaho potatoes, peeled,
  cut into 2-inch dice
1 onion, diced
1 large carrot, diced
Salt and pepper
1/2 cauliflower in smallish florets
1 tbsp. salt

6 oz. egg noodle "flakes"
Soup greens (parsley, dill, parsley
  root), tied up in a bundle
1-lb. container sour cream

Shake the diced potatoes, onions, and carrots with the salt and pepper. Wait for the vegetables to sweat. Fill a pot with cold water. Put in the potato cubes, the diced onion and carrot, cauliflower, and salt. Bring to a boil. Add the egg noodle flakes and soup greens. Cook the vegetables about 15 minutes, or until potatoes are soft. Taste the broth; it should be well flavored.

With a fork or whisk, beat the sour cream. Add a large spoonful of hot broth from the pot to the beaten sour cream. Stir again. This will keep the cream from breaking up when you add it to the pot. Pour the cream slowly into the soup pot, mixing as you go.

Yield: 8 servings

The Cauliflower

Cauliflower florets
Pinch of salt
Pinch of sugar
1 egg
Breadcrumbs (commercially pre-
   pared seasoned breadcrumbs or

homemade: Heat stale bread
and rolls in the oven till hard.
Hand-grate, not too fine. Add
salt, pepper, parsley flakes.)
Oil for deep frying
Piece of bread

In a pot, put florets in water with a little salt and sugar. Boil until soft. Drain and cool. Beat the egg in a bowl. Dip the florets in egg. Roll each floret in the egg, then dip in breadcrumbs to coat thoroughly.

Cover bottom of frying pan with oil. When oil is bubbling hot, slide in the cauliflower. Add a piece of bread in the pan to absorb the burnt bits and keep the oil clear. Fry cauliflower until crisp.

The Fish

4 large flounder fillets (Miriam
   says, "I look for the thick
   flounder fillets, or I take a
   fillet of sole.")
1 egg

Breadcrumbs
Paprika
Oil + 1 tbsp. butter ("just for
   the smell")

Dip the fish in lightly beaten egg, then in breadcrumbs mixed with the paprika. Fry in oil and butter. Don't forget to add a piece of bread to the frying pan to keep the oil clean.

Yield: 6 to 8 servings

CHEESECAKE

Filling

3 lb. hard farmer cheese
4 eggs
3 tbsp. sour cream

1¹/₂ cups sugar
2 tsp. potato starch
1¹/₂ packs vanilla sugar (see p. 157)

Combine filling ingredients until thoroughly mixed.

Dough

3¹/₂ cups flour (more if needed)
2 tsp. baking powder
1 stick (¹/₄ lb.) butter, softened
1 stick margarine, softened
1 cup sugar

2 packs vanilla sugar
1 level tbsp. sour cream
2 eggs (reserve ¹/₂ egg for
   brushing top of cake)

Sift flour with baking powder. Add rest of dough ingredients. Knead (add more flour if needed). Cut dough in half. Line pan with half of dough.

To assemble:

Preheat oven to 350°F. Pour cheese mixture into pan. Roll out other half of dough. Cut into strips. Lay strips on the bias over the filling, forming a lattice. Brush egg on top of cake. Bake for about 1¹/₂ hours on the bottom rack.

NOODLE KUGEL

*T*here are many ways to make a noodle pudding, *lukshn* kugel. It can be sweet or savory, crisp or creamy. My grandmother made hers *pareve,* neither meat nor dairy, using fruit and eggs. She liked thin noodles that would curl and brown on top, and there was that special chewy taste of raisins exposed directly to the oven's heat.

The fruit made it sweet, but not dessert-sweet. It could keep warm company at Friday night supper with a roast or a *polkele,* a little chicken thigh. Or it could be eaten for lunch the next day, as the Sabbath puddings were intended to be—room-temperature puddings for *Shabbas* lunch, a day when cooking was not allowed.

"Kugel" translates as "pudding," but *lukshn* kugel seems more casserole than pudding, a different texture and purpose. It is a different breed of thing than tapioca stirred atop the stove. A kugel is baked and substantial, mixed in advance, then left to the heat. As puddings go, perhaps a baked rice pudding is closest to noodle kugel.

For noodle kugel, noodles are first cooked, then mixed with other ingredients that bind and flavor. Primary among these is the humble, maligned egg. The progress of the egg in our kitchens parallels the evolution of our religion: The grandmothers believed in eggs; the daughters took them for granted; and I enjoy them, but my affection is complicated by science and the times. I eat far fewer than my grandmothers ate, and serve my children eggs less often than their great-grandmothers served theirs.

Maybe science—dare I voice it?—will one day find that eggs are what children need.

My grandmother's kugel had autumn in it: chopped apples and raisins, and sometimes walnuts and other times lemon zest or a dollop of orange marmalade melting into the beaten egg. It was like a toothsome crustless apple pie with silken noodles sauced in apple spice. I can remember my grandmother at her kitchen table thoughtfully wielding a short, sharp paring knife. She never seemed rushed or frazzled, she was elegant and deliberate in her kitchen. This was her life and she was consistent in it. Kitchen work was not something apart from life or distinct from what counted, not something to get through in order to get to the life you preferred.

Miriam, my mother-in-law, says *kigl,* not kugel. Her accent is different, and her *kigl* is different too: a lush, custardy thing. Broad egg noodles bake slowly, absorbing and melding with cottage cheese, sugar, and sour cream. She makes it for lunch in Catskill country summers, placing it out on the porch table. Here is the table: white napkins, the *kigl,* a bowl of damp strawberries and blueberries—*malinkas* in Polish—and a jar of Queen Anne's lace picked from the meadow, set in clear water.

"You should take that recipe," says Miriam of the dairy *kigl* when she sees I want seconds, and I do take the recipe down.

"My family likes it," I explain to myself.

The last time Miriam made *kigl,* I took it home. I ate half the pan after the children were asleep in their beds, dreaming their cinnamon dreams.

Once my aunt asked her mother for the kugel recipe. My father's sister Millie sat down with her mother at the kitchen table with a cup of coffee, and paper and pen. My grandmother gazed into the middle distance and recited a formula that could have been plucked from a page in a women's magazine: so and so many eggs and apples and bags of noodles. She gave precise measures, detailed ingredients. She prescribed seasonings, baking heat, time. She was specific. My aunt, in her fanciful handwriting, took down every unequivocal word.

Later that day the daughter watched her mother make the noodle pudding, and the making bore no relationship whatsoever to the recipe. The daughter was accusatory. The mother gave no quarter.

"You must have made a mistake," my grandmother said.

"She was going for a certain look," explained my father, when he heard of this episode. "Those women didn't cook from recipes."

MIRIAM'S DAIRY NOODLE PUDDING

1 lb. medium-width egg noodles,
   cooked
1¹/₄ cups sugar
6 eggs
1 can (20-oz.) crushed pineapple
1 tsp. vanilla

¹/₂ cup margarine or oil
1 large container (16 oz.) sour
   cream
1 lb. 4% cottage cheese
¹/₂ cup crushed cornflakes or
   cookie crumbs

Mix these ingredients together, spread into a greased pan (9 × 14-inch). Cover with crushed cornflakes, sprinkle with sugar.

Bake 1 hour at 350°F.

IRENE'S PAREVE KUGEL

8 oz. medium-thin egg noodles,
  boiled in salt water 5 minutes
  and drained
4 tbsp. margarine or oil
2 eggs, beaten
$^1/_2$ cup sugar
2 large peeled and grated baking
  apples

$^1/_4$ tsp. cinnamon
$^1/_8$ tsp. ginger
1 tbsp. orange marmalade
$^1/_2$ cup raisins or currants
$^1/_2$ cup chopped walnuts, if
  desired

Mix together all ingredients. Bake in greased baking pan 35 minutes at 325°F.

GROCERY SHOPPING

$\mathcal{M}$y father did most of the grocery shopping when I was growing up. He rarely took a list. He had his regular stops, and he selected that which looked good. Staples at a price were acquired at a certain super-market, while another sold superior fruits, smoked fish, and cheese. Milk was freshest at a small local store. The delicatessen for corned beef and pickled tongue, the kosher butcher for raw meat, fresh fish at the fish market.

He liked one bakery for rye bread, salt sticks, *ayer kikhl,* onion rolls. A rival bakery won his custom for its seven-layer cake and challah. Bagels, *pletzls, bialis* were only procured at the bagel "factory." Before the fall holidays, Dad found his way to an old A&P store in a worn part of town, and bought cases of club soda and ginger ale there.

He looked for bargains and quality. He enjoyed the search, the bustle, the human contact. There was a town square feeling to it. He ran into old friends at the market, kept up with who was building houses, buying cars, gathering signatures for a petition, running for office, managing illness, moving back east or out to California.

My father's shopping skills were a matter of some pride, especially the selecting of produce. As a child he had accompanied his mother to the pushcarts of East New York, down a steep hill from their house and over the long blocks beyond. What a consumer's education this was, the boy's view of arguing, bargaining, impugning, insisting, the exuberant dead-serious throng of Jews and Italians choosing only the finest vegetables and fruits.

Then came the shlepping of heavy *peklekh,* packages, home a long uphill way. He and his mother, Irene, had a deal: The bus cost a nickel, but so did a grilled frankfurter, slathered with brown mustard in a soft roll, its hot casing popping in juicy joy at that first hungry garlic-laced bite.

"You can have a frankfurter or take the bus," Grandmother would say.

"I always took the hot dog," my father told me, shaking his head at the boy he was. The aftertaste, taste memory, the satisfying heaviness in the gut had to carry the boy over the long blocks, up the long steep hill. They carried pounds of potatoes, grapefruits wrapped in tissue paper, onions in net bags, prunes, cabbages, the largest unblemished colorful specimens Irene could procure for the lowest price. String handles left red marks on their palms.

Irene in her hat, lisle stockings, and walking shoes offered the choice freely. She accepted his decision and trudged without regret. She took pleasure in the son's eating, laughing to herself at his predictable choice. This sort of thing, chalked up to martyrdom, gave Jewish mothers of the old school a bad name. It was nothing of the sort, martyrdom, but only a fable of motherhood, ancient, universal, direct.

MIKVAH

I am going to the *mikvah*. I drive my car for an hour in the rain, pouring rain. It is night, it is dark. It is late. I had to put the children to bed first, and wait for my husband to get home. Married women use the *mikvah* at night, after sundown, eight o'clock and later this warming time of year.

The *mikvah* is the ritual bath. It is a small pool constructed in a special way to blend still and flowing waters, according to ancient principles. Immersion in the *mikvah* is commanded in the Torah, the written law. In Talmud, the oral law, the commandment is ordered, described, made practical. There is an architecture of *mikvah,* and a spiritual purpose: dip in this special pool to attain ritual purity. This dip once was required of both women and men. It was required after childbirth and menstruation, after contact with a dead body, after illness, after nocturnal emissions. In biblical times, priests officiating at the Jerusalem Temple immersed themselves before performing sacred rites.

Most of the uses have lapsed. A small remnant of the people retain the tradition, remember the *mikvah*. Mostly, it is a subset of observant women. These women refrain from sex during menses because that is specified in the law. They count days of physical separation from their husbands, and then go to the *mikvah* to purify themselves, to renew themselves as sexual beings.

It's not in my racial memory. It's not in my lexicon as a woman. I had heard of "family purity," but never desired to know more. It was well cast aside, I always thought, something like animal sacrifice, with no reasonable use in our days. Too, I felt uncomfortable with the categories—pure, impure—and I still do. "Female impurity" resounds harshly on the modern ear. It sounds like a primitive blood taboo: fear of women and their cycles. It sounds as if men abhor a woman's blood.

I was surprised years ago when the rabbi we chose to officiate at our wedding suggested I think about going to the *mikvah* before marriage. My fiancé and I were in a restaurant meeting this rabbi, deciding if he were the one to oversee our matrimonial rites. He spoke to us of blessings and good deeds, of ritual, of mystery.

As the rabbi discussed these things, he ate from a bowl of barley and mushroom soup. His glasses slipped on his nose. The soup dripped from his spoon, down his reddish beard, and onto his tie. He was oblivious to such quotidian concerns—clearly a man who occupied a more spiritual plane than I. In the old Chasidic tales, it would have been he who chose us. However, we thought we chose him. We booked him for our wedding.

I thought of my foremothers, who went to the *mikvah*. I looked up *mikvah* in the telephone book. This was years ago. I went to the *mikvah* and started off my marriage that way, just to do it, to cross that particular "t." I never went back. Until now.

I drive in the rain, in a state of strange excitement. I've wanted to try this again for a while. After each child was born, I thought about it. Renewal, demarcation, punctuation. But I didn't go. Many things held me back. The notion of purification, against a woman's monthly "impurity," rankled. No, menstruation is not "unclean," say the modern explainers—apologists?—but only renders a woman "impure" in a ritual sense. The unfertilized egg expelled from the body is a small death, they say. As with everything in life, one ought to be conscious, to treat the body's cycles seriously, and to mark the transition from that small death to the possibility of new life again.

Explanation or apology? Clearly there is a connection between clean and pure, if only in our common perception. I went to the *mikvah* before my marriage. I said my prayer, I dipped in the pool, and I can still hear the *mikvah* lady, the officiating figure. "Kosher! Clean!" she exclaimed. Clean is what she said, not pure. Translation problem, perhaps. Perhaps.

The parking lot behind the building is full. I circle the block, peering through the beating windshield wipers. My station wagon, a traveling dump of rolling soda cans, crumbs, overdue library books, and crossword puzzles, follows one-way streets. I make out few street signs in the night mist. Street lamps are dark, broken maybe, or turned off for economy or for energy savings. I find a spot for my car and park. For a moment I sit. The rain lets up. I lock my car door under dripping trees in the dark.

Strange and excited, I walk the narrow sidewalk, turn as indicated by a small arrow and handlettered sign. Beyond a chain-link fence is a back staircase. My heart thumps under a black T-shirt. I am dressed in a way that for me is ordinary—sandals, jeans. My head is uncovered. I would never guess I was going to the *mikvah*.

I open the door and feel warm, clean air. In the waiting room, a large woman in a green dress sits by a telephone. She must be the *mikvah* lady, I surmise.

"What do you need?" she asks me.

"*Mikvah,*" I say, a bit puzzled. Is there any other reason to be here?

"Yes, but do you need a bath or a shower?"

"A shower is fine," I venture. Wrong.

"So, you'll have to wait. We're busy."

"O.K., I'll have a bath. A bath, a shower, whatever is free first." I shrug.

This is a discreet, mannerly place. No one looks up, but all must be listening. So far, I have made a number of mistakes, realizing nothing.

I sit in the waiting room, trying for nonchalance. I perch on an unsteady vinyl stool, turning away from my reflection in the polished mirror. Worn, green industrial carpeting is under my feet. The *mikvah* lady is up, down. She is down a hallway, through a doorway. She is back, speaking on the telephone. Over her head, information is posted. A late fee will be charged after closing time, eleven p.m. It is now past ten. "*Thank you for your donation of $18,*" I read.

Eighteen dollars. Of course. Eighteen is the lucky number. The Hebrew word *chai* means life. Spelled with the alphabet's eighth and tenth letters, the word also signifies the number 18.

In the tradition, Hebrew letters have mystical meanings and even personalities. Each letter seems significantly placed in the Torah. Stories and superstitions have grown up around the letters and the numerical values of letters that make up the words. Men have spent their lives studying such things, and felt the richer for it.

Here on the sign, "18" is used in an off-hand, casual way. Write out your check for eighteen dollars, and gain one more useful jot or tittle of good luck. Not a fee but a donation. Not a service, either, but a *mitzvah,* a word that may mean both "good deed" and "commandment."

I actually remember that I have to remove my contact lenses. I have a lens case and a pair of eyeglasses in my purse. I switch from one to another. There is supposed to be nothing between the body and the waters of the *mikvah*.

A woman enters carrying a gym bag.

"What do you need?" asks the *mikvah* lady.

"Just a shower. I'm completely ready, I bathed at home."

Oh, I think.

"Excuse me," I say. What I need is a bath.

"Yes, I know," says the *mikvah* lady, but kindly. "You'll have to wait."

I sit, waiting, beside a long, clean, Formica counter. On the counter sits a basket of hair dryers. A rack of magazines hangs from the wall. In one corner, hats are displayed and may be tried on, the sort of hats one wears to synagogue in the Orthodox hat culture. A large bulletin board is tiled with business cards and advertisements for apartments and vacation packages. Attendants whisk about, women in housedresses and slippers, keeping things spic and span. Their faces are sun-creased, their accents foreign, their lives a mystery. I have heard they do this as volunteers.

This waiting room is similar to other places I have been: changing rooms at community centers, health clubs, locker rooms, doctors' waiting rooms, hair salons, cosmetologists in second-floor offices, massage studios, the steam bath, but this has its own peculiar ambiance. Like those places, this place is self-directed, but it isn't exactly about health, or beauty, or pampering the senses. There is something here I can't quite taste or recognize. It doesn't feel like religion, either.

I am stealing glimpses at a woman reading a book nearby. She is my age, fortyish. I cannot see much about her but thin hair, pale skin, thick glasses, and run-over shoes. She glances up. I look away, and it strikes me: She is here for a reason and the reason is to purify herself before permitting her husband to touch her, to prepare herself to admit her husband entrance into her body, in anticipation of that primal instant of merging and losing control. Suddenly the whole plain, dowdy, modest, quiet, archaic place reminds me of nothing so much as sex.

Are they all thinking about sex right now? I try not to scrutinize the women waiting with me, each in her private moment. But I am so curious. I want to know everything. Here are two women, late forties, I guess. One is plump and tall, with a wry expression on her face as she chats with the *mikvah* lady and leafs through *Newsweek.* She is dressed up in a shiny printed frock and high heels, and on her head is a *sheytl,* a marriage wig. The other woman is wiry, petite, shaking her damp, short hair as she heads out the door in a sweat suit and rubber sandals.

Here is someone I surely have seen on the commuter train into the city, wearing a navy suit I might wear to a business appointment—but her skirt is shorter. And two young women who seem to have arranged their trip here together, wearing something I recognize as a kind of uniform for one branch of the people: everyday long skirts, short socks, slip-on shoes, and pull-on headscarves, to keep the sight of their hair from all but their own husbands.

I can't stop looking and wondering, how had all these women, different as they are, come to this? Did their mothers take them to the *mikvah* before they were married, and they just kept going? Because that is what one does? Or had they found their way here on their own, like me? Have they been living this rhythm of sex, abstinence, *mikvah*, sex every fertile month all the years of their married lives? What is the experience for them? Is it everyday, nearly unconscious? Self-conscious? I have a million questions I wish I could ask each one. But I can't. And one doesn't. People don't talk about going to the *mikvah*.

As with much in life, all I can know for sure is my own experience. And I am edgy, new. I don't remember much from that sole visit as a bride. I look within and find only a question: Why am I here? Contradictions flood my mind—the primitive fears, the magical construction, the flowing water, the weights and pulleys, the *halakhic,* or legal requirements, the difference between sanitary and spiritually pure, the hair dryers, the parking lot, the telephone, and my own imperfect state: something is missing, so I am here.

There are only three commandments specifically enumerated for women in Jewish law: challah, candles, and *mikvah*. When you bake your bread, you should throw a bit into the baking fire, to echo the Temple sacrifices. You should light your Friday night candles. And you should go to the *mikvah*. Of the three, only *mikvah* is mentioned in the Torah. A rabbi told me this. So now that I know it, shall I ignore it?

I am willing to try, but I look for logic and benefit, possibly a blasphemous approach—"Maybe there is something in it for me." Here are the points others have made in support of *mikvah*: Monthly renewal, consciousness of life and death, connection with foremothers, greater appreciation of sex for both husband and wife, and respect between spouses. You must work out relationships in impure times, without sex to solve problems.

I'm listening, but not buying. I'm distinguishing, too, between *mikvah* and the whole complicated package in which many observant women wrap up their fertile lives. Some will not hold their husbands' hand, or sleep in the same bed, during menstruation or for seven days after. Whether to avoid the risk of accidental tangling, or because they think pollution is actually transmitted from woman to man, I don't know. This probably varies. After a while, all you know is that certain things "feel wrong."

I don't like legal thinking, myself; you accept a structure, then think within it. Do I want to keep this law above all else? Do I want to be actually observant—or only traditional, transmitting my children's birthright as I believe I should, but leaving the question of spirituality for the next generation to decide?

At last I enter a sparkling clean, private bathroom. Paper slippers on a paper mat rest on the floor. A faded terrycloth bathrobe hangs comfortably on a hook on the door. There are thick, fresh towels, mini-soaps in paper wrappers. Here is a shelf stocked with containers of alcohol, shampoo, toothpaste, cotton balls. *"Just a reminder . . ."* reads the sign on the wall. This is a checklist, amounting to specifications for preparing for the *mikvah*. Reading the list, I realize I will have to race. It is a half hour until closing time.

How can I possibly do it all? I have been in the garden this week, and my nails are layered like mica, with grit between the layers. I have walked in sandals through urban dust. Every bit of visible dirt on my body must be cleansed away. Every nail must be bare and neatly clipped, all traces of makeup, lotion, perfume, deodorant, ink stains wiped away. Rough skin must be smoothed. Jewelry must be removed, earring holes cleaned with alcohol, hair washed and combed over all the body, teeth brushed and flossed. I must take a bath and after I am really clean, I must take a shower to rinse any residue, dead skin, loose hairs.

I crack open the door. A sweet-faced woman with gold teeth wearing a housedress and slippers is instantly on the other side.

"I didn't bring a comb," I apologize.

"So?" she asks. "I get you it."

Russian? Romanian? How did she come to be here? She fetches a comb, manicure scissors, and nail file from a series of beakers of blue antiseptic solution arrayed on a plastic cart. While I peer out the doorway, waiting for these items, the thin-haired ordinary woman I studied in the waiting room emerges from her bathroom, dressed, post-*mikvah*. She catches my eye for the second time tonight—and I am overwhelmed.

The woman glows. Her skin is radiant, the thin hair is filled with soft light, the eyes behind her thick glasses are doe-like, deep. She smiles slightly at me, passing in the narrow hall, and I catch my breath, stepping back from the radiance, the sensuality, the intimacy of this encounter. I try not to think of her going home, stroking her husband's back . . . after not so much as touching his hand for many days. . . .

I close the door, soap and scrub and snip in fast shorthand. I can imagine taking my time at home, with pumice stones and natural sponges, Dead Sea mineral salts, orange sticks, cotton, and Sea Breeze, before coming to the *mikvah* and saying, "Just a shower." That's the way to do it. For now I race, noticing for the first time the mosquito bites, scratches, calluses, freckles, veins, scars, cuticles, a small green bruise. I have been oblivious to this my body. Hello, body. This perception seems important, I need to think about this.

In the shower there is a sign informing women to examine their breasts for lumps, just like in the showers at the gym. The best time for breast self-exam is the week after completing the menstrual cycle, note the instructions: imagine that, exactly *mikvah* time.

At two minutes to eleven, I press the buzzer, to tell the ladies I am ready. Wrapped in the *mikvah* bathrobe, I turn the doorknob in my hand, and I see my hand, palm, thumb, fingers, clean nails, circlet of gold.

"Oops, sorry, I forgot something," I say to the attendant, and close the door, feeling daft.

I don't know if I have had my wedding band off in this dozen years. Maybe once or twice? My finger has gotten larger, or my knuckle. The ring is too tight. I grasp the ring, turn it, pull. This hurts. I try again desperately—nothing. I apply soap, hazardously working at the ring over an open sink drain under fast running water. My knuckle, growing red, is beginning to swell.

From the pocket of my jeans, thrown over the hamper, I wetly fish out my wristwatch. It is now after eleven, the *mikvah* is officially closed. I panic. I am in a small, silent room, I can hear silence waiting beyond the bathroom door, I am the last person left in the world, I am ridiculous. I cannot remove my wedding ring.

I'm plucked like a chicken, clean as a new broom. I am nude under the robe. I can't go in the *mikvah*.

Rummaging among the vials on the shelf I find baby oil, and flip off the cap. I slip the greasy ring into my jeans pocket. I have to soap my hands again, and rinse them once more. I check the pocket just in case. It would be just like me to lose my wedding ring at the *mikvah.*

"It was a long time ago, I've forgotten—" I admit to the *mikvah* lady, following her to another door, and the inner chamber, the ritualarium itself.

"I'll hold your glasses," she begins.

I hand her my glasses. Without them, all is blurry. I can just make out a square pool with steps and a handrail. I place my robe on a chair. I am naked and completely clean, not at all embarrassed. I don't actually feel naked, but somehow—prepared. Nearsighted, I descend carefully down the hazy steps, feeling my way down the handrail, with tiles underfoot, and into the bath. The water is warm. It reaches to my chest.

"Go completely under water, without touching the walls or anything," she instructs.

I do. I feel my hair drift in the warm, slightly moving water. As I emerge, the attendant hands me my glasses, so I can read a prayer off a laminated card. I bless God for commanding me to immerse. I give back the glasses and dunk twice more.

Last time, the attendant pronounced me "Clean!" This time, the *mikvah* lady tells me, "You did great!" Then, she says, "Your glasses," and hands them down to me. A strange thing happens, standing there. I begin to weep and I can't stop.

I climb the stairs and slip into the robe, still sobbing. The *mikvah* lady has vanished, leaving me that moment for emotion and release.

I pad in paper slippers to my bathroom, and close the door. I don't know what has happened. The tears have stopped, just as suddenly. In a bit of a trance, I get dressed, count out eighteen dollars, using every greenback and quarter in my purse. I seem to have come with exactly eighteen dollars. I walk to my car in the dark, damp night.

I drive home, guided by instinct, in some sort of heightened state. There is traffic on the highway, but it is quiet, there are lights and there is neon, but it is muted. The skin on my hands, usually sandpaper, feels smooth. My hands feel the way they used to feel, before daily laundry, dishes, finger-painting, children's baths, weeding the garden, dumping compost, lugging briefcases, before assembling bookcases, before scraping the barbecue rack.

The world is padded, or softened, or something, a pleasant feeling.

And when I get home, my husband is there, not yet quite asleep. I am not at all sorry to have gone.

Next month is another country, and the month after that. We shall just have to see.

June

THE LIFE FORCE

June

*I've finally gone out and bought a set of dairy dishes to replace my blue
odds and ends, and I've put together a white meat set. It feels good. I look
at the stacks of dishes on their shelves, at the cutlery in their drawers, at
soup ladles in two plastic colors, each a code for a different phase of life's
appetites. Meat and dairy. There is a difference, in the essence and in my
kitchen. This gives me a tidy, settled feeling. I look at these dishes and feel
happy.*

*I still need a dairy soup pot and a few meat saucepans. I could use a
matched set of dairy tableware instead of the odd lots I have commandeered.
Generally, though, I feel content with this, fortunate and whole, but not
complacent; aware that equilibrium is dynamic. A sense of balance this has
given me.*

*"You are what you eat." In a society of excess, this is true. Consumption
by choice is different from consumption out of need. I make choices based on
my view of myself on the planet, and in the end I become the expression of
those choices. Should I adorn my home with rare woods harvested from a
shrinking rain forest, should I tour the tender tundra, shall I pit my own
green yard against tomorrow's groundwater? Are curiosity, aesthetic standards, a desire for new experience, financial wherewithal the right criteria for
gathering up handfuls of the earth? I can have almost anything on my plate.
But should jets fly, barges course, trucks lumber, should oil wells pump and
atoms split, so I can eat fruits out of season and swim in a distant sea? How
important are the words "I want"?*

Kashrut *is the place where I think about what I will eat, with reference to something beyond the words "I want."*

It is inconvenient, this kosher keeping. I drive my hungry children past the fast-food outlets, I do not drive through to emerge with a Styrofoam box of fried chicken. I lose convenience and time, and time is precious wealth. I have to explain it to my children, sometimes firmly, sometimes faltering and evasive. Once my son, five years old, cried: He wanted to stop for fried chicken.

I was evasive. "Well—" I said. I wanted to minimize the appeal without banging shut the door. Maybe we would try it one day; maybe he would go with a friend. I was not yet ready, and still am not ready, to sit stolidly behind the wheel of my station wagon and say, firmly and finally as we pass the chicken place, "We don't eat that. It is treyf.*" I didn't want to engender revulsion and disgust. What others eat should not be scorned.*

But it was unkosher chicken, not fed or killed or examined according to Jewish law, and then it was maybe dipped in milk and fried in I don't know what, and served with macaroni and cheese and a roll with butter and string beans with bacon bits and a complimentary ice cream for dessert. Solid food, not to be scorned, but not what I wanted to allow, just then, even just this once.

Here is the difference between those returning to tradition (me) and those securely rooted but not absolutist in life. My husband could have taken the kids and said to the teenager behind the counter, "Chicken, please, and fries, and Coke—no bacon or butter or ice cream." Good enough, shoyn, *already.*

My husband wasn't there. I was piloting our boat through the shifting tides of subjectivity. What we did instead was this. We came home and fixed dinner, the children helped or had to wait longer, and at last we ate, looking at one another around our own kitchen table. I knew what went into our bodies that evening, and I could feel good about it. Not such a loss, perhaps.

But we also cemented one more brick into the rising edifice of our life as a family. We eat at home, mostly, and less and less often dine out. We don't make spur-of-the-moment food decisions. We pick and choose and have a certain consciousness about it. We don't have a fast-food life.

Exploring kashrut *is my way of bundling up all the broken twigs that belong together. I can tie up my past, and transmit to my children something that, if not unbroken, is patched and coherent. They will receive the tradition. It is something to leave behind, perhaps—that will be their choice, later—but also something on which to build.*

SHE WANTED A GIRL
TO HAVE THEM

*H*ello, hello!

It is a spring morning, a dairy food holiday. In Miriam's kitchen all is ready. The curtains are washed and ironed—white eyelet, re-embroidered on white nylon sheers, made in the small curtain factory Jacob once owned. The porch door is open. The curtains billow in the cool, fresh air. Light reflects on the wallpaper, yellow and orange flowers splashed on a background of shiny white. Basking outside on the sunny porch, the egg-carton seedlings are green and bushy. Summer's zinnias and marigolds are on the way.

We are going to make cheese buns, what Miriam calls *danishkes* or sometimes, *danishlekh*. Whether this is real Yiddish or affectionate English I do not know. But oh, they are good. Brown and shiny, flat and thick, each yeast dough pocket will hold a heavy sweetened cache of rich vanilla-scented cheese. We will have them as breakfast, and as illicit snacks, and as lunch, before they vanish for another year. Today, when the *danishkes* come out of the oven, Miriam will make a percolated coffee, and we will have a danish as soon as we can, right away, warm. Most years, that would be the moment I arrive, in response to Miriam's phone call, and carrying a large plastic storage box.

Today, however, I am going to record the recipe. I rummage for paper and wash my hands.

"I am getting the toys," murmurs Jacob, disappearing down the basement stairs. He has a special place to keep playthings for the children, and retrieves them immediately we arrive. Mixed feelings bubble in my breast. *The Barbies.* As a mother I was going to ignore or subtly discourage those high-busted no-hipped long-legged icons of impossible male fantasy we girls played with and measured our pubescent bodies against. But when my daughter was three, Jacob brought up a case from a basement closet, black and shiny as patent leather, splashed with a familiar pink script. Inside, Barbie dolls.

These had belonged to Miriam's daughter, Tamar, who is gone. She was twenty years old when she died.

Miriam must have put them away, with care, a lifetime ago, when Tamar grew too old to play with Barbies. The ordered contents bore her handprint. Who but Miriam would have straightened the jointed doll-bodies and brushed their synthetic hair, attired them in coordinated ensembles, strapped the figures into their proper compartments? Only she would have hung the little dresses and suits and formals and raincoats on little hangers, delicately pushed tiny purses and shoes and pink curlers and filmy bits of lingerie into tiny cardboard drawers. It was she, certainly, who buckled the storage case and set it aside, and then wiped down the case with a damp cloth a few times a year.

Neatness, conservation, comes naturally to Miriam, but there was more to it than this. How could she not foresee a granddaughter thrilling to Barbie dolls? Miriam must have imagined continuity: Tamar engaged to be married, Tamar a bride, a mother, and then, in the fullness of time, Tamar's baby girl.

There never will be that baby. Aunt Tamar for my children will never be. My husband's sister, his only sibling, the sole human being to share his childhood compass points, is lost forever, mourned forever, gone to dust.

Tamar went to high school, wrote her reports at the library, helped her mother and grandmother cook, for she loved to cook. She sat babies on weekends for pocket money. I have seen the school papers Miriam kept, written in Tamar's neatly slanted, clear hand. Coiled within that careful script was breadth of mind, curiosity, hopefulness, wonder, poised to spring.

One day, the mail brought a full scholarship to attend a most famous university, and Tamar went away, a circumstance Miriam and Jacob barely could understand. It was not easy at the famous university—How could it be?—for this tall daughter of immigrants, a public school graduate with a serious and dazzling mind. Already, an opaque pool of illness was growing in Tamar, an illness for which was never found a cure.

Once she must have placed this red flocked skirt next to this striped jersey and flowered hat, sighing with happiness at Barbie's perfectly ordered world. Sitting cross-legged, she slipped the stiff little sandals on Barbie's pink, high-heeled feet. She worked the doll's legs, puppetlike, to mince across the living room carpet, on her way to a rendezvous with Ken, attired in zipless toreador pants. To set off the wedding gown, Miriam made a pipe-cleaner bouquet. It remained in the Barbie case, saved all these years.

As the illness rose, there was a leave of absence from college, then a hospital stay. Tamar's clarity slipped away, and then her hold on life. Miriam's arms ached for Tamar. Her yearning would never end.

"It was my grandmother's recipe," says Miriam, surveying her set-up, cheese and grater, basin and bowl, sugar and soup spoon and eggs. "My mother's mother. She was some cook, even better than my mother. She knew how to cook things, you can't imagine. And all her five girls learned, each one could cook."

"She taught them?" asks my daughter, innocent, sidling up to the counter, Barbie doll in hand.

"They helped her!" exclaims Miriam, with surprising vehemence. For a moment I question the fashion in which I am raising my kids. I should be cooking and cleaning, my children beside me, so they also can learn the ingredients of everyday life. "How else would she manage, with nine children?"

We have no answer. There is no answer to be had.

The great-grandmother showed her five daughters how to do, and they were to transmit the knowledge to daughters of their own. The four sons might have brought home four wives eager to learn Poland's best cheese danishes, wives who too would have passed the recipe along. By now, if the world were a just place, dozens of kitchens, genetically linked, should have been busy, this prefestival Friday, with rolling pins, graters and spoons, turning out these very *danishkes*. Instead, it has come down to this: Miriam, an only child, who came out of the war with a mother, two aunts, and an uncle, showing me on behalf of a single grand-daughter.

Miriam holds a rusted, broken chain. Imagine that chain, once burnished and whole. Miriam trying so hard to fasten and fix with her small hands. What else might I have done today, on this balmy Friday, simply cannot exist. The pronoun "I" has no importance. I have to be here doing this, that's all. And now that my girl, the granddaughter, so good with her hands, is old enough to learn and help, I don't know what to hope for. That she will like to cook? That she will drop everything once a year, to make *danishkes*? That she will remember? Or only a mother's heartfelt eternal wish, that she should live and be well?

We make the filling. Miriam pushes the farmer cheese through a grater. She mixes the farmer cheese, half a beaten egg, vanilla sugar, sour cream, sugar, yellow raisins.

"With cheese, you always use yellow raisins," says Miriam. If the mixture looks too stiff, she adds the other half egg.

The yeast dough, needing time to rise, was made the day before. Miriam tells me about it. She made what she calls a *roshtshinye*. She heaped flour on a board, made a well in the center, filled the well with crumbled yeast, and dissolved it with warm buttermilk. Then she added sugar, salt, shortening, sour cream, eggs, working a dough with her hands. She set it to fluff up on the stove, over a warm oven, and stored it overnight in the refrigerator.

My mother-in-law takes the dough now, pulls and pokes a bit, judiciously esteems it ripe. On a floured board she cuts off a piece of dough the size of a large walnut, and shows us how to roll it flat, thin, round, about six inches in diameter. Each chunk of dough becomes one pastry.

The assembly is precise. The cheese filling is spooned into the center, a tablespoon or two, and smoothed flat. Miriam stretches strips of dough across the cheese, and seals the pastry shape with flour and knife and quick patting hands. She brushes beaten egg on top. We copy her, clumsily. Miriam does three for every one my daughter and I complete, and then Miriam repairs our creations.

We let the formed pastries rise a bit. A pan goes into the oven.

We never will know what the blonde, hollow Barbies could say to a dark-eyed immigrant daughter raised by two driven women who cooked. My three-year-old girl who at last was Miriam's granddaughter, though, knew their language at once. There was a winter coat with a spotted fur collar, a muff to warm the posed, cool hands, a vinyl raincoat, umbrella, hat, and matching knee-high boots, dresses for many a party or daytime event, a negligée with matching panties, daring swimsuits and demure uniforms, even a tiny pepperoni pizza for several Barbies to share.

There were clothes from Mattel, tiny replicas of pre-Vietnam American fashion when women were not supposed to stride or perspire, and outfits made by Miriam, sewn from cloth scraps or crocheted with leftover strands of yarn. There was a hair care kit, complete—curlers, a brush, wee elastics, and original instructions enclosed in a small, yellowish plastic bag.

To look at that case and its contents was to know it was well played with. Indeed, Tamar had owned few other toys as her parents and grandmother struggled for financial security. To look was also to know that never were these left out in a naked tangle for days, or even overnight, but picked up, smoothed, ordered. Each bit of wardrobe, each little spiked heel slipper must have been searched out before the set was ever tidied away. The case held no odd gloves, no single shoe, no misplaced crayon or chewing gum wrapper closed up by mistake.

Yet this was no Barbie museum. Rather, it was a caught moment, a well-cared-for fragment of 1965. I was ideologically opposed, but when the case was opened, there was nothing to do but gasp in a sort of awe. Yes, my feminist training ill-disposed me. Yes, my parents scorned the phenomenon, the consumerist values, the insatiability of Barbie's fashion needs. I had worked at acquiring my own sort of scorn, which was a mixture of trying to please my father, anger at having to do so, superiority, jealousy, uncertainty, and longing for a straightforward glamorous model of femininity. Yes, I hated Barbie.

For a long time I only remembered being too old, too sophisticated, for Barbie, hating Barbie, and I vowed to protect my child. But then Miriam flipped open the case and my daughter exclaimed. Forgotten feelings bubbled up, cracking the surface of my acquired scorn.

We had owned a few Barbie dolls, my sister and I. We bought a few outfits at Kiddieland, and others we fashioned with scissors, squares of dime-store fabric and lanyard sashes. How I remembered suddenly the tempting packages, coordinated fragments of wardrobe, hanging from hooks in the Barbie display. I remembered the expanding Mattel villages in bedrooms of fourth-grade girls, the arrival of Ken, the perfect escort, and good-natured Midge, in a phalanx of cars, boats, dreamhouses.

What I had wanted most, I suddenly recalled with near terror, was a bald-headed doll whose look could be varied with three distinctly styled wigs—yellow, titian, brunette. One day, visiting the New York variety store of our Great-uncle Abe, my sister and I saw what must have been the Japanese knockoff, a Barbie lookalike with three interchangeable heads that popped off the one body with a small sucking noise. We were allowed to take it home. The thought of playtimes beheading and recapitating our ersatz Barbie until the plastic necks were stripped, is almost too much to bear.

My Barbies were gone with the wind long ago. I had a long, unbalanced childless adulthood before my own children arrived. My life was nearly free of even a glimpse of old person or child; my days were spent unnaturally, year after year, with my peer group. Under the illusion of eternal youth, I was in fact losing the ability to look at the world as would a child. I saw Tamar's old dolls that first time, and I thought, *Why, they're priceless, they are collectors' items, first-generation Barbies in mint condition, put them back wherever they've been preserved. . . .*

"She's only three," I complained. "She'll wreck them, they're too valuable to play with."

Miriam looked at me with disdain. "So what?"

My values were questionable. She wanted a girl to play with them, and it was long enough, already, to wait. And in truth, my daughter didn't wreck them, she studied them and loved them. She told me that they were more beautiful than the new Barbies in the store. She styled their pony tails and walked them down the aisle on Friday nights and Sunday afternoons. She spoke to and through them, cross-legged on the living room rug in her grandparents' house, as we orbited year after year, in that rotating galaxy of apples and honey, potato pancakes, gefilte fish, *danishkes.*

I am struck, as always, by the small things. How to crack an egg and use every drop of albumen, the pinch of flour to seal pastry seams, the warm water to soften the raisins, the advance thought and preparation.

"Someday I will have to watch you make the yeast dough, to get the recipe," I say to Miriam. I have never made yeast dough, the part of this two-day affair that seems most mysterious, least controllable. Yes, I have begun watching the cooking, noting down the precious recipes, trying to do something to anneal the chain. One chain of countless chains around the world and in every century: the way someone once canned peaches, placing their syrupy halves gently into a glass jar in a Georgia summer; and someone else stacked up tortillas on a clean white cloth, and then, in one place and one time, cheese danishes.

In the scope of eternity, preservation of this kind is futile. In this personal moment at the middle of my life, it is the only thing I can think of to do. So I watch and try to learn, and I hope against hope that life will always be as good as it is right now.

"You have recipes there," remarks Miriam, gesturing at a cardboard binder. I had not noticed it, resting beneath the telephone. The small binder is packed full of paper, held shut with a thick rubber band.

I snap off the band and open the binder, I flip gently. There are brownish leaves of newspaper, magazine clippings, index cards, an orderly array. I see measurements for cakes perhaps tried once or tasted at a party, economical casseroles that seemed a good idea—dishes that, containing no history, fill me with no desire.

What takes my breath away are the narrow loose-leaf sheets, covered in neatly slanted script. "Granny's Cheese *danishlekh*," one page is entitled. The ingredients are listed, dough and filling. Tamar already did it. She stood at this counter beside her grandmother, who baked from memory, and Tamar watched and measured and wrote down the recipes.

She found time for this, after laying aside the Barbie dolls. Miriam's daughter, she wrote into the future, saving a bit of what was important as best she could, no matter what was going to be.

GRANNY'S CHEESE DANISHES

Dough

4 cups all-purpose flour
1 yeast cake
1/2 cup buttermilk
1 stick margarine, softened
1 stick sweetened butter, softened

1 tbsp. sour cream
3 eggs
1 cup sugar
2 packs vanilla sugar
Dash salt

Make a *roshtshinye*: measure out flour. Make a hole in the middle, and crumble the yeast into small pieces. Warm the buttermilk, and add into hole. Mix in rest of ingredients with a fork, knead together using hands. Cover with a towel, set in a warm place (atop the stove is good) for about 10 minutes, until it doubles in volume. Refrigerate overnight.

Cheese Filling

Yellow raisins
1 lb. hard farmer cheese
1/2 to 1 egg (depending on consis-
    tency of cheese)

1 pack vanilla sugar
1 tsp. sour cream
1/2 cup sugar

Grate farmer cheese. Pour warm water over raisins, pat dry. Mix ingredients together until smooth.

For each danish, cut off a piece of dough the size of a large walnut. Roll it out flat, thin, round, about 6 inches in diameter on a floured board. Spoon 2 tablespoons of cheese filling into the center and spread a bit. Fold the ends in and seal up. Let rise for a few minutes. Coat with lightly beaten egg. Grease pan (margarine). Bake at 400°F.

"If there is dough left over, make a jellyroll with jam, nuts, raisins, cinnamon, or whatever else is handy."—Tamar.

DRUGSTORE

$\mathcal{H}$ere is a photograph, a brown Brooklyn print taken in the 1930s. It is a picture of Isaac, my grandfather, balding, his posture straight, in the accustomed three-piece suit, high collar, and tie, posed in front of his pharmacy.

It is the closest I can get, through visual record alone, to the intense world of The Store my father knew as a boy. No photograph, as far as I know, ever was snapped within the walls. If I want to see Isaac measuring and mixing with tiny spoons and brass weights at his pharmacist's bench; if I want to see my father's sisters bringing their dad a midday meal wrapped in tea towels; if I want to follow the son down dark steps to the cellar to sit alone in punishment for some misdeed, I must conjure these images.

Edward, my father, had jobs to do in the store. The chores were necessary, part of making the living. They were not assigned to teach responsibility or earn an allowance or any other such contemporary conceit. You didn't do them mechanically, either, you made them yours. There were better ways of doing, and worse, and you took pride in engaging your mind to find the better.

Every day there were boxes to unpack, shelves to stock, crates to store in the dark, spidery cellar, under the metal sidewalk cellar doors. There were canisters and syrups to lug upstairs. When his sins were extreme, Edward was sent down cellar to think about morality and justice for a while.

Edward took money and made careful change, and he got fast at arithmetic. He wiped fingermarks off the woodwork. He mopped the floor at night.

He ran the soda fountain after school and on Saturdays, mixing syrups with carbonated water, scooping ice cream, wiping the counter, and washing the pumps. He washed thick cocoa sludge from the bottom of crockery mugs, and he thought about that sludge. The directions had been followed: one packet of cocoa mix per mug, then whip it up with the malted milk machine. But directions are writ by man, not God.

"Half a pack of chocolate, Dad," he said after trial and error. "It's just as good."

Ever after, my grandfather, hearing customers order cocoa, would whisper, "Remember, half a pack of chocolate, son," as if he had invented the proportion. In my time, my father would recall this story and laugh. It seemed pertinent to so much in life. Indeed, an Ivy League education in human nature was to be had in his father's store.

Over the years, I learned secondhand a few salient points of curriculum. It interested my father that people sometimes don't know what they think they know. At the soda fountain, they could never taste a difference between the cherry flavor and strawberry flavor, insist though they might on one or the other. There were different sorts of folk; he came to know and accept it: some people paid their bills; some had excuses. Then there were the small cunning acts that folk concoct when they have too much time, and little money. Years later he would describe one, a Depression classic, as thirsty men and women stretched a soda through long bankrupt afternoons.

"They would drink half, then say it was too sweet, so you'd add more soda water. They'd say it was too sour, so you'd add more syrup."

We children, listening, were fascinated, resolving to try this ourselves with ice cream and hot fudge at Sanders, our local sweet shop.

"They'd drink some more, and it was too sweet again, and so on and so forth." You couldn't boot them out. Your Brooklyn neighborhood was your small town.

My father and his two sisters worked in the store. It was there that Edward learned to wrap packages, an important skill, for there were no shopping bags to give away. Perhaps paper shopping bags had not been invented, or maybe they were too dear. So the children wrapped tidy bundles in brown paper and tied them with string, for the purchasers to carry home.

They wrapped patent medicines, prescriptions, ointments and creams, hair dressing, eye wash, pencils, notions. Druggists' children must be polite, neat, friendly, helpful, and yet, in a way, impersonal. Working in the store, they knew what children must not know—who has the dandruff, the bunions, the hemorrhoids, the menstrual cramps. My father, the adult, would speak frankly of such things: Indeed, my adolescence was one long mortified blush. Puberty as I knew it could not have survived my grandfather's store.

On slow afternoons, my father and his sisters wrapped twelve-packs of sanitary napkins in plain brown paper, to meet the customers' preference for discretion. It wouldn't do to be overly delicate, but still, the younger aunt refused.

"I can't," she told my father.

"I'll show you," offered he, four years the elder.

"I don't want to know."

Another life lesson, my father said, the distinction between ability and will. But I felt for my aunt. I heard this story in my blushing years.

My childhood, papered with such gleanings, also came wrapped in my father's packages. Edward took pride in the drugstore skills. He never shook salt and cinnamon from their shakers, but tapped precisely, imitating the druggist's careful forefinger. We grew up on frothy egg creams, Brooklyn concoctions devoid of egg or cream, but rich with Brooklyn-made chocolate syrup sold in but one Detroit supermarket, and but once a year, at Passover. And my father wrapped the best packages.

He approached each packaging problem pleasurably, from a design sensibility tempered with a sense of history and thrift. In the method, his youthful experience was reflected, but also his adult trade. My father worked as a tool-and-die man in the automobile industry, designing the stamps and presses that would bend and fold metal into doors and fenders and quarter-panels for new model cars. He stood at drawing boards nine feet tall and as wide as movie screens, working the trigonometry in his head into delicate pencil tracings of angle and arc.

If a design was particularly complex, he would model three dimensions out of paper for the toolmaker to consult—beautifully taped and folded structures, imaginary and mechanical, filled with fluorescent light and coded with arrows and dots of Prussian blue ink. When I imagine my father's death, I am seized with panic and dread for all that will be lost, even beyond the love that I have for the man.

My father would assemble his exciting packing supplies on the dining room table: grocery bags cut to lie flat and hemp cord to knot, manila envelopes to reuse and newspaper crunched up for protection, shirt cardboards rolled into cones, shiny coffee-colored paper tape, corrugated cardboard he might carve into useful shims. He worked with my mother's big chrome sewing scissors, or the red-handled kitchen shears, and with the always handy pocketknife my father has carried since a boy.

He packed hand-me-downs for cousins, or a gift of new walking shoes for a grandmother. These things went to the post office, wrapped taut and secure, using as little tape as possible. Thus bundles of chocolate bars, socks, and books arrived at our camp bunks in summer; thus gifts for our children arrived later in life.

Edward knew a lot about his father, a knowledge gained from working beside him all the years. My children see their parents dress for the office and vanish, to reappear after a span of time: the actual work is theoretical and hard to imagine, and has little to do with what they are learning from us. My grandfather's work was something different—comprehensible, tangible, and tied in with the rhythm of Edward's own life as a boy. The son talked to the father, but also he breathed in his father's substance like atmosphere—the exactitude, the honesty. He was surrounded by the respect in which his father was held. You never got rich in the pharmacy, but my father's father was honored in his time and place, and he gave all he had to those around him.

"We talked about all sorts of things," my father has said to me. My grandfather died before I was born, so I grasp each reference greedily, press each dewy recollection between leaves of memory. "Your grandpa believed in God. . . ." He identified firmly with the traditions of his faith, did Isaac, and he belonged to the synagogue. But he distinguished between faith and synagogue, the politics of which he did not like.

A friend of Isaac's was, for a while, rabbi in the family's synagogue. He stepped down from his post in the 1940s, disgusted with the unspoken agenda of having to please the *shul's* powerful *makhers,* the synagogue's wheelers and dealers. The rabbi gave up his pulpit and opened a hardware store in the neighborhood. He was still a rabbi. He married my parents. He said the Seven Blessings over my mother and father in 1950, in my grandmother's living room. The rabbi who ran a hardware store became my father's paradigm for all that a rabbi should be.

Growing up, and for many years later, I labeled my father's parents "Orthodox." My grandmother's unalloyed *kashrut,* her Friday night candles, her slightly sardonic invocations of the evil eye set a religious standard for us, away in the precincts of postwar Detroit. Still, it was understood that in America, a store that served the public could not be closed on *Shabbas,* the Sabbath, if you wanted to make a living. As formal as Friday night dinners might have been in Brooklyn—and these, they say, were as serious as chicken soup, kugel, crystal, silver, wine, mahogany, candlelight, and a little black *siddur,* or prayer book, can be—my grandfather opened his store at eight on Saturday morning, and my father worked beside him there.

It was a community, after all, and the store was part of that. My grandfather took in film, and gave back photos. He ran a lending library, with mysteries and adventure tales to borrow for a dime. He sold chewing gum by the stick and cigarettes one by one, to anesthetize tough times. There were a couple of tables for checkers and chess, with a wooden box of game pieces stored on a shelf. When things were slow in the economy, or at the firehouse nearby, idle men would drift in. They would sit outside on a sunny day, and inside when it was damp, kibitzing and playing.

My own careless household has gone through countless sets of plastic checkers and chessmen. We can never find fifty-two cards for a deck. My father, however, still has the wooden box with the embossed checker disks, the carved wood bishops and rooks, that once helped pass the long Depression afternoons when neither storekeeper nor client were making ends meet. When my grandfather died, and the store was sold, Edward threw in with the inventory the brass scales, the gilt-trimmed cash register, the bronze mortar and pestle, the oak apothecary chest, and all the other solid, picturesque equipage that later turned up on the pages of collectors' guides. The chessmen, the checkers, he packed to take home. These games he had learned from his only father, in the store.

There were games within games as the father taught the son. Isaac won most of the time, Edward once in a while. One day, Edward suddenly perceived a pattern, in which he was winning one game out of every seven. He bit down his sense of deflation—his father was letting him win—worked at his game and kept count, until the time came at last when, of seven games played, he won two.

"Your grandpa never said anything about it, and neither did I," my father told me. "But I knew then that I really had won on my own."

Thereafter, the victories were random. Father and son contested in earnest, approaching equality as the boy grew up.

In the cellar of the store, during Prohibition, Isaac kept a few working crocks. For the family's use, medicine and sacrament, he brewed blueberry wine and a kind of hard liquor from the ethyl alcohol a pharmacist could get. Once, when we were visiting Brooklyn, my father paused with me under a concrete overpass and told a merry tale: In the early 1930s, a vessel of hooch on its way to the house slipped out of someone's hands right there, and it broke. Edward was dispatched home for mop, soap water, and pail.

Passing there then, you might have seen a boy at the overpass, mopping in broad daylight, anything but inconspicuous. He scrubbed away the telltale signs of illicit production, as if the scent could lead to their own upright door.

Errands and such were my father's job. His was a wide open world. The neighborhood sprawled and stretched, rose to steep hills, clattered over cobblestones. It was a new neighborhood, a suburb of the time, built in a way that seems urban today, with its tall brick houses and apartment blocks. But woods, farms, and water stood at its edge, and from the highest point, a boy on a scooter could see Jamaica Bay. Isaac never owned a car, but Edward had a wagon, a scooter, and roller skates; they were treasured toys, and they were more: the family's capital equipment, in Edward's charge.

At the store, there were deliveries to make, prescriptions and standing orders. Telephone messages, too: The pharmacy's telephone was one of the neighborhood's few. Neighbors placed calls there, and they gave out the druggist's number as their own. Calls came in. Messages were taken. Edward strapped on his roller skates and went forth.

I can see it, the boy and the store, the boy in knickerbocker pants and kneesocks and a peaked wool cap on a curly head, his daredevil skating tricks down the steep hills of East New York, his slower progress up the inclines, tracing diagonals from curb to curb. The mix of sport and speed and the importance of his errands must have been magnificent. And there were nickels and dimes deep in his pocket, tips for his trouble. This was Brooklyn; these were New Yorkers, immigrants, people of the world, though they might be living on pickles and sauerkraut, they knew what was what. A boy brings you medicine, you give him a tip.

My father took all his tips home to his grandmother, who was busy making life miserable for her daughter-in-law during the long hours Isaac spent in the store.

"She told me I should give her my tips so I did," Edward marvels, with a self-mocking shrug. "That's the kind of stupid kid I was." But the way he says this, it actually means, "I was well brought up." The ostensible purpose was safe-keeping, but he never recovered the principal. Occasionally, Great-grandma would dole back a penny, with elegant flourish: This was the grandson's tip.

As my father grew older, there were distant supply runs as well as local deliveries. He took the subway to Manhattan, to the wholesale markets, to purchase the makings of powders and potions. My grandfather, a practical chemist, used chemistry every day, more so than a druggist need do today, when dispensaries rely on ready-made drugs to fill prescriptions. My grandfather worked from scratch, following formulas and accounting for customers' histories and tastes.

He stood at a chemist's bench, fit out with scales, weights, droppers, and spoons, glass vials, cork stoppers, cotton, crucible, mortar and pestle, Bunsen burner. He spooned and poured, tapped and measured, mixed, dissolved, and flavored. Here was science knowledge, medical knowledge, on which a community relied. They called him "Doc." He told them how to cure their ailments, from sour stomach to sore throat.

There were Grandfather's mixtures and medicines, and then there were the brand-names. For constipation there was Ex-Lax. I was shocked, first encountering the photograph of my grandfather in front of his store, to see right there in full view under the family name an advertisement for Ex-Lax. My father explained that your big brand vendors would require a store owner to display such a sign. You had no choice about it, something like keeping your store open on the Sabbath.

There was a cure for every ill. For a sore throat, it was elixir of turpenhydrate with codeine, taken by spoon, and argyrol, to paint the throat. These medications, and others like them, eventually faded from drugstore shelves—but not from my father's lexicon, nor from our family's life. Throughout my childhood and adolescence, and even young adulthood, there was an ongoing search for the increasingly difficult-to-obtain formulas, the elixir of turpenhydrate, without codeine by then, the argyrol. The demon was capitalism, and we knew all about it: their exclusive patents having expired, these *perfectly good* treatments were dumped by drug producers seeking the holy grail of new, patentable formulas.

We could find them, though. On a dusty bottom shelf of a worn-out old drugstore, the one failing after the big chain store had opened down the street. My father would always talk to the owner, lingering there, and later in the car, he would speak sympathy. In Windsor, the Canadian town just over the Detroit River, you might find turpenhydrate, and for a long time, nonprescription codeine as well. Elixir of turpenhydrate was clear, strong-smelling. It tasted dreadful. The brush full of argyrol painting our throats made us gag. But the argyrol linked us with the hoarse throats of my father's childhood, and the mysterious secrets of the dead grandfather. And no one could say these treatments did not work. Every sore throat went away.

So it was with the many solutions to pain and illness I grew up with, treasured vestiges of my father's boyhood in his father's store. I had gooey, tarry ichthymol, a brown-black ointment from the stinking pits of hell, to spread on an allergy rash. We rubbed down fevers with alcohol, and fumigated congestion with Vick's. Delicious Coke syrup settled our stomachs. We never had bags of camphor hung about our necks, polio having been tamed, but we knew of them. My father spoke of such things.

We soaked cuts and splinters in Burrow's Solution, cleaned our scabbing sores with peroxide, gargled with salt water. We had an eye cup for rinsing out errant lashes and specks of dust. We doctored our earaches with sweet oil, and slept with warm cotton stuffed in the ear. We used Merthiolate or iodine, which were burnt orange in color and burned the raw skin, but never Mercurochrome. Mercurochrome, bright pink and painless, obviously could not be trusted to fight germs. We dressed our wounds with Bacitracin, and never with anything advertised on TV.

Our medicine chest was uncompromising: aspirins and Q-tips and chalky liquids for the digestion and bicarbonate of soda. In high school, I venture to say, only one other girl shampooed her long tresses in tincture of green soap, and that was my sister. Noxema was allowed, but deodorants were frowned on. Body odor, I understood, was an invention of Madison Avenue in order to create a market for a product, and at the same time, an indication of indifferent hygiene.

We had basic Band-Aids, the flesh-colored strips, never the ouchless novelty shapes. My father had taken the drugstore with him, as it was at a pristine and exemplary moment of social life, before commodity fetishism had its way with American values. And then too, my father preferred to make our bandages himself. He stocked a cardboard box in the hall linen closet with gauze rolls and adhesive tape and a tiny scissors, and he cut and folded and expertly taped as occasion arose.

There was a passionate subspecialty around colds, coughs, and sore throats, maladies of the chest and the nose. There were colds in the head and colds in the chest, colds in the stomach, and colds in the bladder. The cure in the end was simple: bed rest and fluids, warm garments, warm air. The fluids were orange juice, hot tea with lemon, and chicken broth, drunk clear and ambrosial from a large, off-white, Woolworth's china cup. At the first sneeze, my mother started the soup. She stood over it, skimmed it of every tiny globule of fat, so you could drink it like tea.

If it was flu or fever, you drank hot water with milk, possibly with sugar, as grandfather's mother, who lived to be ninety-three, had daily done. If it was sore throat, you dripped honey into lemon tea. There was one variation. When I was a teenager, my music teacher, a cellist and chess player who had grown up in the Bronx, prescribed whiskey, honey, and lemon juice mixed together, one shot each.

"I don't know if it cures you, but you feel better," my teacher told us. This was the only time I remember my father augmenting his medical repertory, and sometimes he thinks he invented it. *Half a pack of chocolate.*

If it was a cold, you did the obvious: you got warm. You jacked up the heat so the radiators spit and moaned, you put on pajamas and father's big white sweatshirt, and a loose, heavy pair of socks. In the kitchen, where the windows were shut tight, your mother started the soup boiling, and the steam drifted into the plaster, into the curtains of every room in the house. You put on the most comforting garment in the house, and that was my father's long, blue-and-white-striped terrycloth bathrobe. And you wrapped a towel around your neck—his father's advice, dispensed at the store with the argyrol and turpenhydrate.

It was a kind of religion, this. My grandfather was a modern man, his days were full of chemistry. This produced in my father a worshipping love for science, and science, I think, came to replace religion in my father's life. As an adult, Edward read physics and biochemistry, relaxed with science fiction, turned over theories of life's origin in his protean mind. God was the Creation, and not the Creator. It didn't matter if God was, or was not. Yet at the same time, in some way, Isaac's science became part of Edward's religion, to be respected, practiced, preserved.

It was—and still is—a proselytizing religion, and even if you did it, you wrapped the damn towel around your neck, but you did it with less than fervor and full commitment, my father would shake his head, sad and injured. His father's medicine, from a time that seemed to him certain and secure. If you ignored it, you deserved your scratchy throat.

But you didn't ignore. You heard the summons, the distant heartbeat of a tidy family business long ago, and you obeyed. You pinched your nose and opened your mouth for the argyrol, and you put a towel around your neck. You went to the linen closet where there were boxes of extra toilet paper, Ivory soap, Band-Aids, light bulbs, shoe polish, rags and brushes, vacuum cleaner attachments, sheets, tablecloths, and folded towels. You looked for a towel of a certain size, bigger than a face towel and not too thick, a thin, pliant grade of terrycloth, just long enough to wrap around your throat once and tuck into the lapel of your PJs. This lent a buxom, middle-aged appearance to a ten-year-old girl.

The towel was warm; the girl felt cosseted. She took her aspirins and throat medicine. She gargled with salt water, drank chicken broth and tea and juice. Sloshing with liquid and surfeited with every comfortable feeling, she got into bed with her book, heaped up the extra woolen blankets, and drifted away. No one bothered her, no one, and she would heal.

We were protected by invisible spirits, the drugstore spirits, and my father was the shaman, channeling our ancestor and bringing the old magic to bear.

ISRAEL

Yesterday I was boiling corn on the cob. Miriam, who never cooks it, watched me. She remembered buying corn in Israel, roasted corn from a vendor on the beach in summer. She used to take her son, my husband, to the beach with a cousin, when both were small children. This meant packing up her little boy on the bus, traveling two towns over to her aunt's house, collecting the cousin, taking another bus to the beach. At the end of the day, the two boys slept at her house, and next morning, she traveled back to the aunt to bring the little cousin home.

"I used to go three or four times a week with them," she recalled, and she didn't dwell on the schlepping, the packing and carrying, the long nauseating diesel-rocking bus rides. "They were so good, those boys," she said.

"That corn on the beach was so good," my husband remembered.

Such a picture this gave of the mother Miriam was and their life as a brave little family in the new ancient place. She was young, early twenties then, waking at dawn for her day at the beach. Everything would have been prepared the night before, and the two rooms where the family lived in that first house left in perfect order, when she took her little boy in hand to meet the rumbling bus spewing exhaust into the evaporating dew, the best transportation a poor country could afford in 1954 or so.

She would have carried scrounged playthings, spoons and cups, a canteen of drinking water, a few coins. Perhaps a towel and lunch, or would the boys' little bodies have dried brown in the warm sea air while they ate hot ears of corn to the sound of the vendor's cry and the hot roasted smell?

"I'm sure the beds were made when you left, and the breakfast dishes washed," I said, mulling over Miriam's logistical feats, her energy as a young mother. "Maybe I could have managed the beach before ten a.m., but not the dishes too."

"And what about your husband's dinner?" Miriam's son asked with a teasing air. For fifty years, Miriam's husband came home from work to a ready meal. "Did you forget your husband?"

• • •

"We ate our main meal about one or two o'clock. Jacob came from his work and the children home from school. At night, dinner was like lunch here," Miriam said. "Mostly salad."

To go with the corn, we were frying fish and making what I call "red salad," a sweet–tart standard of Miriam's, dressed with lemon juice, sugar, salt, pepper, and oil.

"This is an Israeli salad, I learned to make it there," she said. "We used to eat this for lunch, for breakfast. There was very little to eat there that time."

She showed me how to shred the red cabbage, the green cabbage very thin, using a cucumber slicer. She chopped carrot and scallion in tiny bits, diced red tomatoes. She mixed and added her flavors, in a certain special order.

"Maybe that's why we don't have cholesterol," she murmured. "We didn't eat meat for thirteen years."

Life was different there then, in every small way. When I wash dishes, my toddler is up on a chair by the sink, turning the faucet on and off, drenching himself with happiness. Miriam walked half a mile for water in the early Israel years: each drop was precious.

My older children pour milk, gulp, and fly, usually leaving an inch or two in the drinking cup. I grab a fistful of ice cubes to chill a drink that is already cold. Miriam remembers making thin gruels from dried fruits for her son to drink, and cornmeal-and-water porridge with a few drops of lemon juice, when milk could not be had. She remembers the struggle to keep the milk, when she had it, from spoiling in the Israel heat. No refrigerator, and often no ice.

"If I had milk, I didn't have ice," recalled my mother-in-law. "If I had ice, I didn't have milk."

Once in those early days, she told us, right before Rosh Hashanah, the autumn New Year, Miriam and her mother prepared the holiday fare. They improvised menus known back in Poland, with scant Israeli ingredients. Miriam made noodle sheets with an egg from her backyard henhouse, kneading and rolling and cutting the silken dough on a wooden board. She had a fowl slaughtered, and this became soup and a filling for kreplekh, dumplings; she baked a savory pudding and a sweet dessert. And then the mercury rose.

"It was very hot that time. I was afraid all the food would go bad," she said. "So my husband went out on the bicycle, the day before yom tov— the holiday—looking for ice, here and there."

Three towns over he found some. He returned, pumping slowly over the sizzling sand and gravel, with the parcel on the handlebars.

"A little piece of ice like this it was." Miriam held her hands a scant eight inches apart. "I put it in a basin in the ground, between some rocks, with the food I had prepared on top, and then a wooden board over all." She stopped a moment. She shook her head.

"And then the neighbors started to come." The whole street had heard of Jacob's coup, and all shared Miriam's predicament. One brought a cholent, a thick casserole, one brought a *meym tsimes,* a sweet carrot stew, one a *kompot,* cooked fruit. "Each one brought something. Everything went into that basin." She shrugged: "We were neighbors."

"At the very end one family brought borsht—beet soup. They put the bottle on top, under the board. When I went back later to get my food, the bottle had turned over, and there was borsht on everything, all over. Everywhere." She closes her eyes.

I too am visualizing a kerosene stove, an erratic flame, the long forays by foot, bus, and bicycle to market, the queuing up for ingredients purchased with tightly gleaned funds, the long hours of preparation. And then I see pots and dishes, covered with cloths—no plastic containers with airtight tops, no foil wrappings, no Ziplock bags—and the whole thing dripping with viscous red borsht.

"A little piece of ice like that it was," Miriam moaned.

They were pioneers, survivors. They cleaned up the mess and went on.

RED SALAD

2 quarters each green and red cabbage, washed and patted dry
Salt and pepper
1 large carrot
1 scallion

1 tomato, diced
1¹/₂ tbsp. salad oil
Juice of 3 lemons
10 tsp. sugar

Shred cabbage as fine as possible; sprinkle with salt and pepper. In a food chopper, chop carrot and scallion very small but still discrete.

Combine tomatoes with other vegetables, mix gently with the oil. Mix lemon juice with sugar, pour over all and mix well.

Yield: 8 servings, as a side dish

SEX

The work, the work was never done. In my grandmother's house, the housework churned like laundry viewed through a front-loading washing machine.

My grandmother had a washing machine with a round porthole in front. The capacity was not large. She was annoyed to see things return to the laundry soon after seeing them there before.

"But it smells," I said once, of a peach-colored sweater. I was embarrassed.

"If it smells, you air it. You don't wash it," she said, exasperated. "Do you have body odor?" she added in surprise, as if the possibility made me genetically inferior.

When the washer completed its cycle, she squeezed the wet things through a handwringer. For laundry, she didn't bother with the dumbwaiter, a rope-drawn lift that brought heavy loads from basement to upstairs hall. In her blue-and-gray felt slippers, she ported the basket of wet wash, up the hard cellar steps.

She leaned out her bedroom window to hang the wash, pulling a length of clothesline through the pulley, snapping on the clothespins, pushing the cord and garment away into breeze and sunshine, where it would dry.

My mother did housework when we came to New York. My father made repairs and ran errands, we children happily in tow. My mother cleaned the bathroom, changed beds, scrubbed floors. She washed dishes in hot, soapy water, and when she was done, she scoured the kitchen sink.

She worked beside her mother-in-law, hoping to please and also because there was so much to do. There was furniture to wax, and silver to polish, and candlewax to carefully scrape from candlesticks. There were rugs to vacuum, and *shmates,* rags, to shake outside and then soak in bleach in a bucket downstairs. The corners of closets, smelling of mothballs, could not be neglected. Glass jars were useful; they had to be washed and dried. One never threw out a mayonnaise jar.

We have environmentalism, they had thrift.

My grandmother rose at dawn. When I got up, she already was stirring the oatmeal, already lifting out skillets and saucepans from cupboards, and bringing butter and eggs from the icebox in the hall. Fresh oranges had to be squeezed every morning. She would cut them in half and squeeze them by hand, working the fruit on a ribbed glass dome until every liquid drop was released. She would strain the juice and pour it into the red-and-green-striped juice glasses.

When my father was a boy, the many half-sphere rinds, cupped one inside the other, were set out at the curb for daily garbage pick-up. "Mrs. Ehrlich's accordion," was the neighborhood's name for this matinal orange display.

The preparations for dinner commenced after breakfast. The kitchen table, fully extended and layered protectively with newspapers, received a succession of peelings, pits, trimmings, offal, eggshells. There was chopping, dicing, rolling, slicing, mixing. Bowls and pots and implements came out, were used, got washed and dried, and were stacked securely once again. Burners were lit, ovens heated. Soups must be stirred and puddings timed.

Before Passover my mother and grandmother turned the house inside out and put it back together. The books came off shelves. Furniture was angled away from the walls. Rugs were rolled up, floors were polished. Every strip of molding had to be dust-free.

Boxes of Passover dishes rose in the dumbwaiter; boxes of everyday dishes were packed and sent down. The Passover housewares, smudged from their newspaper wrappings, must be washed, dried, put away. *In mitn d'rinen*—in the middle of everything—the women stopped to make everyone lunch.

Toward dinner hour, the work became frantic. Coordination of courses and children and table, keeping the sink always empty to receive the next lot of soiled pots, dishes, ladles, and spoons. My grandmother had, with two daughters' help, done all this for years for a sizable household: a husband, three children, her mother-in-law, and my dad's youngest uncle, who slept on the living room divan when the family was young. My mother, as a child, had helped her own mother in much the same way.

There was serving and clearing and wrapping up food after the evening meal. They washed, dried, inventoried, put away. The table was wiped, the floors must be swept, the garbage put out. The clock was ticking. The time was late. The women were exhausted.

They didn't know I was at the door when my grandmother, reminiscing, spoke: "And then, you get into bed, and you're still not finished."

July

COMMUNITY

July

I want to create a home of rightness and wholeness, to establish the percussion beat of work and Sabbath, Sabbath and work. I want to infuse the minutiae of everyday life with something more—meaning or history or awe—and to experience it without too much sentimentality or irony.

Then on the other hand, I know, I now know for a fact, that this sort of thing must become a priority mission for someone in the household, and that person would have to be me.

Let me explain. If you are going to light candles on Friday night and have it feel like Sabbath, the house should be clean on Friday afternoon and the table dressed and the meal cooked by sundown. It's a satisfying feeling to have made ready, to have cleared away the detritus of a whole workaday week, sure it is. But then Friday is going to be about cleaning and cooking.

I can't cook on Friday, I'm working on Friday. I can cook on Thursday night after the children are in bed if I'm not too tired, or I can cook at five in the morning on Friday. My husband could cook, but he can't cook. If I have the money, I'll have the house cleaned.

I have to shop before cooking, and when will I do it? I will shop on Thursday evening, if I have the strength. Or my husband could shop, if I made up the list on Wednesday.

Friday's meal is not all I must plan for. To have a traditional Sabbath of rest, in which you neither drive, shop, light fires, nor do anything that resembles work, Saturday's meals should be prepared ahead. One could begin cooking Saturday dinner after sunset, if it is not summer when days are long, but all the ingredients should be in the house by then. Or one could go out for pizza. We will go out for pizza, post-Sabbath.

What else must be done? We all should be home and our bodies bathed by the onset of Friday sundown. That is 4:32 or so on those winter afternoons when sudden dark falls early. It's a foregone conclusion that much of the year, I will fail to hew to rabbinic timetables. If you're late lighting candles, the rabbis say, you'd better not light them at all. You'd be lighting a fire, forbidden on Sabbath.

I will deem Sabbath begun when mother is ready. Or I will light candles on time, and bask in their light, surrounded by clutter. I will welcome the Sabbath, and bathe children later. Or maybe they'll go to bed dirty. We'll have our imperfect Sabbath, our soupçon of grace and peace.

Then there is Sunday. Sunday's plans may need preparations, cash transactions. I cannot achieve spiritual refreshment and retreat from the material world, and still pop out to the A&P on Saturday afternoon. I must think about Sunday on Friday.

There may be a birthday party Sunday, with a present to buy. We mean to plant tulips and fix a faucet, but the garden center is closed on Sunday and so is the hardware store.

I or my someone must buy things on Friday, but Friday I'm cooking—no, working. Thursday night I am grocery shopping. On Wednesday, then, the Sunday errands somehow must be done.

And then comes the week. A child needs a library book Monday at school. The library is open late only on Thursday. I could go to the library Thursday night, and get the groceries on Wednesday. Will the avocado hold up from Wednesday to Sunday? We promised guacamole for a neighbor's Sunday brunch.

If Sunday is our day for going and doing, for children's sports and family activities, all the myriad house chores must get done during the week. Even if our cleaning is done Friday, and even though we no longer mend and sew and iron and bake, there is still yardwork and laundry and reorganizing a closet and fixing a door handle and paying bills—all those tasks that the rest of the world does on Saturday. When to do these things? Some of it can't get done. Or the family runs on overdrive. Or else it all falls on the wife.

The Sabbath is a gift: you give over twenty-four hours to contemplation, rest, and praise. It is regenerating. It punctuates the temporal world, or, as the sages explained it, provides a glimpse of the world to come. Also, it is a good deed to make love on the Sabbath.

Not that I believe in a world to come. But a roasted chicken on Friday night after candles are lit and lights are turned low and blessings are said, in a clean house, is for the moment, paradise enough. So I will roast a chicken on Monday and freeze it, then on Friday defrost and reheat. Or order in. Like a mad escapee from an unknown century, I explain myself to myself, hoping for the right answer.

KOSHER DAY TO DAY

*W*hat's for dinner?

This question gets asked in millions of homes, and answered in millions of ways. Roast beef and potatoes. Pizza. Pasta putanesca. Soyburgers, miso soup. Whatever you want. I don't know yet. Same as yesterday. Let's go out.

To which children respond in many ways. "I'm not hungry. . . . Not polenta! . . . Can I have cereal instead?" So it is in my house. Once I cooked a veal stew, brought it to the table, and lifted the cover of the dish with a flourish.

"Voilà!" I crowed.

"I hate *Voilà,*" wailed a three-year-old boy.

In my house, there are other layers now. At busy dinnertime, my six-year-old, who once hated *Voilà,* opens the refrigerator to choose a beverage. "Is this a meat or a dairy meal?" he asks.

"Meat," I reply. So he can't drink milk with his dinner, or have butter on his potato, or a cream-filled cookie later. On the other hand, meat goes with ketchup.

"I don't want meat. I want milk to drink. I never get to drink milk."

"Milk!" demands our toddler.

"Why are we having a meat meal?" *kvetches* my daughter, age nine. She is trying to go vegetarian, making exceptions only for tuna fish, for the split-pea-turkey-and-matzo-ball soup that Miriam, my mother-in-law, makes, and also, for schnitzel, Miriam's boneless chicken breast, pounded flat, breaded, and fried. Stretching the logic of our *kashrut* to tensile extremes, she refuses the broccoli that has touched a bit of meat.

"We're having schnitzel," I say, trying not to take it personally.

"Did you make it or did Grandma?"

"Just try it, won't you?"

"Plump, juicy chickens on the farm," comments the vegetarian's brother. "Buk Buk Buk Buk Buk. Flesh. Living flesh. Plump, lively chickens. Here chick chick chick."

"Ugh! Mom!"

Grumbling, banging cutlery a bit more than I have to, I fix a tuna salad sandwich. Since it is a meat meal, I use a spoon, fork, knife, and dish from the *fleyshik* set—*fleysh* meaning meat, as in "flesh." I do this so the dishes and utensils can be tossed in the dishwasher with the rest of the dinner things.

The alternative would be to mix tuna in a *pareve* way, in a glass bowl, with neutral implements, and then to wash the bowl, the fork, the knife, the spoon separately and by hand. So I'll make it *fleyshik,* and tomorrow, at dawn, I will reject the leftover meat-made tuna for a lunchbox sandwich to be consumed with chocolate milk—or do I have to? This is a cold tuna salad, nothing was cooked, anyway there's no rabbi in the kitchen to ask. . . .

My parents visit. We're comfortable in the lives of one another, and thus in our kitchens. In fact, with my parents here, we live in the kitchen. We sit around the table with oranges and tea and coffee and newspapers until we can't talk or sit or delay anymore. My mother always found her way around my kitchen easily, which has pleased me. I was proud, in a small, unimportant way, of having cups and glasses just where you would want them, waxed paper within reach, dishtowels near the sink and pots by the stove. This is a traditional kind of female pride, but paradoxically it made the kitchen less mine, less female, and more general: anyone could walk in cold and fry an egg. I set it up, then renounced stewardship.

My mother's arrivals, in particular, have set me free. She is no kitchen drudge, nor would I desire her to be. But when she picked up a sponge to blot spilled milk, or buttered a grandchild's bagel, I could take a sip of coffee (still hot!), read the front page, or dial the phone. For a moment, I could disconnect the complex mental wiring that runs our family switch-board: the beeps and flashes, the warnings against citrus allergy and cream cheese phobia, the scheduling of intramurals and favorite jeans in the wash, the synthesizing of homework problems, the filtering of necessary sounds from static. For a moment, a blissful, appreciative moment, I become but one member of an extended family tribe in the Kwakiutl longhouse. And my father always did the dishes.

But no more. This was in the days when my kitchen was organized on principles of logic and not on those of *kashrut.*

Mother has not been here for a crucial while, a period of time in which I instituted divisions and definitions. Now you can't just reach for a skillet and fry an egg. You have to say to yourself, *Meat or dairy meal?* The boys are eating chicken nuggets; let's call it meat. The dairy pots are in the corner cabinet, but the meat ones cower across the kitchen, stuffed into a pantry shelf—not enough room near the stove. There, you must take everything out to look for a small *fleyshik* frying pan, the one I'm not sure I ever got around to buying. "The children have marked the cabinets with colored stickers, Mom, follow the red dots."

As the egg fries, I hunt down a spatula.

"Not that one, Mom, this one, and use these plates. The green containers are *pareve,* so they shouldn't go in the sink with all that other stuff."

"*Oy,* I've got a *rebetsin* here," says my mother.

A *rebetsin*—a rabbi's wife, a term falling out of favor among women actually married to rabbis, women who may be doctors or teachers or rabbis themselves, or who simply chafe at definition by their spouse's status or profession. Something like "Mrs. Doctor," it's a Jewish anachronism. I was brought up to date on this point by the woman wed to the rabbi at our synagogue, a teacher, artist, and friend to whom I have often griped about inequalities in our tradition.

"May I introduce," said I in a crowd, "our *rebetsin.*"

She turned to me, aghast. "You! Of all people!"

But a *rebetsin* also signifies a woman of domestic piety, someone who consistently sets her standard above the rest of us mere mortals. When applied to a woman of obviously lesser virtue, or newfound virtue, such as my mother's daughter, this term *rebetsin* has the humorous force of a gentle put-down.

"I'll master this," says my mother. "Tell me about the sponges."

In a way, it was easier for my mother, and for her whole generation, the children of Jewish immigrants. My mother's mother lived by the rules reflexively. Thus, the divisions and distinctions were marked indelibly, and without a lot of meditation, in my mother's heart and mind. In the 1920s, in Toronto, in the home of a neighbor, the little girl my mother was surreptitiously slid a sunny-side-up egg with ketchup into the pocket of her pinafore, because she didn't think it was kosher. In domestic science class, she perfected the baking-powder tea biscuits but wouldn't eat them.

However, she brought the biscuits home for her father, a man who by then had serious doubts that God gave a damn. And he ate them.

Later, when my mother left home, she dressed in a black dinner suit

and a hat with a net veil, tried to smoke cigarettes, and ate shrimp cocktails. But it didn't matter: her soul was kosher even if the food was *treyf*. I
sometimes suspect that I am the opposite. Thus Mother is truly bothered
to think that her single sponge that wiped a milk puddle today will soap a
steak knife tomorrow. I have separate sponges, atoning for her misgivings.

"It does feel good, to know that everything is the way it's supposed to
be," says my mother, surveying the blue, red, and green dots punctuating
my white kitchen cabinets. "I never stop thinking about it. It has bothered
me for forty-seven years."

After dinner, when my father steps up to the sink on his busted left
knee and his bum right foot, I scurry around hiding the wrong sponges
and dishtowels, putting things away, separating this and that. I feel strange
explaining to him that he can't just wipe the counter with any old rag. I
hover, I oversee. The kitchen has become a woman's kitchen, my
kitchen—a side effect I don't desire.

It took me a long time to tell people we were doing this, and still it is
something I volunteer infrequently. It puts off, it drives in a wedge, or so I
worry it will. Invitations to dinner I approach with some delicacy. Often it
is easiest to imply that we are reborn vegans, or mostly so—fish and ovo-
lactarians. Somehow that seems more acceptable to others or easy for me
to say.

We have two-decade friendships that have not been exactly totally
informed of the directions in which we have moved. We turn down
Friday night movies and come out for brunch on Sunday with the kids.
We say no to beef chili with sour cream; we attend to the *saumon fumé*.
We ask for pizza *sans* pepperoni, snack on carrots rather than blue cheese
Buffalo wings.

I am getting around to talking about it, I really am. But most of the
people I love serve secular humanism at mealtime. They would never
dream of choosing sashimi over jambalaya, falafel over sweet potato pie.
To say I have chosen might seem a slap in their dear, decent faces.

In the meantime, icebergs surface. Our children are in private school,
Jewish parochial school; most of our friends have made different choices.
"Is the chicken kosher?" the children will ask. Their clear piping voices
stand out in a conversational lull at the Christmas party at work.

At a restaurant we order noodles and bean curd, cabbage and rice,
while our dinner partners feast on spare ribs, lobsters, won ton, roast pork,
duckling, shrimp, and seasonal soft-shell crab. Do we split the check four

even ways? My aunt arrives for a visit, bearing a gift of Canadian bacon, which her husband would appreciate for tomorrow's breakfast. I stammer and stutter and try to explain. This is the aunt, you see, with whom I once dined on *pied de cochon,* and it was Passover.

And this question comes up: "Do you believe in God?" It was easier when my answer was firmly no, instead of this wonderment or appreciation or wishy-washy version of deism or something more I sometimes get to now after a quiet Sabbath, reflecting on how much better a God-fearing, ten-commandment-observing world would be. So I have been embarrassed, I suppose. Loath to get into it anyway. It might seem as if we have made a judgment against our friends, that might hurt our friends, when we really have not. And I don't wish to seem—odd.

Are we indeed kosher? After all of this, would a rabbi sit at our table, and joyfully swallow our soup? It would depend on the rabbi, of course, but not only that. No, there are flaws, there must be, mostly because I will not stand there and do it all myself. My dishwasher alternates loads of meat dishes and dairy; the last rinse cycle is over 200°F.—good enough for me, but not for some. Whenever we have house guests, my bread knife—*pareve*—floats in the dishwater with an ice cream scoop. I throw the bread knife in the dishwasher, too. Two hundred degrees is good enough for me.

So I cut a few corners and make my peace. In the wee hours, furtive, I sort out misplaced cutlery, I don't bury it in the yard. I douse with scouring powder here and there, and hope for the best.

I watch my kids grab cookies of a summer evening, on their way out the door to watch fireflies. They always share with the neighbors' kids, and this makes me happy, this is pleasure that, for me, outweighs any worry that the cookies might be dairy, when the dinner two hours ago was meat. I can't worry about everything.

And what's to worry? Yesterday my kids broke bread down the street. My son, served chicken, asked politely for water when the other kids were drinking milk. "It's a kosher law," explained the six-year-old, sweetly, when pressed. That's the thing, that awareness, carried out into tomorrows when my body is gone. That is all I really wanted, anyway.

BUNGALOW

"*C*ome for the weekend. Come up with the children on Friday, early. Come right in the morning," said Miriam's voice. The line crackled with country static. "You won't have to move a finger, you can just rest with the children."

I said something vague, and said good-bye. I hung up the phone, gripped by useless emotions. It was unfair of me, this I know now, but denial was what I heard in her voice, denial or wistfulness—for a different sort of daughter-in-law, one with perfect nails and a house to match. A daughter-in-law who didn't work, who could spend a whole Friday, indeed a whole summer in Miriam's bungalow, watching the Catskill days drift by with her pretty children and their eager grandmother, while the husband, the *fardiner,* the breadwinner, came up for weekends. A daughter-in-law with time to spend, who was organized and careful with objects and money, who never would have lost a gold necklace, say. An old, long, gold necklace given her by Miriam.

Instead, she got me, a mad circus juggler keeping too many plates aloft, while which ones were crashing I did not know. I went to work; my nails were dull and ragged; money slipped through my hands. I did not even remember the necklace. And to whom could Miriam complain?

Friday would be a regular work day. I would greet the sitter, zip my heart into the closet, kiss the round faces of two small children, and close the apartment door. I would descend eleven flights on the elevator, disappear into the subway under a blazing morning sun, tunnel south under fifty blocks of pavement. Emerging from the depths, I would buy a cup of hot brown coffee, ascend fifty flights on the elevator to my office, and enter a world of printers and telephones, copiers and metal desks, important meetings, artificial light, fluorescent buzz and hum. Nine hours later, if I were lucky, I would reverse the course and meet my children after their day in a parallel universe under the open sky.

This was the frank reality of my life, and I wished it to be acknowledged, perhaps praised, by Miriam. Praised? All day long to leave two *kinderlekh* of that quality? a *meydele,* a *yingele,* a little girl and boy like this?

"Come early, and rest," urged Miriam. There was infinite generosity in this, the door was open. But you need ears to hear.

The next day, Friday, New York was melting: 90 degrees already, reported my clock radio, broadcasting into my uneasy, guilty sleep. The apartment, smelling faintly of kitchen refuse, surely was hotter still. On reflection, everything seemed possible, even a day off work.

So I called, and I packed, and I double-parked the car in front of the building.

Into the elevator I schlepped suitcases and strollers, swimming pool floats, sun hats, sun lotion, insect repellent, extra sweaters, juice cups, portable crib, *Goodnight Moon*, Fluffy Bear, Mr. Turtle, Baby Pillow, Octopus, and Duck. Outside in the brothlike air, I packed the car, I got the children in, I wiped up a juice spill. I set off with a credit card and seven dollars in my pocket. Logistics being as they were, I could not think of a way to stop at the bank. I would have to borrow from Miriam.

Out of town Friday morning! Henry Hudson Parkway, George Washington Bridge, the Palisades—and since the old, borrowed car had no air conditioning, the wind was in our hair. I raised and lowered windows, trying for balance between temperature and noise. I sang! I called attention to birds and trees!

Bear Mountain approached, and the children were asleep. Juice cups fell from their limp, sticky hands. There would be no afternoon nap now, no breather for me at all. . . .

Shah, let them sleep, I imagined Miriam to say. . . .

I found highways and exits; I found myself enjoying the green view, the subdued breathing of two little ones. The office could wait. The best and most important job in the world seemed less important. It blew away. My mind wandered, perhaps too much. In general, I have always been lucky to get where I get in one piece.

The last leg of the trip is a long crooked back road littered with the history of the lower Catskills: nineteenth-century farmhouse close to the road, empty; abandoned chicken coops, trailer homes, economic depression, soap suds spewing into mountain tributaries, a Ukrainian resort, a drug treatment village, rabbits for sale, fishing boats to rent, a summer camp for girls.

And then we are once again at Green Gardens Lodge, parking in crunchy gravel amidst many large Fords, Chryslers, Cadillacs, one Yellow Taxi cab, and also a Mercedes. They have millionaires here, and taxi drivers.

"How can a Jew drive a Mercedes?" Miriam has asked me, more than once. She has not forgotten the German military-industrial complex, and will not forgive.

A ring of forty spruce little cottages, freshly painted, encircling a razored lawn and a few shade trees. There are common rooms and out-buildings, a hotel turned condominium, patches of flowers and shrubs, a tennis court, and a pool with a fence that is locked until after lunch. This is the bungalow colony, my in-laws' summer world.

I turned off the motor, cracked open the car door. It was nearly as hot as New York City. But the hot air was clean, cleansed in the mountain night, and by this time on a Friday, nearly noon, the air was redolent: chicken soup boiling in country kitchens. And Jacob had seen us; he approached over the lawn ready to hoist luggage into his spare, bony, surprisingly strong arms. As far as I can tell, he never changes, never ages.

My little warm ones slid from the car and ran, looking ahead, not back. They belonged here—and still do—among the grannies and uncles and grandpas and aunts, the visiting grandchildren, the Polish and Yiddish conversations, the piped music, the card parties. They ran. The hammock to swing in, the flowers to water, the screen door to bang, lunch all prepared and a huge box of homemade cookies: they ran toward these things.

We ate, I unpacked, the children ran. Ladies in housedresses gathered and greeted, questioned, scolded—barefoot children in an era of deer ticks. I hunted for little shoes and socks in the grass. I took the children to the pool, and Jacob came to watch. I bathed the children after their swim. Miriam fixed ice cream cones. All was in her knowing embrace.

Later, Miriam's Sabbath dinner on the screened porch, and, with the fading sun, the lighting of her Sabbath candles.

My husband found his way there that night. We all slept in the two small rooms of Miriam's bungalow, under fresh line-dried linens warmed by Catskill sun and ironed to silken smoothness under Miriam's practiced hand.

● ● ●

Twenty years ago, Miriam, Jacob, and their circle, acquaintances, family, and friends, bought this place. A few years later I, fresh from the midwest, was feted here with my fiancé. Ten years ago I brought my first baby, to rock in the hammock my husband installed between two shade trees and to feast on the admiration and surreptitious sweets a colony of grandparents could provide in full measure.

Then I brought my two children, escaping a cramped city apartment and frenzied work week to stretch out in Miriam's hospitality amidst the pleasant green. Later we moved to the suburbs, and I left my office job: escape was less urgent. I don't come as often these days. Still, a few times each summer I arrive with my children, three children now, neglecting my own house and garden for two days or three or five. The three children fan out in all directions: this is their place, deeply, completely, and always. They love it. How lucky they are to be here.

Here Miriam cooks her country dishes. If we arrive at lunchtime, lunch is ready. Eggs and onions, perhaps. Before we arrive, Miriam slices five or six onions. She peppers them, softens them over a low flame, adds plenty of oil, and fries the onions to a caramel sweetness. Then she scrambles the onions with five giant eggs, adds a pinch or two of salt, heaps it all on a warm platter, and brings it proudly to the table.

The table is *gemakht,* ready, with barely a centimeter to spare. Here is a plate of sliced melon, blueberries, strawberries, and a bowl of sugar for the berries. There may be ripe tomatoes cut into chunks with raw Spanish onion, oil, and wine vinegar. Perhaps a herring in cream sauce, or a tin of smoked sardines. If there is *mizerya,* finely sliced cucumbers dressed in sour cream beaten with lemon juice, salt, and sugar, there will be little dishes and spoons to nurse the tangy sauce. There are fresh little challah rolls, or heavy slices of corn rye bread festooned with caraway seeds. Cream cheese with scallions.

In my honor, the old coffee percolator spits and taps stovetop. Miriam and Jacob drink instant coffee, a cup each at dawn. I drink high octane coffee all day.

These are jolly grand country lunches on the breezy screened porch crowded around the small porch table.

Neighbors pass by. "Good appetite!" they call, in accented English.

"Send the children over later, I have something for them!" orders *Tante* Sonia at the screen door. Probably chocolate and gum and Polish wafers and lollipops from Aunt Sonia's bottomless supply.

"Sonia! Come in, eat something!" urges Miriam. "Onions! A roll! Why not?"

"I cannot! I ate already, in *mayn bungele!*"

"Grandma, do you have any *plain* cream cheese?"

"*Oy, ye! Ikh hob fargesn!* Yakob, *oytser*, treasure, *nem der* plain cream cheese *fun* Frigidaire. *Un* a seltzer *oykhet*," as well.

"I'll get it," I say. "I'm closer!"

"Why? I am there already!" Jacob rises from his chair with a large gesture.

"He is there already!" explains Miriam. *"Es, mame sheyne!"* Eat, pretty mama, this is your job now. Try to be good at it.

This is a kind of utopia: a glimpse of both idealized future and past. Forty couples, many of them children together in Poland, spared in the war and determined to live with spirit, bought their colony for a future. Each inhabits a neat and perfect summer dwelling where one's own standards, language, and cooking reigns.

There is pride of ownership and independence in *mayn bungele,* and at the same time it could well serve a socialist's dream: A cooperative community of rules and order, where universal committee membership accomplishes maintenance, religious observance, improvements, and entertainment year after year. Hard work done willingly.

Yet no democracy is this. There are officers for life, male only, and each allotted a precious, status-conferring golf cart. Among these, my husband's uncle, the redoubtable Uncle Fred, prime mover and organizer of this place, is mayor, holder of the keys, maintenance supervisor, quality-control man. He books the musicians, handles the taxes, orders the corned beef, buys the Saturday newspaper in town for our Jacob, his loved and respected older brother. Jacob does not drive on *Shabbas*.

Uncle Fred—still Fishl to Jacob—takes his wife, Pearl, shopping, and out to restaurants, and here and there. They like to go and do. Pearl is a perfectly groomed and certain sort of person, whose legs at seventy-something look better in shorts than mine, who once informed me that I was definitely not too young to have children, and again, later, that this was the final correct moment to buy a house, and so we did.

Fred motors about Green Gardens in his golf cart, seeing to a leaky faucet or a fallen tree. He takes in the harness races with a visiting son, who calls this place *Greeneh* Gardens, *greeneh* being Yiddish-English slang for "immigrants." Uncle Fred can do anything, and he knows everything.

After the war, Pearl had the first winter coat and the first warm boots, of Russian army issue, and the first temporary apartment in Germany and then the first visa to New York: Fred's doing. Later Fred schlepped paint cans on the subway from job to job until he could buy the first car, the first house.

It was Uncle Fred who explained at last this crowd's aversion to the buffet meal. "I was in a concentration camp five years," he said. "I don't stand in line for food." I blanched and cringed: my wedding. No one had told me, and I never understood for ten long years what was the matter quite, what . . .

At Green Gardens, Miriam and Jacob and Fred and Pearl have neighbors, real neighbors. They do informal favors for one another, they share food, they run to town for bread, they offer rides. The support network is there for them now as they age, as the number of widows grows, and the mid-summer trips to doctors become more frequent. They meet for *davening* in the synagogue by morning, they have their tennis players and their card players, their golfers, their avid shoppers, their regular walkers. They have their gardeners, like Miriam, whose green thumb has splashed the front of her bungalow with gorgeous color each and every year.

Afternoon, when day's work is done, they gather on the greensward to chat in Yiddish and sometimes in Polish. The women wear loose casual frocks and slippers by day. They dress after dinner. Every evening, there is coffee and cake in the card room, and Saturday night they throw themselves a party—splendid food, dancing, singing, entertainment.

It is a bit like going to Poland for the weekend. In a *shtetl* echo, peddlers pull up to the lawn in their Fords and pop the lids of trunks stuffed with pocketbooks or bath towels. A fish man from the Bronx stops by each week to sell herring and lox.

Down the road, a *frume*—religious—colony runs a kosher store, its moldy shelves stocking pickles, salami, shampoo. Fresh bread is displayed in a cardboard delivery carton, and endless children drip ice cream on the floor. A little store, as Miriam says, "like in Poland."

This is where the walkers go. They have their route, these twenty years. From Green Gardens to the *frume* store is half a mile. Back is one. There and back again is two miles. In the sun, in the rain under an umbrella, after breakfast, before dusk. Never the other way, never up the road past meadow and butterfly, abandoned barn, overgrown graveyard, blackberry bramble, and cattail swamp, to where the running creek empties into pond, full of algae, bobbing beer cans, visiting birds, and a last few frogs. Always the same, reliable two-mile course, punctuated by the comforting sight of the *frume* store.

One woman, her son in the garment center, sells sweaters in her bungalow. Sweaters and dresses and men's polo shirts, stuffed into closets and drawers and boxes. Another woman runs to her neighbor offering a *maykhl,* a savory morsel: stuffed turkey neck or calves' foot jelly, with hard-boiled egg slices suspended in the sturdy aspic, a lemon slice on the side.

Once Miriam made potato latkes in the evening cool, and a dozen people managed to drop by. My children slathered on sour cream, sugar, applesauce. *Tante* Sonia waved her latke as the golf cart zipped her away to a committee meeting, Uncle Fred at the wheel. He likes to help out the ladies. He does whatever he can.

It is secular, our colony, and religious too: live and let live, a virtuous stance. There are ladies in hair-rollers hitchhiking rides on golf carts to the laundry shed on Saturday, and grandchildren whose ritual fringes hang out of their soccer shirts. There are men in skullcaps playing cards on a Friday night. There are women at the beauty parlor on *Shabbas,* while their husbands read Torah with tears in their eyes. There are grandfathers out to Pizza Hut with the children, while their wives make two sets of dishes somehow fit on a bungalow shelf. Two sets of dishes, two sets of spoons, two sets of pots in a tiny little country kitchen.

Comes a knock on the door any day at dawn, and Jacob makes his way to the *shul* to fill out a *minyan.* The little *shul* is lovely, peaceful, filled with colored light. The members built and furnished it. One, a talented artist, crafted the stained glass windows. Another is a rabbi, still another a trained Torah reader. That man bought the prayer books, that one contributed the *bima,* the pulpit. This one donated the Torah scroll.

It is a bit of the fabled Borscht Belt on Saturday night. At 8:15 sharp the whole colony is in the casino, with any friends, children, grandchildren spending the night. The women are coifed, the casino is decorated, everyone is dressed to the nines. The band is playing, perhaps an ensemble of keyboard, percussion, and sax. Start with a *forshpays,* appetizer—chick peas, chunks of pumpernickel-and-rye marble bread, schmaltz herring.

Each fine herring bone was tweezed from the velvety fish flesh by this week's ladies' committee on Friday at 7 a.m. in the big kitchen that once served the hotel. I saw them. The ladies in their housedresses worked together, slicing the herrings, dressing them in oil and chopped purple onion. Two men run an open bar for exactly one hour: vodka, whiskey, scotch, orange juice, soda, ginger ale, Coke, ice.

"That's it," say the men as the ice melts down. "The bar is officially closed."

There is a sit-down meal, delicatessen or smoked fish, salads and cookies and cakes. A singer may belt out in Yiddish, French, Italian, Hebrew, or English, and where did these people learn all the words? And is there a language they do not know? for they sing along unapologetically and with feeling. They laugh at a raucous comic spiel, and dance waltzes, Israeli circle dances, Russian dances, two-step, disco. I dance with my children, and dance with my father-in-law.

Until one in the morning they dance, long after we, the visiting children, tired out by our frantic middle-aged lives, have rolled into embroidered bungalow beds.

Miriam's place, Green Gardens, recalls the region's Jewish heyday, already past peak in the 1950s as these folks got back on their shaky but determined feet. It is New York, with its sense of escape from the oppressive heat of immigrant urbana. It conjures the *kokh-aleyns,* the housekeeping cottages of Rockaway Beach, that my father knew as a Brooklyn child. It reverberates with the spirit of the grand resort hotels. It is a last hurrah for all of that, in the Jewish style at least—for the Catskills are still to be discovered by newer groups of immigrant strivers, Korean, Jamaican, Chinese, Dominican. They, the new *greeneh,* will find that the real estate is cheap and plentiful, the air is fresh and the children can run, and that a bungalow colony can be imagined any of a thousand perfect ways.

Miriam's bungalow colony is socialist, private, foreign, American, New York, past, and present. It is work and vacation, reality and idyll. It is the apotheosis of valuable Jewish things in my past as I knew them. It is an oasis out of time. All my roads have led here. But I am only a facilitator after all. This place belongs not to me—who gets cranky sharing two rooms and a bath with six other people and sitting down to eat on schedule—but to the grandparents, and the grandchildren too.

By the time she was three, my daughter was staying here for stretches of time on her own. She swung in the hammock and watered the flowers. She went to town with her grandparents to shop, for a frilly dress, a little toy, a book of puzzles. She went to the beauty parlor with her grandmother and had her nails painted red. She went to the card room. She dressed up for the parties. There was no bedtime. Mornings, she slept in, watched cartoons, had chocolate milk for breakfast.

"It's not a wholesome environment," I complained once to my husband. He laughed.

"Give her a bath and wash her hair tonight," I told Miriam by phone during one of these visits. Later I learned my daughter had stormed out of doors, leaving an angry note: "I COME TO BUGLO TO BE FREE." The E's faced backward, as in my own printing at six years of age, when I also longed for freedom.

I close my eyes and I see: that six-year-old girl on the screened front porch, making *kreplekh,* filled dumplings, with her grandmother. Miriam showing her how to place a glass, precisely so, on a rolled-out sheet of noodle dough. Lifting the round with a butter knife, placing on it a bit of sweetened farmer cheese or blueberries. Folding the circle in half, pinching the edges together, effecting a succulent dairy won ton. She, the girl, totally absorbed, eager to be good at it. Learning a small bit of lore. So it shouldn't be lost. Blueberry *kreplekh.*

Once when I was a new bride we sat on the porch of the bungalow talking into Friday night, as the Sabbath candles flickered and fireflies danced outside. Miriam spoke of Poland, and childhood. Her village, hard by the town of Radom, was shadowed by forest. She and her mother used to go to the woods in May to pick mushrooms. There were so many kinds of mushrooms, she told me. One kind for drying, for soups, another for cooking fresh—the best mushrooms in the world came from her forest in Poland.

Especially one kind she remembered, that she had not seen since the old days: a little yellow mushroom, like a chicken's foot, a mushroom called a *kushinushki,* a Polish name. She rhapsodized over those yellow mushrooms.

"My mother used to cook them with sour cream, to eat with potatoes. You never tasted something like this."

Back home that week, I recalled the discussion. At a fancy Manhattan produce boutique I rooted. There, in the tempting fungal array, was a bin of precious chanterelles. They fit the description, yellow, small, shaped like a little chicken's foot, plump and eager. I would bring a bag to the bungalow, I decided, although I could never tell Miriam how much they cost. She had never even seen them in her America: they were not to be had in the Northeast Bronx.

But week after week, rolling into months, there was no intersection between market visits and trips to the Green Gardens colony. As I rushed out of town on a Friday, a billion things to remember pushed any thought of mushroom from my mind. If I went to the market, it meant we were staying in town the weekend. At the market I remembered. Making my country lists, I forgot.

That summer went by, and the next, and the next. In between, Miriam cooked mushrooms from supermarket tins, cooked dried mushrooms from plastic wrappings. Many a fall, winter, and spring went by with mushrooms. Miriam sautéed mushrooms with onions and chopped them finely into hard-cooked eggs and mayonnaise and dill to spread on fresh breads and rolls. With drippings and garlic and a bit of flour, her stewed mushrooms swam in a luxurious gravy over veal meat balls.

Darkly crisped mushrooms and slivered onions festooned her *farfel,* a kind of steamed and fried pasta used as a side dish. In winter, when Sabbath comes early, we sometimes sat down on a Friday eve to Miriam's slow-roasted *dekl,* a cut of beef softer than brisket, that in Miriam's kitchen is baked under a mellifluous crust of sliced mushrooms, oil, garlic, parsley, pepper, paprika. And served on a silver-rimmed meat dish beside a heap of kasha *varnishkes*—buckwheat groats with bowtie noodles.

"These mushrooms are nothing," Miriam would say from time to time, as we swooned, "compared to the little yellow mushrooms we used to get in Poland." She would pause, alone in the memory. "Little yellow mushrooms, like a chicken's foot."

The comment would prick my complacency, reignite my resolve. *Chanterelles.*

One summer Friday at last I remembered. The luggage for the country was already packed, and I was leaving work early with time to spare. I stopped at the market and filled a bag with tender yellow gleanings, a plastic bag, wondering idly if paper wouldn't be better, but they were out of paper bags, then I forgot about it. Forgot, walking home twenty blocks in humid summer heat; forgot, packing the car, forgot while driving, and

in a traffic jam, and stopping to change diapers and fill the gas tank, and—
I squirm to recall—parking under hot summer heat in an asphalt parking
lot while I explored a newly opened factory outlet mall on the way to
Green Gardens.

Unpacking, I remembered. There they were in their plastic bag. I set
them on the table.

"What is this?" asked Miriam, holding up the warm, damp bag.

"Yellow mushrooms—but I think—"

"These are *kushinushki!*"

"Are they?"

"Where ever did you find them?" Miriam bundled them into the
refrigerator, behind something, under something.

"*Ema,* I don't know if they are good."

"They are good!" assured Miriam.

Just then a baby called, a child needed me. I meant to get back to the
mushrooms, those perishable fungi, but I always have too much on my
mind. We left early on the Sunday . . . and it was the end of the week
before we spoke.

"Those mushrooms—" Miriam began.

"Oh, no."

"They aren't the *kushinushki.*"

"No?"

"We went and bought all the things for the mushrooms—sour cream,
potatoes," recounted Miriam.

"You didn't—eat them?"

"I prepared them for the *Abba.* They looked the same, but they didn't
taste good. They were terrible. Nothing like *kushinushki.*"

I might have killed my husband's parents. Thank God, thank luck,
thank evolution and genetics, that I did not.

Such are the dangers of careless daughters-in-law, and the perils, perhaps? of trying to go home again, as I vicariously was.

Once I suggested barbecue. Some of the bungalows do it, cooking up
minute steaks without soiling or heating their always immaculate kitchens,
fixed up more in the manner of miniature subdivision homes than 1940s-
vintage Catskill bungalows.

"Probably they learned from their children," remarked Miriam, with neither curiosity nor envy in her voice as she watched smoke rise from a charcoal burner a few doors down. Miriam, who could not afford a bungalow makeover, unknowingly made a virtue of preservation. Her bungalow is authentically beautiful. The walls are pine paneled, and she keeps them polished and clean. Accordion folding doors separate the two rooms. The children lay their hot faces on the cool linoleum floor. Mothballs scent the closet, vinyl valises are stowed under the white and gold bedroom furniture, hidden by dust ruffles of eyelet and voile. There is a big white freestanding stove in the pink-and-aqua tiled kitchen, and a plaid sleep-sofa hospitably placed along the far wall, under a sunburst-shaped electric clock ticking summer moments.

We eat our meals on an old metal table on the breezy screened porch, and our meals are the mythical food of vanished Polish summers.

When I said barbecue, my husband looked at his mother with mock interest, his eyebrows up, and mouth turned down, as if to say: "Why not try it, *Ema?*" They exchanged that merry, sour, mutual expression, mother and son.

"It's too dirty," I accused, and Miriam did not deny.

It was also wrong, I see now, the wrong aesthetic, to cook at the last minute over a hot fire, or worse, to see her husband standing on his feet in an apron tending black lumps of meat with a *groyser gopl,* a big fork, breathing carbonized fat.

So at other summer places, such as on my own patio back home, let hot dogs broil for dinner, among the mosquitoes. At Miriam's we snug around the porch table at dusk as a faint breeze rises, flowered plates on our vinyl placemats. Miriam serves a pickled corned beef, simmered all day with pepper, garlic, cloves, bay leaf. She serves Israeli potato salad, made with cucumber pickles and onions and peas. We swallow stewed plums and cherries, chocolate marble cake, and a comforting cup of tea.

In the bungalow I am crowded, and I grow irritable. This is the bungalow: a porch, a front room that includes the kitchen, a bedroom with two double beds, a bathroom. When I come with the children and their belongings and my husband, we have seven people in this space, though it doesn't look it. Miriam knows how to manage. She squirrels away everything, finding places where there are no places, so that the surfaces may appear clean, as they were. Still, rainy days are tough.

I'm on a short fuse here, and this makes me feel guilty. I think about the small cramped spaces occupied with dignity by Miriam early in her life. So she had to live, with others, several families sharing a room or two during the war.

After the war, there were transitional apartments in Germany and Israel, and later the immigrant digs in New York, always kept tidy and gleaming with a sense of worthy pride that no external darkness could extinguish in Miriam. And here I am complaining. I wish to arrive and spread out, be messy and relaxed. I'm an American, spoiled and despoiling. Despite myself I am the product of a frontier heritage and prosperous times.

"You shouldn't know from it," says Miriam, "how much a person can take."

It took me too long with the yellow mushrooms.

I finally got to the country this year with chanterelles in a cool paper bag.

"We will cook them," said Miriam.

She chopped onions and dried them with pepper over a high flame and added oil and fried the onions golden. She cleaned the mushrooms and added them whole to the hot oil and softened the mushrooms and tossed in a pat of butter too—"for the smell." With a fork, she whipped up a whole pint of real sour cream, and she mixed it into the pot with a pinch of salt, a dash of paprika.

Miriam peeled Idaho potatoes, cut them into chunks and boiled them soft and dry. She dressed those steaming potatoes in that sour cream and chanterelle sauce. She had fish too, baked salmon; she had summer squash cooked with peppers and tomatoes; she had buttermilk for drinking. The hot, dry potato flesh absorbed the creamy sauce, and the mushrooms—

I looked out through the porch screen, pleasant and pleasured, removed from the clang and rush of the great world. Something basic and simple and splendidly civilized here. A respite if I want it. A gift. I made resolutions to try to be better.

You never tasted something like this.

"Are these the *kushinushki*?" I asked Miriam.

She paused.

"I think it's the same ones," said Miriam. "I don't remember."

I was stunned, shocked. Three dangerous words for Miriam, who is—

suddenly I see—more tired than I have ever seen her. Then I noticed the garden, beneath the porch, for the first year barely abloom. It was always the prettiest.

Every year, clematis vines twined up strings, petunias wagged their bonnets, dahlias pushed forth from bulbs. Every spring, right after Passover, Miriam starts her seeds in egg cartons under the sunny Bronx kitchen window—seeds saved from last year's garden. She plants the seedlings Memorial weekend; by July, the bungalow is dressed in daisies and marigolds and asters and zinnias and mums and impatiens and black-eyed Susans. Nothing fancy, always beautiful, planned and tidy and reliable, the result of invisible effort, always eager to give delight. The kind of flowers she would have.

She barely gardened this year, Miriam. The flowers are sparse. Miriam is growing old.

In my life, I have said things, and done things, that I regret.

POTATO PUDDING

*W*hen your child marries a non-Jew, it is as if that child is dead. You forbid your child to see you again. You gnash teeth and wail, and you say *kaddish,* the mourner's prayer.

Such is the anguish and fear with which intermarriage has been regarded by a besieged and defensive people.

When Aunt Selina, my father's sister, married Uncle Charles, whose forebears were every sort of Christian, Selina was banned from Brooklyn. She had been the adored eldest, the beautiful, the smart, the mother's mainstay, the father's pride. But rules are rules.

Rules are rules, but human beings are another kettle of fish.

"We fought, and we lost," said my grandmother to her husband. "Let's not lose her, too."

My grandparents agreed to meet Charles. It was Passover, and my grandmother invited. Selina and Charles came to Brooklyn for a Seder, the ritual Passover dinner. Charles shook the hand of his father-in-law. He shook the hand of his mother-in-law. He said something gracious. His manners, as always, were perfect. He sat down to his first Passover Seder.

Candles were lit. Blessings were recited. The story of Passover was told in fast Hebrew. Charles read the story to himself in English, turning pages in the Haggadah from right to left. Charles was interested. Hands were washed, blessings were said. The festive meal was served.

"Do you remember Grandma's potato kugel?" Selina asks me, pouring tea into our cups. "For Passover, she made a potato pudding, and it was gorgeous."

Selina has never been able to copy this pudding, quite, this savory, elusive combination of grated potatoes, matzo meal, seasonings, oil, and egg. My grandmother poured the heavy batter into a large glass pan for baking. She cut the hot pudding into squares—substantial, crisp at the edges, sticky within, gray in color—and arranged the squares on a gold-rimmed Passover plate.

• • •

"Will you have a piece of potato kugel?" my grandmother asked Charles.

"Oh, yes, thank you," replied Charles.

My grandmother watched him eat it. This was not mashed potatoes and gravy. This was no soufflé. This was a discovery, a moment. In which Uncle Charles the Good came face to face with the essence of his quest.

Uncle Charles praised the kugel.

"Have another piece," said my grandmother

"Thank you," said Charles. My grandmother, hands in her lap, her face expressionless, watched him eat a large second piece of potato kugel.

"This is superb," said Charles. It was superb. I do remember the potato pudding. It melted in the mouth, a foretaste of the world to come, and it sank in the belly, dead weight.

"Do have more," my grandmother said.

The family sat around the mahogany table, silent, expectant, tense. Already, Charles had been served a dish of fruit salad, a whole hard-cooked egg floating in salt water, a crisp board of matzo, chicken soup with many matzo balls, gefilte fish and horseradish, chopped liver, and three glasses of wine. On his plate at the present time was a large joint of roasted chicken and a slice of pickle.

"I don't know if you remember," Aunt Selina says to me, taking my measure from the corner of her eye as she sips her tea. I sip mine. "My mother could be—devilish."

"Well, I—" said Uncle Charles, at the Seder table. He, Ivy-educated, Brooks Brothers attired, high-minded, landed, and correct, would be a model son-in-law. Inhaling deeply, Charles took a third piece of potato pudding onto his plate, and thence into his body.

I do remember my grandmother. I can almost hear her laughter, perhaps the very laughter she suppressed that judicial evening fifty years ago, behind her impassive face.

"There's a little bit of savage in everybody," my grandmother used to say.

• • •

"Charles must have eaten five pieces of potato pudding that night," says Aunt Selina. She sets down her teacup carefully, for her hand has begun to shake.

"They were friends after that—good friends," gasps Aunt Selina. I set down my cup with a dangerous *ping* and mop my eyes with a napkin. "But it almost—killed him."

Thus tried, found guilty, punished, and raised up was Charles MacIntyre. I must ask Selina if he, nearly sacrificed on an altar of love, ever ate potato pudding again.

SITTING *SHIVA*

I don't remember the funeral, but I was there. I was thirteen, and I watched as my mother's mother, the *bubbe,* was buried. Buried: the box that held her body was set in a hollow dug for that box, and her remains covered with earth. We never said "laid to rest," or resignedly, "It was her time." My mother was angry, she felt cheated, and the hole torn in her heart so many years ago still is a fragile mend.

In the spring of 1969, my mother ran for the northbound train. In Toronto, beside the sudden hospital bed, my mother cradled her mother's hand, powerless, trying to will a failing heart to hold the gentle spirit. My mother felt the final breath. With fear and panic she saw the beautiful skin of her mother's face settle, saw the perfect straight nose grow sharp as life's bloom fell away, an image that haunted my mother's bad dreams for a year.

The weeping phone call we dreaded came into our ringing night, and everything took its course: our hasty packing without Mother to tell us how, the key-turning, the hurtling drive from Detroit into space with my father at the wheel and children bracing themselves at highway speeds in a time before seat belts.

I don't remember the funeral, but another memory appears: another Toronto funeral, three years before. Then, the *bubbe* was burying a son. She strained toward my uncle's open grave, trying to throw herself in. Her other sons held her back.

We shivered in the cemetery. Our unhappy group huddled in the shadow of our little matriarch and her shrieking passion. I dug my nails in my palm and moved close to my sister, my father. I was hearing something ancient and deep and huge, and I was scared.

I looked at my sister. Our faces were wet. From his height, my father's face struggled. This raw Jewish emotion alarmed him. On the frozen cemetery soil, we seemed to be standing a distance away, we the Americans. My Canadian cousins drew close to our *bubbe,* familiar. It was her kisses, her cooking, the perfume of her braided hair, that kept their essential clay pliant and moist. We saw her but rarely, knew her less than we wished.

Suddenly the small hands of our *bubbe* rose. Her crooked fingers grasped the collar of her blouse, on the right side, as was proper, having lost her child. Weeping, moaning, with the shocked strength of grief, she tore her garment, ripped the woven cloth. As mourners rent their clothes in Bible times.

The ripping cloth stays with me, an image that serves the *bubbe* as well as her son. Did anyone tear their clothes for her? I do not know. Perhaps such ripping would have helped our healing. We wept, I know. We are a weeping people. In the funeral home, in a little room off the main chapel, and in the cars that followed the hearse to the burial ground, the family wept together. We wept, during the ancient graveside prayers, and as the casket with its unthinkable contents was set in the ground.

The casket was lowered, beside the husband and near the son, near the father who had deserted his daughter, our *bubbe,* near the stepmother who had resented her, whose hostility had pushed her into marriage too young—a genealogy of heartache. Then there was the bleak and hopeless trip from the graveyard to the home of my youngest aunt.

Here in my aunt's house, the survivors would "sit *shiva*." *Shiva,* from seven in Hebrew, names the week's span of hardest mourning, after the washed, shrouded body is placed in the silent earth. The week is commuted for feast days and fast days, and suspended for Sabbath. The bereaved mourn hard and sad, but they mourn according to rule and rite—minutely detailed, immortal, and fixed—not as they might choose to mourn, or ever might devise.

For the *bubbe's* religion envelops death, as well as life. There are instructions and warnings, some in the Torah, some codified by generations of teachers, and some, the most mysterious, passed from one *bubbe* to another. I ask you, where is it written that there must be a dish of hard-boiled eggs on the table when the mourners, stricken and stunned, return home from the burial ground? Yet so it should be, and so it is.

With her scourings and scrubbings and separations, her whisperings and prayers, her hiding things away and bringing others forth, her penny-filled *pushke,* the charity box for orphans and paupers, with her modesty and humility, her visits to the sick—the *bubbe* hallowed the everyday, according to her tradition. Likewise the tradition makes manageable that which is tragic or sublime. There are rituals around death, requirements incumbent on those who have lost their closest ones. There are responsibilities to the mourners as well, debts of duty and honor the community must pay.

When our *bubbe* died, the world reeled with shock and fresh grief, but someone made calls, someone made arrangements. You are not allowed to mourn in that moment of loss, but only to prepare. The body is washed. Burial must be quick, and dust returned to dust.

There is a funeral service, and ancient prayer at the grave. "Man is like a breath, His days are as a fleeting shadow . . ." As the body is set in the ground, mourners tear their garments. This our *bubbe* knew, in a way that is beyond knowing: so ingrained was the tradition, it had become, for her, pure expression.

In these days of restraint, funeral homes will give you a bit of black grosgrain ribbon, a notch snipped symbolically away, to pin on your lapel. Probably my mother wore one of these after her mother died. Our fears of death, our sadness and guilt and cosmic anger are unabated, but we have lost the chatharsis of shrieking and ripping, that paradoxical means by which one may begin to again grow whole.

Until the burial, say the rabbis, no one may comfort the bereaved. Those who have lost close ones may not mourn or pray, lest they curse God. But after the cemetery, and for a span of seven days, the family will sit together, surrounded by the balm of human comfort. And you have to accept that balm, whether you want it or not, because it is good for you.

During *shiva,* the mourners—sons and daughters, brothers and sisters, wife or husband, or, God forbid, the parents—eschew vanity and luxury. My aunt's mirrors were covered, cushions were removed from her chairs. Sex was banned, though I didn't know it then. My uncle's beards went unshaved. Meanwhile, people came, the second cousins, the friends, the neighbors. They wrung out their salty handkerchiefs and did what had to be done.

By the front door, after the cemetery, someone would have placed a basin and pitcher and towel for ritual handwashing, before entering the house. Inside, the table would have been laid for a meal by women, who came straight here from the service at the funeral home, letting their men drive to the cemetery and witness the emotional farewell. The women would have boiled the eggs and peeled and rinsed them, found tablecloths and dishes and cups and knives tucked in unfamiliar cupboards, and set out food they had prepared.

The bereaved, though sick at heart, should bless the food and eat. At sundown, there must be a *minyan,* the traditional ten-man quorum, to recite prayers and say *kaddish,* the mourner's prayer.

And then there is more food, and tomorrow the same thing, morning and evening the *minyan,* the *kaddish,* a meal. On the fourth day, mourners must join the *minyan,* the formal expression of community. They must begin to return to life.

People come. The family must not be alone, even if it prefers solitude. There will be visitors, a stream of murmuring, kissing, weeping relatives, friends, and neighbors, colleagues, members of the synagogue. They will bring gifts of food and drink, serve the mourners with heaping plates, and, naturally, help themselves. Trays will arrive from the delicatessen, bags of bagels and rye breads. Baskets of fruit will be set out, boxes of chocolates opened, cakes sliced and arranged. The women will be busy, clearing, setting, washing, wrapping and unwrapping, making coffee, making tea.

I have never yet been to a *shiva* where women were counted in the *minyan.* I am unlearned; were I counted, I would not know what to do. In other settings, this worries and offends me, but not in this one. *Shiva,* for me, still is about that old-time female web, the embroidery with which women build and embellish.

The pattern was set for me at my first remembered *shiva,* in the old-fashioned style familiar to the *bubbe,* in whose honor it was held. My impulse, on a *shiva* call, is to draw close, hold a lonely hand, fix a chopped liver sandwich for a grieving friend, that is all. Still, I hope that a *minyan* will gather when I die, and that it will have women in it.

I have wondered at times if the rites, being standardized, are in some sense to be regretted. The *bubbe's* tradition is fixed, impersonal. Original feeling is compromised. The mourner may not roam the beach all week, let's say, scattering the dead one's ashes, or sail off alone for distant seas. One must confront death in this particular way, among these people, even if you don't like them. Others must try to comfort you, with their presence, their words, their food, though they don't understand, can't understand, all that you feel or don't feel. You must accept this comfort for seven days.

Seven days of waking to the reality of your close one gone from the earth. Seven mornings of brushing your teeth and putting on clothes, though you don't feel like getting out of bed and you couldn't care less. The doorbell rings early, and well-meaning arrive, to ask how you are, to bustle about, to gather for prayer, to press on you a bagel *mit* lox and a cup of coffee, to ask you how to work your toaster and where you keep the clean hand towels. You crouch on the cardboard box you are using as a mourner's chair, with your paper plate in your lap and a big slice of raw onion on the lox, and you don't like onion for breakfast. They are right there with you, pulling over a chair and reminiscing about the dead.

Seven days of sitting *shiva,* with a break for the Sabbath. Seven nights, except Friday night, for a *minyan* to gather and pray and join you for a meal and a glass of wine and a piece of pastry and sit up with you until you are ready to fall into bed. You are never alone.

Yet every day is different; the week evolves. Midweek, you find yourself smiling at something, forgetting yourself. You pull out a photo album. It hurts every time you think, but still, there was that day, that pleasure, still yours to recall. There is an emptiness here, but the doorbell is ringing again. The day comes when you think, "Please, let there be no more cinnamon coffee cake!"—thus you know you are going to live.

The formula offers a way to experience personal sorrow, and return to the fold. It acknowledges pain and need, and stabilizes the community over time. How might we mourn without *kaddish*? Perhaps there would be more creative responses, more Jewish poetry or music—but then, it wouldn't be Jewish. There may be something to miss, some high or some low, some soaring creative upswing, but then, some free fall of despair. If I lose my footing, I have the woven web of centuries, with all its compromises, even banalities, to fall into. I admit, this is comfort of some kind.

Intense mourning for parents is in the culture, as is the ripping cloth. Our *bubbe,* mother of six, left four sons and daughters to mourn her. One son was dead, one daughter away in a rest home, unaware of change and time. The four sat *shiva* in my aunt's house. The house was small and cramped, packed with things there was never time to sort through, things too good to throw away. This had been the *bubbe's* second home. My aunt was a widow, poor and young; her mother had been there for her, to cook and keep house and soothe three children when my aunt went off to work.

The visitors crowded in, remembering the *bubbe's* cheerful, generous nature, her kind, loving heart. We, her grandchildren, were too green at death to know what we would miss: her great soft hug and her big bosom and her long black braid with just one streak of white and the quick ways of doing and slow ways of moving and her patient warm hands, and her smell like fresh bread, and her yeasty accent, the *colt slaw* she made, the *kitchen floyer* she walked on, the way she understood that children are always hungry and that satisfying such hunger, among all human imperatives, always comes first.

We were sad and fearful and confused at her death. We were excited at this family reunion and commotion. We were dangerous as bare electric wires. We cousins prowled the kitchen for bananas and cookies and sweet carbonated sodas we never usually got to drink. We sat daintily at table and were served by ladies with voices and hairdos and aprons and lipsticks and flowery B.O. As days went on we giggled at names and made jokes and at last shrieked with manic laughter at the peach pie one er brought.

My cousin Yvonne started it. She was out to get her mother's suitor: Of course Yvonne's spirited mother had a boyfriend—she, the young widow, oval of face, with her eye shadow, long legs, and ebony hair—and of course the eldest daughter, on the brink of puberty, would detest him. He was a marked man, and it was he who had brought the offending pie, straight from the supermarket in a gray box with the price still on it.

"Peach pie! Peach pie! Loblaw's peach pie! Just like homemade! A dollar twenty-nine! Peach pie!" exclaimed the cruel Yvonne.

I knew it was wrong but I had to laugh.

We flew upstairs to the cousins' rooms. We crashed through furniture, bounced on beds, overturned baskets of wash. The civilized veneer crumbled, the tension snapped, the dam broke. A rumble began: The boy cousin with no father taunted my brother. My brother, oblivious, at nine, to psychodynamics, put up his dukes. There was punching and yelling. Eight or nine cousins full of cola drinks, cookies, and sweets, in two small rooms under sloping eaves, bereft of their *bubbe* and her unconditional love: explosive.

Then there was my father, angry at the door, blaming me and not the fatherless lot who lived here.

"You," he smoldered. "You're not even sorry your *bubbe* died."

I was the oldest girl and should have known better. I was thirteen, a great age, and I had let my father down.

Seven days of *shiva,* and three weeks more of standing apart in mourning: no parties or haircuts, and then you join the living. Except for those who mourn parents. They mourn for eleven months; during this time, observant mourners recite *kaddish* daily in synagogue, and avoid music and celebration.

In all of life to come, a person must remember the parents, lighting a memorial candle on the anniversary of their deaths, the *yahrzeit,* and at other special times throughout the year. The *yahrzeit* candle is lit at sundown, when the new Jewish day begins, and it is made to burn for twenty-four hours. Sometimes, it flickers longer still, jogging memories of the life and stirring up the embers of pain from a time when that pain was fresh.

My parents have chosen to make their own way in the world. They live and let live, from one Yom Kippur to the next. But death is a different matter. When I visit them, there it is, right over the coffee pot, taped to the kitchen wall: a memo page with *yahrzeit* notations, initials and dates in my father's hand. In this fragment of some perpetual calendar, the number of candles grows with time. For my parents now light for their parents, but also for those in their families whose parents and children no longer observe.

Our *bubbe's shiva* ended with Friday night. Someone sent over a *Shabbas* dinner, and the family gathered in. The table was opened to its full size, spread with a cloth, and set. Grownups and children squeezed up to the board, straddling table legs and sharing chairs. The visitors were gone.

It was a good hot dinner, after the days of sandwiches, cold cuts, and salted fish. We spooned it out. There was roast meat, roast chicken, potato pudding, *kishke*—the stuffed cow's innards that made savory virtue of *shtetl* necessity.

From what or whence our appetite, I don't know, but we were hungry, and everyone ate. There was that eating silence. Then an uncle spoke.

"This is a meal that Mother would have enjoyed," he said.

There were nodding heads and glistening eyes, and a pause of remembering, before the dinner resumed. But the pause, and the words, and the grammar itself had done it for me. Would have enjoyed, and never would again. I got it then. Good-bye, dear one, *bubbe,* good-bye.

August

WORDS AND DEEDS

August

It is nice to live in a world of bright diversity, with many forms and colors from which to choose in designing a life. It is enjoyable to select from among the manifestations of many traditions: Chinese New Year tonight, gospel music tomorrow, a Passover Seder. But the wellsprings must be authentic, or else it is just a museum. Someone, many someones, must keep the sources alive.

We want to pick and choose from the great shopping mall of expedient culture: a certain sandwich to feed a hungry nostalgia, particular communal values when we need them, ritual expertise at times of joy or stress. But when one decides, after all, to celebrate a son's bar mitzvah, *the synagogue and all the trappings must be there, maintained by a community. The old kosher bakery will close without regular shoppers. With no passionate discussants, the valued argumentative traditions of Jewish study will fade away into irrelevance.*

Without commitment, the sources will die. The forms we love to have the choice to return to will wither and disappear, or worse yet, become hollow shells, cultural theme parks. Someone, many someones, have kept the forms alive and vital, have kept the choices available to me. They may have been skeptical; they must have had moments when their preferences were elsewhere.

It is my turn now.

MOVING

*A*fternoon: our front-room windows, which glinted with light before breakfast, have pivoted halfway round the earth's axis. Now the late summer sun is somewhere back of the alley gate, and gray shadows wash the bare rooms of our home.

Detroit, moving day. We have spent this day doing the things one does—disconnecting, packaging. Naked mattresses lean against walls. Furniture legs, unscrewed and unbolted, are piled up like bones. Mirrors and pictures are wrapped flat, knotted with string. Shelves, brackets, and standards lie taped together, their screws and plaster anchors carefully bagged in plastic. The many cardboard cartons we carried away from the backs of liquor stores are stuffed, sealed, labeled. Our boxes and bags surround us. The gas and electric have been turned off. The movers should be here any time.

It does not look like our house. Our home was full of books and conversation and bowls of grapes and shoes reposing under chairs. Our books in their order, our particular stacks of mail, all our objects and uses hid the fact that is now stark and clear. This was a rented flat all along, the empty flat I first saw eighteen years ago as a small child. I remember a spongy carpet and distant ceilings, before the house became smaller, familiar.

Now, the home is gone. Pale rectangles on coffee-beige walls are a map, marking where pictures hung. White curtains, bleached and ironed, bleached and ironed over the years, no longer ruffle against windows. Windows, bare, seem severe and long, under slatted Venetian blinds my mother used to wash in the bathtub, soaking in bleach and suds. The carpet is worn hard as a floor.

Here we had our rhythms—music days, swimming days. We rattled home in the dark on the Hebrew school bus, and were received here. Here was our living room. The bookcase is empty, the one that held classics of fiction. We had books on the arts, histories of science, a yellowing text on chess moves we children refused to read. Once in a while on a winter night, my family would read together in the living room, a play of Ibsen or Shakespeare, taking all the players' parts. The books spilled, in time, into every room of the house.

We rarely ate in the dining room, even on Friday nights; that was for birthday parties and holiday meals. We dusted and polished the dining table, then used it for homework, projects, crayons, and chess. One cupboard was filled with art supplies, another with teacups and trays. An old upright piano stood in the corner. A crystal decanter refracted morning light into small trembling rainbows on the coffee-beige walls.

There in the dining room, my mother's mother, my *bubbe,* had wept to recall her mother's death. She was visiting. I was eleven, and had just yelled at my own mother.

Here was the kitchen. Here was our home. Here, we evolved a Sabbath rhythm, ours alone. On Fridays, we came home from school to the smell of cleanser and soup. At the living room mantel, my mother would cover her head, to light candles and recite prayers in English. She had never learned Hebrew. We, thrilled children and then hostile adolescents, witnessed this on a lonely island of echoed tradition.

On a Sabbath evening in summer, we might hear a radio through the open window, a rhythm and blues tune from the planet outside. In later years, we ignored the sounds of gunshot. I kept telling myself they were blown-out tires, the noises of careless cars.

Concentrating, I can still recall my neighbors of the first few years, all of whom were gone a decade later. There was a bakery nearby that sold *babka* and custard donuts, a market where the shopkeeper knew my mother's name. Then, suddenly, there was bulletproof glass and a muffled voice behind it, or there was nothing, just a cracked and emptied shell. How often I've dreamed that I am walking along Six Mile Road, trying to find missing stores that I thought were there.

Our lone house was dark on a street dressed in Christmas lights. Our windows were closed against Fourth of July barbecues wafting the fragrance of searing pork ribs. Waiting in a dwindling small clump for the Hebrew school bus, my brother and sister and I were harassed; walking home we were frightened targets, ashamed to tell our parents of our inability to cope. Once my brother Izzy, a seventh grader with an anachronistic name, was beaten to a pulp in a schoolyard by a gang of boys, while a teacher watched from the window, afraid to intervene.

Of course it was only the few, the angry or troubled kids, a roving stranger, but it was enough: We experienced the weird, dehumanizing, soul-corrupting definition of ourselves by race. We had been whatever we were, then we became honkies; we had a label, White People, not an identity, even among goodhearted folks, neighbors who trusted us.

Then one day our landlord, long gone to Palm Springs, sold our house. The new owners moved into the upstairs flat. Joyous with property, they ripped out the back hedge and planted a country garden of spinach and collard greens. But the bushes had been a lilac hedge, and when it bloomed purple and wildly perfumed every spring, blocking away the sight of garbage cans and roaming alley dogs, it was my mother's greatest solace.

For my mother, the new back view was decisive. She had been mugged, robbed, and taunted on her way home from work; had suffered the refusals to visit from friends and cousins. The rooms were cramped; in the winter, the house was cold. "I can't live here anymore," she said at last. And my father agreed, "It is time."

The new landlord was upset. "You just couldn't stand paying rent to a black man," he told our dad. He must have been crushed, the new owner, a decent, hardworking man—a long-standing tenant deserting. But it wasn't that at all, it wasn't that. . . .

So my sister and I, having just finished college, convened in Detroit, to sort, pack, and throw away, and to find a place for my parents to move.

All this strange summer we have said good-bye to our childhood. Days became weeks in the basement, sifting the years' gatherings one last time. The basement was full of keepings, forgettings, wishes and passing interests.

We went through the bags. We had often cleaned house with a fast, mad, "company's coming" sweep of out-of-place objects and papers into large shopping bags, and then moved the bags to the basement. After years of such housecleaning the basement was chockablock with the green, spotted-paper handle bags once given out at Detroit's big department store. There were no consistent efforts to sort through the contents after the straightening sprees. The bags, resembling large spotted frogs, became permanent features of a magical landscape of discovery. Chance sightings of forgotten belongings, basement reunions with favorite toys, and the sense that objects had lives that could not be entirely controlled by human beings, characterized my childhood.

In the basement we sorted and packed and tossed—and we looked and grew dreamy, reliving. There was our old record player, brought downstairs when stereo came in. There were children's records, and folk songs from my parents' union days, and *Oklahoma!* and also a rack of 78 rpm platters, which had belonged to the old bachelor who lived with his mother in the flat above ours, during the early years of our tenancy. The 78s had songs like "I Live under the Viaduct," and "Roll 'Em Girls, Roll 'Em"—a title, according to my mother, that referred to the silk stockings of a distant epoch, daringly rolled down below the kneecap on garters of quarter-inch white elastic.

There were our basement books. A great bookcase housed engineering textbooks, my father's high school readers, a huge stack of *Scientific American*, and forgotten treasures of the Progressive Book Club. Here you would find histories of imperialism, biographies of inspirational figures, political cartoons. My favorite was titled *Please Sir, I Need More Money*. Its cover depicted a proletarian wearing a barrel suspended from shoulder straps, beseeching a fat cigar-smoking capitalist in top hat, spats, and tails. This bookshelf also held a copy of *Fanny Hill*.

In the green shopping bags we found long-lost school permission slips, notebooks, and savings bonds. We read the books, and found a closet we had never known, filled with wondrous old clothes.

"What's going on?" asked my father, descending the stairs into our dim July day. He was dreaming at night that the basement held him fast, that he had to burn down the house to escape the family's collected unconscious. He hoped for the best from his two daughters, but he found us dressed up in our grandmothers' hats, listening to Paul Robeson sing "The Peat Bog Soldiers."

We packed away, sorted, and filed. We filled three boxes for my brother, who was away that summer. We were sad and excited, determined, unsure. We both, my sister and I, were on the brink of a new kind of life—she was off to medical school, and I, who had graduated college a year late, was going to try my wings, or possibly coast to disaster.

We decided what would be thrown away, and what was worth taking.

At last we loaded a jumble of giveaways onto a Salvation Army truck. Some of our choices we would later regret. We would think of a lost object, and wonder. But we couldn't keep everything. In the end we had to burn it down to the ground.

For me, it was tinged with heartsick unfinished business. Sorting and sifting the accumulated material of our life, I have worked through little of my blind ambivalence. Living in this house on this street has been a point of both righteous pride and also angry resentment. I don't know if I belonged here or anywhere, and this was my only childhood.

Finding a place was so easy. We saw a townhouse to rent just beyond the city limits, and my parents signed the lease.

It grows dusky and the lights cannot be turned on.

"Am I really moving?" says my mother.

We look at one another in dawning shock. The movers have not shown up. My mother has insisted on hiring the mover who brought our belongings here eighteen years ago, for closure and luck. We thought we had an appointment, but he has not come.

Tomorrow is Sunday, then Labor Day comes after that. The stores are closed, our refrigerator is empty, our sheets are packed. We are abandoned, forgotten, in our communities old and new. *Der mentsh trakht, un Gott lakht;* "Man plans, God laughs," in my *bubbe*'s proverb. The universe is laughing at us.

Then the doorbell rings, and it is Beverly from down the block, with a foil-wrapped platter.

"Ma sent this," she says proudly.

Ma is Beverly's grandmother, Mrs. Henderson to us. She owns the yellow brick two-family house a few doors down, where she has raised Beverly and her siblings these last ten years or so. The oldest son, married and separated, lives in the upstairs flat, and Mrs. Henderson also looks out for his two little boys. Beverly calls her own plump, childlike mother, who goes to work in a uniform, by her given name, Alpha. There is no resemblance. Beverly, wiry and alert, a sharp student with an open smile, favors her grandmother.

"There's more in the kitchen," Beverly reports.

"Go help," says my father. At the door he reminds us: "Thank the grandmother."

My sister and I go. Cheryl was in Beverly's class, and as kids we played together on the street. But I had never been in the house while the Hendersons lived there. Before, it belonged to the Rubins, old people with numbers stamped on their arms, a grandchild in California, and a sewing machine in the back room. Their house was dark and familiar, with a comfortable smell of furniture wax and boiled onions.

Now I enter the front hallway of this house, into the kitchen. Mrs. Henderson, wearing a grandmother's apron, is covering dishes with foil. "I thought you folks would be starving . . ."

There is a pot roast, and string beans, and mashed potatoes, peach cobbler, and iced tea. ". . . Probably nothing to eat at home . . . Moving day is like that . . ."

Moving soft on slippers like my grandmother used to, she stacks dishes and cups on a tray. She and my father are fond of one another. Over the years, she has sought his advice on schooling and summer jobs for her grandchildren. My father, home from work for long stretches, has been a presence on the block. He taught the Henderson boys to clear autumn leaves away from the sewers and how to change spark plugs.

My father, I suspect, has enjoyed the small layered world of our block. Possibly our being there was no accidental overstay at all. Perhaps the ambitious and sometimes troubled black community we came to live in reprised for my father the dynamic of his own old Brooklyn neighborhood of immigrant Italians and Jews. Among Detroit Jews by the 1960s and '70s, he would not have found neighbors out on their front porches of a summer evening, or growing tomatoes by the back fence, or living the kind of complex family lives that he thrived on parsing, analyzing, watching. Here he found the strong female figures that had organized his own extended family, as well as the old elemental drama as neighbors' children grew up to choose school, factory, or street.

Being around the house as much as he has been, he kept an eye on things—he knew who was working two jobs, who was in trouble with the law, who had a drinking problem. Alpha Henderson, good-natured and slightly addled, went about telling the neighbors that my father was a cop, her way of trying to reduce the numbers of break-ins on the street. When this long-standing fib came to light, as we were packing to leave, it embarrassed my father, and I was distressed, to see us unknown, misjudged.

We take home the grandmother's dinner. We peel back the foil wrappings, eagerly dish out food on the Hendersons' plates. The steam rises, carrying a smell of—what? The smell of *treyf*—unkosher—meat cooked without onions and garlic, meat gravy congealing with beans dressed in butter, the cloying sweetness of peach cobbler. My throat closes up, I want to gag.

I hate myself for this. For years I have been cultivating resistance to Jewish reflexes. I have laughed at my mother's residual kosher scruples, her sentimental candles, her wish for me to date Jewish lads. I have eaten White Castle hamburgers, even, greasy gray "sliders" wrapped in a damp, pale bun. I have cracked a lobster's shell and sucked sweet innards from its many little legs.

But perhaps the last taboo is food at home, home-cooked food, in this room—the last reference point, my mother's *ayngedemft fleysh,* pot-roasted brisket, butchered according to law, simmered with bay and prune, served on plates whose history may have been impure, but whose history we knew. Or maybe this unbidden nausea, which I cannot justify and of which I am ashamed, in fact is a severe summation: We have lived here, and defended our staying, but we do not belong. Here or anywhere.

We sit in the growing darkness, a last darkness here that was not supposed to be. No one speaks. My sister is trying to catch my eye, but I, the family trailblazer, refuse to admit to her my failure, the deep and basic conventionality my soul is revealing to itself over Mrs. Henderson's so well-intentioned dinner.

Breaking the stiff silence, my father says, gently, "This is good food." And it is, it is. It is clean, nutritious, and prepared with more kindness and humanity than any meal ever was. It fulfills all that God commands a person to do. I don't want the burden of a Jewish palate, if this drives a wedge between Beverly's grandmother and me.

WHY THERE IS NO RECIPE FOR AUNT DORA'S HONEY CAKE

*I*t was my sister who first asked for the recipe. She loved our father, and she loved to bake. Our father was fond of a honey cake made by his dear Aunt Dora who lived in the Bronx. When tasted, this cake could stop the passage of time.

My sister, Cheryl, wanted to bake this cake for our father. She thought of asking for the recipe, but she did not imagine calling on the telephone. Long distance telephone calls, in our family, still were formal occasions then, to be initiated by adults. Cheryl, who wore two long braids of dark hair and had a round, sincere face, waited to ask in person.

At last our family traveled from Detroit to New York. One day we drove across the boroughs to visit the small, overheated walk-up apartment where Great-aunt Dora lived among antimacassars, slipcovers, foil-lined tins, sweaters, aprons, and paper bags.

Aunt Dora drew us in, explaining the state of her three cozy rooms. Her grandson's boots stood by the front door. His jeans and shirts spilled out of a doily-topped dresser. His razor perched on the bathroom sink. Aunt Dora's grandson, who was studying law in the city, at night came here to eat nourishing dinners and sleep on the living room couch. We visiting children envied him.

The law student's grandmother had, as a young, motherless woman, transported her own mother's secrets of baking from the Old Country. She had baked for her father, a tailor named Moses, whose delicate bearded visage looked out of a brown photograph on the dresser. She had kept house as well for a brother and two younger sisters who also had made their way to New York from Europe in a hopeful, poor, tumultuous time.

Dora married a man who did not deserve her butter horns and lemon nut cookies, cut into crescent shapes and powdered with sugar. This man was a gambler, a card-player, abusive, and no good. Dora, a brave and desperate young woman, defying convention, divorced the husband.

She assessed her resource of domestic arts, and swept her young daughter up a narrow dark staircase in the rich new suburb of Forest Hills. The stairs led to an attic that was the housekeeper's room in the Tudor home of the fortunate family that hired Aunt Dora to polish its candlesticks, darn its clothes, and bake its strudel—strudel served, perhaps, on a silver tray with handles of ebony wood.

After some years, a kind and worthy widower married Dora, who had salvaged dignity from a rum-luck life. Now the dutiful work of keeping house was transposed to her own walk-up rooms. Now Aunt Dora lavished her flaky sweets on her closest own, and too, on an extended family that included her adored youngest sister who was a superb cook but not so much a baker.

Irene, the youngest sister, had fine chestnut hair. She was the youngest of many motherless sisters. Dora, the eldest sister in America, was the essential trusted friend. When both women acquired telephones, Dora and Irene spoke every day of their lives.

Irene's telephone roosted on a marble slab topping a rounded telephone stand wrought of curly iron and green plush velvet. There was a matching chair, high-backed and narrow. The telephone stand and chair adorned the front hall of the solid house in which Irene, our grandmother, lived. She wore gold earrings and promised them to my sister, Cheryl, who, like our grandmother, had pierced her ears.

Irene's household, in her young married years, included her husband's mother, a woman who hid apples in her dresser against famine and want. Periodically, she would exchange the hoarded fruit for fresh apples in the family ice box. My father, grown, would sometimes recall to us the particular taste of apples long stored amidst a grandmother's woolens and camphor balls, discovered only by an unwitting bite. Perhaps Irene mentioned such virtues to Dora in the daily telephone calls.

Aunt Dora had a special affection for my father, her nephew. He in his turn was a lifelong partisan of her baking, which forever evoked for him his childhood among immigrants who never doubted that there was an appropriate way to do, and that they knew it. The religion of persecution and wandering, of Sabbath and synagogue, of ambition and obligation, was for him baked into Aunt Dora's honey cake, mailed from the Bronx to Detroit in brown paper and taken in slivers with a whiskey schnapps of a Friday eve.

My sister, Cheryl, took note of the wistfulness in her father's eye as he savored the honey cake. She longed for inclusion in this emotion through the force of her love and the effort of her hands. When she was nine or ten years old, already as tall as Aunt Dora, she asked if she might have the recipe.

Aunt Dora turned her handsome, care-worn face to my sister, Cheryl, revealing the soul's secret depths in her wide, intelligent eyes.

"Why do you want it?" she asked her grandniece.

Aunt Dora asked, "Do you think I am going to die?"

DOUBT

*T*here is too much to know. What I know is after all infinitesimal.

How did I get so wrapped up? Every new tentative step seems to open another argumentative road. Every road leads toward something and away from something else. I don't see how I can travel this road without diligent commitment, thought, and time. But is the road capacious, or is it narrow and obscure? Will it lead, in time, to everything worthwhile? Or trap me, endlessly parsing the implications of this spoon, that jam, which bread?

Even to find out requires thought and study. I need to read and discuss and find authorities to guide me. I must learn an old language well. It is a lifelong process, and one never completes it. My Must Do list for life is becoming endless, impossible. I am not sure, still, about making the choices the list entails.

My ignorance is deep on so many other fronts. I don't know the battles of the Civil War, and I don't know organic chemistry. I cannot read Russian poetry in the original. I can't reel up the film in my camera without consulting the owner's manual. I would like to build a bird house with my children someday before they are grown, and steer a canoe down a deep green river. I never have gotten around to programming frequently used numbers into the automatic dialer of my telephone.

There is a limit to hours in the day, a finitude of days in life. You must spend the time to have an opinion, but how will I form opinions about how to spend the time?

Largely self-taught, I am at least a rather practiced synagogue-goer now: I know prayers and melodies, when to bend the knee, when to stand. I have learned or relearned enough Hebrew to more or less follow along, by attending the services and standing alongside those who know.

I focus on the Torah reading. Trying to get out of the house on Saturday morning with children, my goal is a ten o'clock arrival, approximately when the scrolls are taken from the Holy Ark and unfurled. First the Torah, or Bible, portion is read, and then the *Haftarah,* a selection from the Prophets chosen to complement the Torah reading. It is exciting, when the reading begins. I often feel a sense of possibility. Secrets of living and understanding may reveal themselves: Insights, meaning, a feeling of coherence and validity.

In contrast, I have to admit that I may be permanently blocked at prayer.

At least, insight and meaning are what I anticipate. Sometimes the reading is filled with numbing historical detail, and the explanatory footnotes seem off the point. Then I wonder if I should take the text simply as symbol that what has been should be remembered. Maybe, in fact, some sections are historical relics, pieced together with no literal meaning for our different time.

Maybe the world would be better off if I spent Saturday mornings cooking breakfast at a shelter for the homeless, or fishing plastic trash out of Long Island Sound.

I have progressed on the ladder, some. I don't skip around as much these days. I used to rewind and fast-forward, turning the pages in English, looking for juicy bits, as if skimming a mystery story. Now I try to stay with the reading. I try to hear the Hebrew, try to comprehend, try at least to augment the translation with Hebrew nuance and phrase. I glance at the footnotes, and look for the place again. I am a beginner, but a familiar one.

So I said to Jacob, my father-in-law, one summer Saturday, "What time is the Torah reading, *Abba*?" We were visiting my husband's parents at their Catskill bungalow. It was early morning. Jacob, at the screen door, scented with cologne, was handsome and trim in silk blazer, light shoes, gray tie, and white yarmulke.

"You want to come for the Torah reading?" says Jacob, as always surprised by the things I say. "Very good!"

At five minutes to ten I open the door of the little shul. I never have joined the services here before. I pause for a moment, a bit let down to realize that I will be sharing a hard narrow bench on the side with the sole other female present, the rabbi's wife. This is traditional style. Men sit with men, women with women, separate but not equal. At least, the quality of seating, the view of the Torah, are unequal. Perhaps the view to the cosmos is equal, but I'll tell you this: the women don't show up.

"You came just in the right time," says the *abba,* welcoming me with

an open prayerbook and a *Chumash,* a Bible. He points to a spot on a page.
I take the books and sit amidst the mumbling and reciting. There is no
coordinated unison. Each worshipper is off and away. No *Book of Common
Prayer* this. The mumbling, emotional *davening,* the garbled layers of high-
speed individual prayer, make for the characteristic remembered incantatory atmosphere, something we are losing as my generation takes to the
front lines. Our congregation at home, as the older men die, increasingly
prays in melodious togetherness, waiting politely to chime in for responsive
reading.

I want to believe that the sound of prayer is a thread spooled from the
dawn of moral monotheism. The thread seems so frayed at times it can
barely be recognized.

Make that, in my hands, a broken thread. No wonder the *Abba* was
startled this morning, when I asked him to fix a time for the opening of
the scrolls. He is kind, polite; never would he dream of dashing a fancy,
but—*oytser,* treasure, there isn't a fragment of English to be had, not on
this page or any other within these four stucco walls.

What did I expect. The little chapel is full of men born in Poland a
long time ago. This one plays tennis. Jacob retired from curtains and bed-
spreads. His neighbor trades stocks and bonds. One man was married
twice, one lives in Florida, summers excepted. One went bankrupt playing
cards. They all, every last one of them, learned to read Torah as children in
cheder, the old-fashioned European Hebrew schools. They learned what to
do in *shul* at their father's side. They were called up to the Torah for
the first time at thirteen years of age. Ever after, the *aliyah*—"going up" to
the Torah—was their privilege, but also their obligation.

They will read Torah now, not because it is their favorite part of the
service, but because Torah comes next in a chain of things that you do in
shul on Saturday morning. You read it in Hebrew, and that is that.

The Torah cycle, in weekly portions, completes and resumes every
year. An observant man born in 1906 like the *Abba* should have read these
phrases from right to left sixty-seven times. Take out the lost years, 1939
through 1945, and a scattered Saturday here or there, and you still have a
number of repetitions large in human terms. Imagine sixty readings of
Hamlet, and many a season of thought and study besides. No doubt you
could follow along, and find any passage you wish.

I, on the other hand, chose Torah at forty, chose Torah at ten a.m.
Ten minutes into it, I still have no idea whatsoever of the subject of this

week's portion. I cannot follow the fast-paced Hebrew, cannot keep the place. As for comprehension—nothing, without the English translation to fill the holes between here-and-there Hebrew words I actually know.

I take full responsibility. I am an adult. Yet, this is not entirely my fault. The boys in my youth at least had bar mitzvah, that first calling up to the Torah, to work toward, prepare for. I do not remember attending a single bat mitzvah, a female version of the boys' initiation, when I was a girl. The girls' bat mitzvah was still relatively new and rare. It had no known roots in tradition; my parents mistrusted it.

Even without a goal like the boys,' it is true that I might have paid attention in Hebrew school. However, none of this has seemed to have much to do with me for the greater part of my life. Not as an American child at midcentury, bicycling into an ecumenical future. Not as a teenager, embracing the radical leftism that appeared, more than anything else, to be my destined birthright. It had little to do with adulthood as I saw it, whereas I *have* reread Hamlet. So far, it seems, I am too much of a rationalist to lose myself in prayer. And as a woman, I have always had a problem with public ritual, the religion of the synagogue.

It has always been the religion of the home that compelled me, not that of the public sphere. My felt heritage was kitchen, and holiday, and attitude, the atmosphere that my grandmothers were able to protect and transmit, against odds, through time. You could have that heritage—practical and charitable, conscious, tasty, and even devout—and still live in the world. Whether husbands went to the synagogue or not, and what they did there, always seemed somewhat beside the point.

And so I am edgy, ambivalent with the public aspect of religious life, with public worship and institutional connection. I bounce between renunciation and the search for my place. Traditionally, men were obligated to play that public role, to make themselves available for prayer assembly and Torah reading at specific times of day and year. Women, with myriad nonlinear responsibilities, were exempted from time-bound rules. No one would expect a mother to show up for a *minyan,* the quorum for prayer, three days after childbirth. Faced with the choice between feeding your nursling and stepping up for your turn to read Torah, the ancient wisdom acknowledged only one possible outcome, and of course it was right.

But obligation came to mean exclusion. For some interpreters, if I am counted in the quorum, I have relieved a man of his obligation—perhaps the very man driving by the synagogue, on his way to the golf course, oblivious. I am not oblivious, and my children are growing up; my husband can attend to a child on Saturday morning as well as I. Thus, the rabbis have been rethinking all this. More and more congregations go egalitarian, with men and women sharing roles.

Meanwhile the old prayerful mumbling fades away—authentic music of the spheres. Must we lose one to have the other?

Having railed against exclusion, what do I really want? I don't know how to *daven*. I'm not sure if prayer matters, or if I want it to shape my life. The heavy, precious Torah scroll, raised high, is joyfully carried about the sanctuary for the people to kiss. If I kiss the Torah I feel like a fraud, and if I pull back I am stiff-necked, setting myself apart from something I know to be a source of resilience and comfort and righteous life.

My children are growing up, after all. My daughter is looking to me for the way. My sons also need to know what men and women can be. And where do they find me? A few weeks ago, in the synagogue kitchen, mixing tuna fish salad for everyone's lunch, while their father was called to the Torah.

The filigree crowns of the Torah scroll were removed with care, the silver breastplate lifted. The scroll was unfurled, the scroll with its heavy parchment patiently lettered by hand without error, ancient letters formed in flowing ink. As my husband, honored to be called, praised the Giver of the Torah, I was adding chopped celery, a bit of grated onion, lemon juice, pepper, and just enough mayonnaise.

It is true that I am better at tuna fish than my husband, and also that I haven't much Hebrew.

I think I want access, I who have nothing to offer.

My daughter has come to *shul* on this country day. She is fetching in her summer dress and pony tail, and she can follow the Hebrew *Chumash*. Jacob, proud, asks her if she would like to lead the *Ashrei,* a psalm of praise, and other Sabbath standards, *Aleinu* and *Adon Olam.* She is nervous, but she will do it.

Squeezing next to me in the makeshift women's section, she taps her toes and hugs me: butterflies. In their ties and skullcaps, these long-known country neighbors now are strangers to her. What? The *Ashrei* goes by, mumbled and unmarked. My daughter gives a silent cheer of relief. I glance at Jacob. He shrugs. It is time for *Aleinu*—and then this too is gone.

Jacob is making his way to the *bima,* the pulpit, then slowly walking back. A rare expression of annoyance strains his face.

"They won't let her do it, she's a girl," he tells us. Last year, he heard a Bat mitzvah girl read from the Torah, first time. He loved it!

"Never mind, *mamele,*" he soothes the "little mother." "They don't know better," he explains.

This is an unhappy first for my daughter. The impersonal exclusion arrives like a slap. Unlike her mother, she *is* capable of participating, contributing. She can pray, and she does, unbidden. At the last minute, packing for sleep-away camp, she slipped her *Siddur,* her Hebrew prayer book, into her trunk.

Jacob wanted her to participate. Jacob was disappointed.

On the way back to the bungalow, I share some of my doubts with Jacob. I don't know what I have accomplished, for I haven't done this and that. I've heard about fine points—do I need them? Is my kitchen really kosher? How much more must I do?

The *Abba* is a man who lost mother and sisters in Auschwitz. He does not drive on Saturday or eat a morsel of forbidden food. He lives with simplicity and modesty, and has never been heard to gossip or to judge harshly another living soul. He joins the morning *minyan,* Sabbath and weekdays, keeps the commandments, mourns his daughter. He washes the supper dishes each night, bent over the sink with aging masculine dignity.

"You have two sets of dishes?" he asks me rhetorically. "Your kitchen is kosher. Enough!"

I may go on tomorrow; I don't know how far. I may try another road. I'll tell you one thing: I never can match the *Abba*'s purity or goodness, or equal him in faith. He doesn't need to do more; I do. If he says "enough," perhaps it is.

BACON?

Our immigrant grandmothers stood for our tradition, but they themselves were not nailed to the past. They arrived on these shores armed with wooden-handled chopping blades, silver candlesticks, tins of buttons, and a certain flexibility. They learned English more or less, and picked their way through the cobblestones of their new world making choices every day. They chose what to keep and what to leave behind, what to forget and what to keep safe in the button tin of memory. And a lot it was that scattered to the winds.

You might say indeed that it was they, the grandmothers, who set the course for assimilation. You even might call them the true assimilationists themselves.

They wanted their children to be of the New World, even as they fought the confusing temptations of New World streets. They wanted their children to have the best, even if it was unkosher, *treyf*. I don't mean that only as metaphor. Somewhere around 1940, my Brooklyn grandmother, listening to a nutritionist on the radio, heard that bacon had special disease-fighting properties, special proteins or amino acids. Thus my aunt insists that from time to time her mother pressed coins in her hands, urging a lunch of BLT on the Brooklyn College campus.

"She could not bear the thought that someone was getting benefit, and her daughter was not," says my aunt with a smile.

My father disputes the story. He has his own stories, his own mother story of the first forty-five years of his life, the plot of which admits no bacon. I find it difficult to imagine my grandmother in the role, yet not quite impossible. I can just put myself into the script. I am no immigrant, true, but I am a mother. Orthodoxies only go so far. Also, you admit things to a dear daughter that you might not admit to a darling son.

SUMMER SQUASH

I arrive at the bungalow colony with a bag of harvest from my garden. I grow vegetables in my front yard, the only flat sunny spot I own. I have brought zucchini, tomatoes, Japanese cucumbers, dill, and round white eggplants.

"You grew this?" doubts Miriam, peering into the bag. "Vegetables don't pay," is her opinion.

"How much are you paying for one tomato plant?" asks Jacob.

I buy the biggest seedlings I can find, with the most yellow flowers, to start the season early. I know it is a pricey way to go, and that I will have to produce hundreds of kilos of big reds and small plummies to break even. I have to tell the truth here, because Jacob already knows. They visited that Sunday when I dug the holes and peeled away the nursery pots. The prices were clearly marked. Jacob has already enjoyed my folly several times.

"Five dollars," I admit, gamely. "But these are organic."

"Five dollars! I am paying forty-nine cents a pound in store!" It is a marvelous rare sight to see: my father-in-law laughs.

"I want to see how you make the squash," I say to Miriam. I am here in the country for a week, and hoping to learn a lot of recipes. And so we begin, with this unassuming side dish I am always happy to meet on Miriam's table. She serves it often, winter and summer, in large quantities, and frequently there is extra to freeze, or to take home.

We take out everything before we begin: one yellow summer squash along with six zucchinis, one green pepper, one red pepper, two onions, small cans of tomato sauce. We dice the onions, wash and dry and dice the peppers. I wash, then thin-slice the squash on a cucumber slicer, scrubbing back and forth to produce transparent rounds the depth, it seems, of a single squash cell.

The slicer is cracked, so I angle it awkwardly. It is actually broken. I think of a smart remark, then think better of it. Miriam is not about to buy a lot of new gadgets for three short months.

She is sautéing the onions now, in oil, with pepper in the top of an old double boiler set straight on the flame, for there is no pot the right size. In fact, it works. The diced onions sizzle, turn golden and crisp. She stirs in the peppers, then adds the tomato sauce, turns down the flame. She balances a large flat lid on the pot, mismatched.

While we wait for the flavors to blend, we wash the slicer, knife, and cutting board.

"This is an Israeli recipe," Miriam remarks. She learned things along the way, wherever she lived.

"I like it cold, too," I say, thinking about the leftovers. "Or warmed up on pasta."

"Really—cold?"

We add the squash and simmer again. We wipe the counter and wipe the sink. Later, we stir in sugar, and after a while, salt.

SUMMER SQUASH

Ground pepper
2 onions, diced
$^1/_8$ cup vegetable oil
1 green bell pepper, 1 red pepper,
 diced
2 6-oz. cans plain tomato sauce

6 medium zucchini, plus 1
 yellow squash, sliced very thin
 (about 6 cups)
$^1/_2$ tsp. sugar
salt

In a saucepan, sprinkle pepper on onions and dry over medium heat (about 1 minute). Add vegetable oil. Stir. Fry onions until brown. Add diced peppers, stir well. Add tomato sauce, stir. Simmer 10 minutes, covered, over low flame. Add squash, cover. Simmer 15 minutes, same low flame. Add sugar. Cook until squash is soft. Salt to taste.

September

CONTINUITY

September

The stories were remembered for a reason. Family stories, they were told
and retold because they contained essential truths. Life and ourselves were in
those stories, whether they were flattering or not, straightforward or opaque,
legend or history. They showed us, in one way or another, how to live.

Religion is a story that tells us how to live. The pious scholars believe
everything is in the Torah, if you know where to look. I don't know
if everything is in it, but a lot is in it. I want to know more of that.

Drawn to ritual, I may perhaps draw nearer to meaning. First principles are
becoming interwoven in the fabric of daily life. I like this dimension, this
reminder, this presence of something timeless, as my own clock ticks.
Random, sparkling, incredible, the world can hold both reason and awe.

I can relinquish, perhaps, the physical things of the past, if I believe that
their essence continues through time. I can go on with everyday life in the
company of ancient values, insights, questions, and doubts.

After all the millennia, I give my doubts another year.

SABBATH

The flier has come in the mail. Summer is over. Today, it rains. School is starting. The air is cool. As the flier proclaims, it is time to register for soccer.

It is a good sport, soccer. My son is ready. He runs down the street with a black-and-white ball, pivots, and kicks it back to the stop sign. It's a nice team sport. I know, because we were registered once. My daughter, older than her brother, has a little gilt trophy on her shelf, and there are shin-guards deep in her closet. I think she would like to play soccer again.

In this town, soccer, like softball and hockey, is a Saturday morning sport. Everyone subscribes. Sport is beneficial. Sport is social. Sportsmanship is a value to be learned, a value tied in with a larger American way to be. Teamwork, competition, doing your best, losing well: The playing field is a training ground for citizenship. And the kids have good clean fun.

But Saturday, Sabbath: a day of sacred time, of human equality, a day for the spirit. A few years ago we joined the team, and then we tried for Sabbath. On soccer Saturdays, we could not find what we were looking for.

We dropped soccer for Sabbath then, an interim strategy rather than decisive play. Sabbath, eclectic and inconsistent as we keep it, has become the necessary high point, the organizing principle, the raison d'être of our week. Still, we don't know quite what to do about it, how far to go, whether to codify and settle into routine. The place where we live, dynamic equilibrium, is inherently unstable. Without consciousness, effort, restraint, everything tends toward chaos. But I can't bear routine.

God rested, that's what the telling is. Fact or metaphor, I have come to respect the mysterious internal logic that made the once-a-week day of rest, that indeed created the concept of "week," a miraculous gift when humankind had no such concepts. If you are tilling the soil or driving a wagon or baking bread or slaughtering meat for six days, how strange and good to stop for a day and face yourself in the mirror of yourself. How much more crucial in our confusing time, when that mirror within seems more elusive. Our gaze is distracted by so much noise.

Even turn off the noise, though: something fundamental has changed since Sabbath arrived on the scene. People still live, weep, love, whelp, and die. But the human condition is no longer the age-old stark dichotomy of work or rest. *Le weekend* has evolved, bastard descendent of Sabbath, and with it, arriviste ideas—leisure, recreation, fun. I have nothing against such notions. I sacrificed my ankle to the ice-skating rink, without regret. I pore through guidebooks for things to do, from apple-picking to rummage sales, wishing to do them all.

However, is recreation work or rest, and is it a mode for Sabbath?

I live in a town where Saturday is for errands, and Saturday is for sport. When I set off for synagogue, *shul,* in blouse and skirt, my neighbors are lacing sneakers and stretching kinks out of middle-aged backs. I face the Ark as the Torah reading begins. Symbolically present for the revelation at Sinai, I miss the chance to wave at a friend at the gym. I pass up the sidewalk sale. I lose out on the impromptu cup of coffee that stimulates community life. Here are my children, in their dresses and *kippot,* skullcaps, learning to pray in the synagogue with a handful of other kids. This is good for them, I think, but so would soccer be.

Why not let them play soccer, their eager cleats piercing the muddy grass? Why not join other good folks to cheer and carpool, to pour juice and keep track of error, free shot, goal? This isn't work, and it isn't routine. It's not washing the car or investing in mutual funds or filling in woodpecker holes in the siding. It is social, it is even uplifting. It is a compelling Saturday ritual of its own. And while it is pagan to worship sport, this I know: If there is a God, God gave beauty to bodies at play on the field.

The high holidays are upon me, calling for renewal of effort and faith. Team registration is upon me as well. There is only one Saturday morning to have at nine o'clock each week.

Is Sabbath objective reality?

If I drive my car to the shopping mall on Saturday and buy a pair of shoes, is it still the day of rest? Maybe Sabbath is the tree falling in the forest. If I choose to go shopping, though, I have willfully ignored its fall. That is not the same, quite, as just not hearing the distant tree.

When I see the house into order and provide grape juice and wine; when I gather in the children and bathe them; when I wash my hands and adorn myself and light candles of a Friday night, do I observe the Sabbath or actually bring it into being? Does observance of the Sabbath create a reality, or—as with a mathematical formula—does it express and symbolize something already out there in the universe? The scientist, the mathematician "discovers" a law, rather than inventing it. Relativity, gravity, calculus, they say, were out there all along to be named and claimed.

Or is Sabbath more kin to the artist's paradox? The laws of perspective are representational, but the painting is its own reality. Spirituality, like vision, is flawed and emotional, shaped by experience. That *Shabbas* feeling cannot be attained from a color-by-number kit.

So what happens to Sabbath, unmarked and unobserved? Does it curl up its toes and vanish? Does it become the property of those who seek it? Is it always there, waiting for consciousness, recognition, choice? Does it matter if we miss a few?

Sabbath, seventh day of creation: God rested. We are to close out the workaday world for a little while. But how? In the traditional mode, women provide the means. In practice, there are dishes to wash and beds to make and babies to change and children to run after at synagogue and meals to set out after the Friday sun slips behind the rising earth and during that rotation of earth and glimpse of moon that we know as Saturday. Only a man, and a rare man today, would say that this is not "work" next to driving a car or flipping a light switch—actions proscribed in the strictest readings.

The vernacular has it both ways. When you light your candles and say *kiddush,* you "welcome" the Sabbath. The Sabbath arrives, and you celebrate. When you wash your floor, dust, cook, and set the table on Friday, however, you "make" Sabbath. So, what exactly is it that women do?

Are women God?

Does the Sabbath exist independently from the preparation, from the tradition? Can you meet your family for a pizza dinner on Friday, relax together for the first time all week, drive home after dark, snuggle up to a video tape, feel happy to be alive, and call it *Shabbas*? Can you go to the beach with your family on Saturday, enjoying the creation on a beautiful day, and fulfill the observance? The rabbis rather firmly say no. A tired man and woman might prefer yes.

Here's a puzzle: If you race home from the office, snap off the cartoons, shake your roast chicken out of a box, and light the candles exactly by sundown; if you bound out of bed next day though you desperately need your sleep, and then head out to services in the rain on foot when driving would be more restful; if you stand and sit in the chapel, your concentration constantly interrupted by children, and then you return home in the rain, exhausted: this might pass for *Shabbas,* and the rabbis would probably confer their blessing.

Possibly religion is not appropriate for parents of young children.

At my house, we are sitting on a metaphoric fence. We go to synagogue sometimes, stay home sometimes, and occasionally, go out and do. We walk to *shul* and drive to *shul.* We have had pleasant Sabbath mornings, at home in pajamas with no TV. We catch up with each other, rest and drift, play Scrabble and read and ignore the phone. We try not to drive, we avoid errands and yard work. Once in a while, though, we get in the car, and head for museum or nature preserve. We have taken a prayer book to water's edge and started our hike with Hebrew words of thanksgiving and praise. So far, we feel, we are getting the spirit of the thing.

Can it hold, however? In the rabbinical wisdom, you must set a standard, or risk a slippery slope. The beach today becomes the amusement park tomorrow, and then the video arcade. If you're in your car anyway, heading back from the museum, you may as well pick up milk, mail a letter, buy shoes. Home on Saturday morning, I sometimes begin to putter about. Why not pull a few weeds, straighten a closet, or—sit kids at the computer and tackle a pile of bills? Soccer season fades to hockey, and then to softball; a year of Saturdays rolls by.

The subjective mental construct collapses, and Sabbath slips from the hand.

One winter morning in the middle of a week I got on a train in Yonkers going north, and I didn't step down until Buffalo. The train rumbled over the frozen bank of the Hudson River. I stared out into the gray river unwinding from its source: St. Lawrence, Great Lakes, Niagara. Here was the watery locus of a hundred years of family history in the Americas, more or less—Toronto, Detroit, New York, with a few scattered outposts, such as Buffalo, along the way. My immigrants followed industry or hunches or others of their tradition to these places, where their names now appear on headstones, chiseled cold.

At Buffalo station a tall sixty-year-old second cousin and his brother-in-law and his father, Sol, waited to meet me. My mother's cousin Sol was almost ninety then, nearly blind. I wanted to see him, I just wanted to see him, and to see his wife, Rita, by then practically deaf.

I hung up my coat. I saw Rita traversing the kitchen in her wheelchair. Once a tall cool walker in tailored skirts, she moved slowly now, pushing back at linoleum floor with heavy feet. Tightly, her hands gripped armrests. On Rita's lap balanced a plate, fused to a yellow stick of butter. This was one of many laborious trips she had made back and forth to get bagels and jam and butter from icebox to table in honor of me.

I saw she had put on lipstick.

"Are you here? Are you really here?" Rita shouted in my ear as I leaned to embrace. Her voice rang loud, gay, moist. Two years had made such a difference.

We brewed tea, toasted bagels. At the table we remained, Rita watching, unable to follow, Sol talking. The son and the son-in-law listened with me, for Sol remembered and still remembers everything, and he told it all in his eerily fresh voice, that of a much younger man.

"We used to spend *Shabbas* with our cousins. We would walk home after dinner, Saturday nights." Sol was remembering boyhood, the 1910s, as the youngest of nine children of immigrants. "It was a good mile and a half, a good walk for little kids. You'd get seven or eight blocks from home, and ask to take the streetcar."

" 'Did you see the third star?' Mother would say.

"No, you didn't. Well, that's it. You couldn't do anything until you saw the third star. It could be pouring down rain."

Sabbath, in the rabbis' view, wasn't over for sure until three stars had appeared in the evening sky. Sol's mother was a devout woman. She insisted that her husband wear a beard, and she herself had a *sheytl,* a marriage wig, although "she didn't wear it that often," Sol said with a little smile. She was superstitious too, and regularly consulted gypsies.

"You just had to walk in the rain," said Sol.

"Cream cheese! Just getting a little cream cheese!" This announcement from Rita, suddenly setting wheelchair in motion again. "Yes, indeed! This is how the other half lives!" she called.

"Three stars," Sol mused. "But it didn't do you any harm."

• • •

For years of my life Sabbath didn't exist. I was unaware of it from week to week. Friday night was another going-out night, a night for political meetings or German Expressionist films. Saturday was all worldly purpose—errands and chores, laundry, haircuts, a jog in the park—topped off by an evening of special plans. I belonged to the universal Sunday, sleeping late, then waking for newspaper supplements, pleasure excursions, pancake restaurants, or that Jewish twist on Sunday, the bagel-and-lox brunch.

There came a day, though, a Saturday morning years ago. I was already, or so I thought, confirmed in my views and ways. I handed my husband a To Do list. Forget it, he said, "It's *Shabbas.*"

This startled me, and it made me laugh, and I let him alone with his coffee and magazines. Saturday rest was a reference point, something that never had left him. His father walked to synagogue every Saturday, and his mother waited at home with a meal prepared the day before. He owned a separate time grid, the ancient lunar calendar, with its periodic soundings and pauses, and this he kept beneath and between his awareness of standard time.

I chortled and let him alone: I shared the reference in a pale, fuzzy way. I did not yet know my husband's parents well, and could not possibly conceive then of an every-Saturday synagogue rhythm like theirs. Indeed, I never thought of it. My Saturdays rarely took me into Jewish precincts. If I happened to see someone walking to *shul,* I registered it as local color. This had nothing to do with me.

Still, I shared something. When my husband refused to take my errand list that Saturday, I laughed but I liked it, and this stayed with me.

We moved slowly forward, shadowed by the past. We sent our daughter to school to learn what there was to learn. She sang her daily prayers upon rising and "Hear O Israel" before bed, when she was scared of dark things in the night. We lit our Friday night candles; she opened her book and made *kiddush,* telling of creation and Sabbath, and blessing the wine in an archaic tongue. She sealed and sanctified our dinner with *Birkat ha-Mazon,* the after-meal grace, which she knew by heart at seven years old.

And then she asked questions. "If God created the world in six days, when were the dinosaurs?" she asked. And soon, "Does Grandpa keep kosher?" We wanted the questions and even dissent. We tested ritual, made accommodations, accepted inconsistency. We wanted form and content too. We wanted Sabbath, a reference point.

We had a year of candlelit Friday nights at home, and then a second, and then a third. My Fridays grew shorter and shorter, as getting ready for Friday night squeezed work from the day, week after week. One hectic Friday we couldn't go on, so we went out. We went out to dinner on Friday night.

The restaurant, perfectly nice, felt strange. We felt strange in it. We ordered our chow fun noodles, our vegetarian spring rolls, our broccoli, bean curd, and rice. It was relaxing, at the end of a long busy week, to just order, sit back, sip ginger ale and Chinese beer. It was relaxing and strange, and we seemed subdued, watching night fall outside and wondering if it was *Shabbas*.

I saw people I knew. Acquaintances, friends I don't see much, also were dining out. Fringed paper lanterns trembled above, fish flickered in a tropical tank. It was festive. It was a relief. I won't have to do dishes, I said, justifying. But we were all aware of Friday night. We were here, not home, self-conscious.

Then we heard singing, the next booth over, a young, deep voice. "What?" said my daughter, ginger ale in midair, shy and dying to look. "Can't be." But it was: *Birkhat ha-Mazon*, the after-meal grace. Two youngish men and their father had set down their chopsticks. One sang, and sang it all, every rich bit of that long blessing, words of appreciation and joy. And why not? Why not live and bring Sabbath with you?

It was dark when we left. We walked home in the dark, under the winter sky. A good eight blocks, and my daughter was singing—*Birkhat ha-Mazon*. She did not know that the words remind us there is a universe out there, beyond one's own sated contentment. She recited by rote, thanking God for the good Chinese dinner, calling on us to feed the poor, praying for the dawn of peace.

She is still young, but someday—soon—she will understand the words she sang.

The form is hers, and form holds content.

SPONGES

*I*t is ten-thirty. I just got home. I paid the sitter, a teenager I find watching TV in a pitch-dark den while most of my house is brilliantly lit. I am tired. I am cold. I am hungry. I take off my coat and resist the urge to drop it on the floor. I pull off my boots and let them fall. Am I more tired than hungry? Should I go to sleep? No, I want food, food, food.

I pad into the kitchen, and I am assaulted. Under glaring lights, a grease-blotched pizza carton yawns open on the counter, containing one last cold slice missing a single bite. Cheesy sauce-streaked plates, knives, leathery pizza crusts, rancid glasses half-filled with tepid milk, an empty ice cream carton, spoons, balls of damp paper towel, and thirty-seven buttery unpopped corn kernels in a large stainless steel bowl teeter uneasily in the sink.

The unwiped table bristles with crumbs. The pantry door hangs open. On my chair, a melted drip of ice cream. One stocking encounters something nameless underfoot—sticky, yet hard.

I open the fridge. An untouched bag of carrots, drawer of nutritious apples and tangerines. Leftover baked potatoes. Leftover baked fish. Lettuce. Bread. Eggs. Three kinds of peanut butter, ginger preserves, mild salsa, green salsa, hot salsa, mustard. Diet Coke, half a can. And—ah, soup.

Good soup. Barley, onions, scallions, parsley, dried mushrooms, carrot, celery, chopped cabbage—clean-out-the-vegetable-drawer ingredients—potato, pepper, boiled and thickened in rich chicken stock. Welcome-home soup. Incurable-optimist soup. Warm-the-innards-and-go-to-bed soup. I raise it from its refrigerator ledge.

Hello, chicken stock.

I have what is at the moment a dairy kitchen, a dirty, *milikhdike* kitchen, and I stand in it, under unflinching electric light, bearing a cranberry glass storage bowl sealed with plastic wrap like some holy grail filled with cold *fleyshike* barley soup. The blue rack is in the sink under the dairy dishes, the dishwasher is half full of dairy dishes, every surface glistens with milk fat—the counter, the table, the chairs. Something nameless is stuck to the bottom of my foot.

There are four different sponges lying in wait on my sink: blue for dairy, pink for meat, green for *pareve,* and yellow to clean the kitchen. Nearby, three kitchen towels—blue, pink, and green. I should wipe the table with the yellow sponge, and thereon set down the cranberry glass bowl. I should wash the dishes with the blue sponge, stack the dishwasher and run it. I should wash the blue rack, dry it with the blue dish towel, and set it aside. I should bag the trash, sweep the floor, use the yellow sponge to wash the counter and scour the kitchen sink. I should rinse the sink with boiling water, and lay down the white sink rack. Then, yes, then, I could prepare my *fleyshik* meal, gently reheating soup in a saucepan, sitting down to soup in a white soup plate, and later wash it all and dry it—saucepan, black ladle, soup plate, meat spoon, cranberry glass storage bowl—with pink sponge and pink towel.

However, life is a fleeting thing.

I know what I will do. I will put the whole glass bowl in the microwave and zap it. I will rummage about for a meat spoon. I will dim the lights, and when the timer beeps, I will peel the plastic lid from the glass bowl, lean against the counter, and eat the soup standing up, hoping my husband will call from Ohio, where he is away on a business trip. Then I will leave the unwashed bowl and spoon on the furthest corner of the counter to deal with tomorrow.

It is as good as any soup I ever have had.

ACKNOWLEDGMENTS

Many people helped me with *Miriam's Kitchen*. I have been lucky with friends, family, and professional associates. In particular, I wish to thank:

Abigail Thomas, for her genius, guidance, and friendship.

Liz Dahrensoff, for her counsel, and for securing a good editorial home for my book.

Barbara Grossman of Viking, for making the book real, and for her acumen and enthusiasm.

The many talented individuals at Viking.

Esther Potok, David Potok, Howard Ehrlich, and Lillian Stocker Ehrlich, for their immeasurable gifts of self. Carol Ehrlich, for her generosity and encouragement; Abraham Ehrlich, for his perspective and sense of humor.

Elisa Petrini and Sally Powell for friendship and support.

Reuben Forbes and Thelma Anderson, for family tales. Seymour Axelrod, for his advice on Yiddish.

The Virginia Center for the Creative Arts, for twenty-five days of uninterrupted writing time.

I write these words in gratitude to my beloved grandmothers, who preserved tradition and recast it for the New World. I write in sadness that Ben Stocker did not live to read this book.

Above all, I thank my husband and children for standing by me with love. I could not have written *Miriam's Kitchen* without them.

Elizabeth Ehrlich
April 1997

A NOTE ON TRANSCRIPTION

Spelling Yiddish words with the English alphabet can be problematic. Some accustomed English renderings may suggest incorrect pronunciations. Yiddish speakers, depending on their region of origin, may pronounce the same word in various ways.

Many Yiddish words have found their way into English. I was surprised to find such words as "daven" (pray) and "cholent" (Sabbath casserole) in *Merriam-Webster's Third International (Unabridged) Dictionary.* Whenever possible, I have used Webster's anglicized spellings. These words, for the most part, are romanized in the text. I chose to italicize certain words, despite their dictionary inclusion, that struck me as unfamiliar to English speakers.

All non-Webster words are italicized. For these, I tried to follow the YIVO/Weinreich transcription system, which standardizes English equivalents for Yiddish letters or combinations of letters. The result may differ from familiar spellings. Thus "rag" is given as *shmate,* rather than *schmatte. Milkhik,* not *milchik,* represents the Yiddish word for "dairy."

I have abandoned consistency in several cases. Where conventional anglicization of certain Yiddish words is so familiar that YIVO transcription may be misleading or appear strange, I have used familiar spellings. "Grandmother" is given as *bubbe,* although *bobe* is technically correct. Similarly, *Shabbas* (Sabbath), rather than *Shabes,* appears.

The text includes a number of words that are identical in written Hebrew and Yiddish, but are pronounced differently. For reasons of personal history and habit, I prefer one form to another in everyday use. For example, I pronounce *kashrut* in the Hebrew way, rather than saying *kashres,* the Yiddish. My spellings reflect such habits.

It is said that a discussion between ten Jews will produce eleven opinions. I expect that some of my spellings will be controversial. My goal has been to bring Yiddish flavor fluently into the text. I can claim neither scholarly expertise nor proficiency in the Yiddish language. I regret any errors.

Elizabeth Ehrlich

INDEX

Page numbers set in italics indicate actual recipes.